الجناح الوطني لدولة الإمارات
بينالي البندقية

National Pavilion UAE
La Biennale di Venezia

بدعم من
Supported by

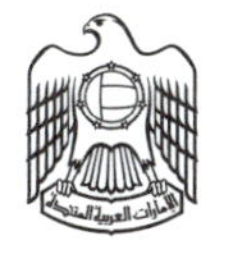

وزارة الثقافة والشباب
MINISTRY OF CULTURE & YOUTH

المفوض الرسمي
Commissioned by

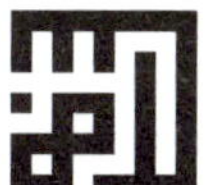

مؤسسة سلامة بنت حمدان آل نهيان
**SALAMA BINT HAMDAN
AL NAHYAN FOUNDATION**

Mohamed Ahmed Ibrahim

Between Sunrise and Sunset

Works 1986–2022

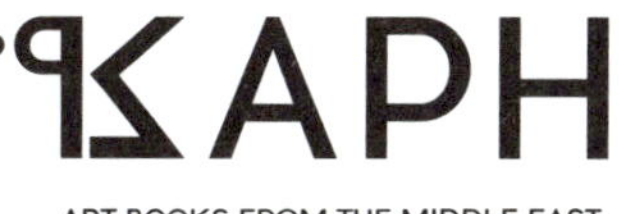

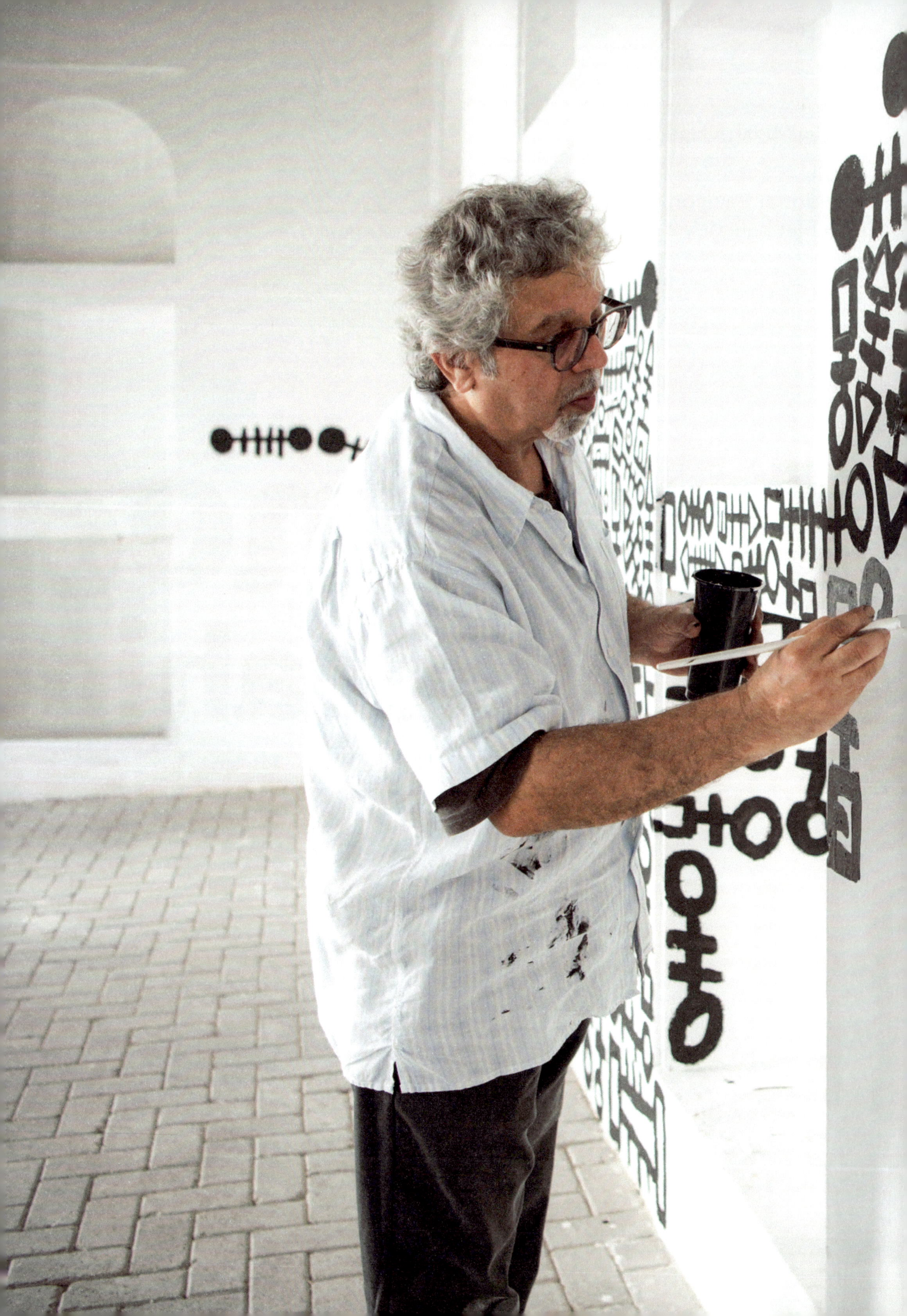

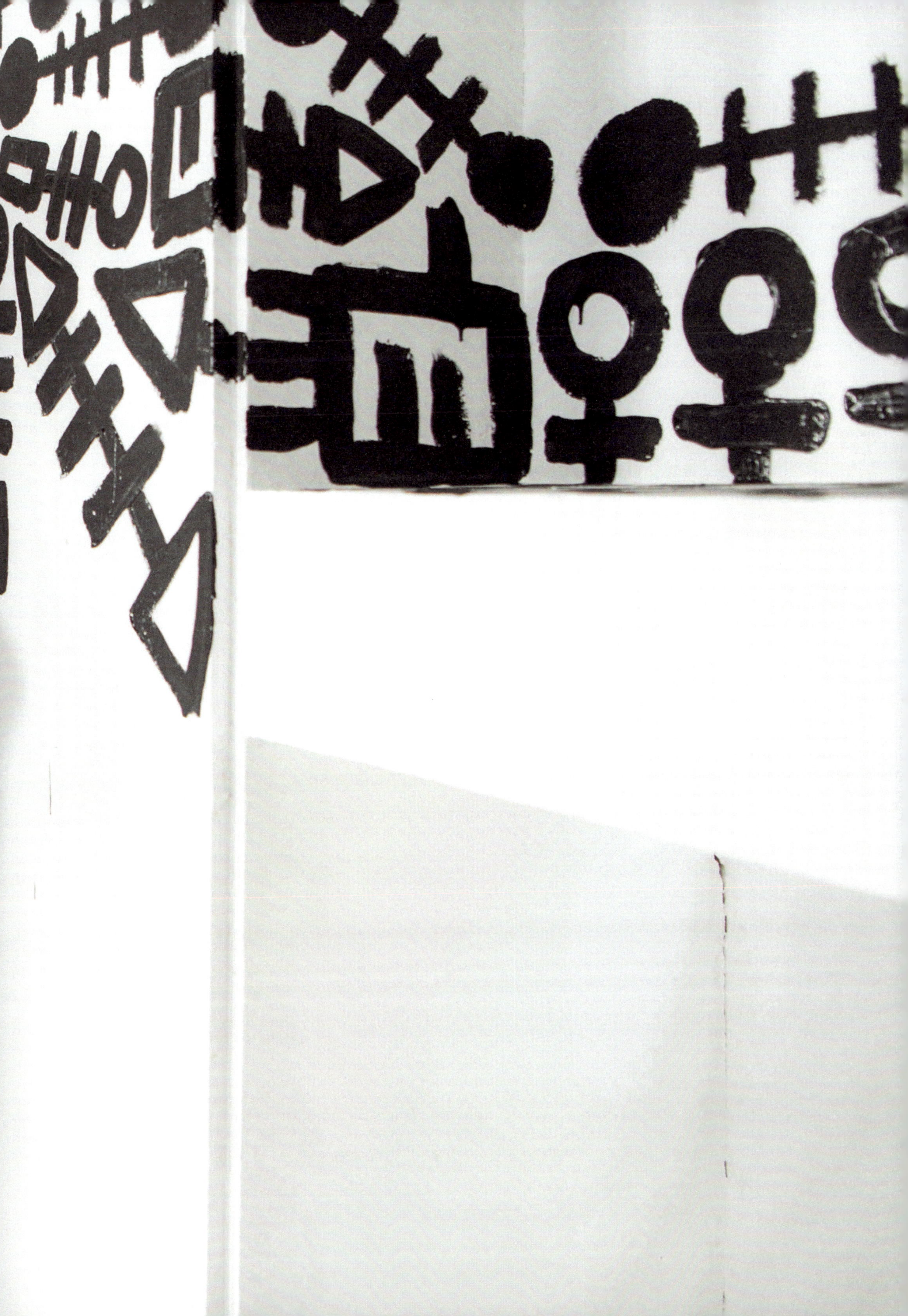

National Pavilion United Arab Emirates 2022

Mohamed Ahmed Ibrahim:
Between Sunrise and Sunset
Works 1986–2022

This book is published on the occasion of the National Pavilion United Arab Emirates' exhibition, *Mohamed Ahmed Ibrahim: Between Sunrise and Sunset*, at the 59th International Art Exhibition – La Biennale di Venezia, titled *The Milk of Dreams*, from April 23 to November 27, 2022.

Commissioner: Salama bint Hamdan Al Nahyan Foundation
Supporter: UAE Ministry of Culture and Youth
Artist: Mohamed Ahmed Ibrahim
Curator: Maya Allison
Curatorial Assistant: Tala Nassar

Editors: Maya Allison and Cristiana de Marchi
Arabic Editor: Alaa Edris
Editorial Assistant: Tala Nassar
Publication Researcher: Munira Al Sayegh
English Copy Editor: Zeina Assaf
English Proofreader: The Content Creation Company
Arabic Translator: Ban Kattan
Arabic Copy Editor: Manal Khader
Arabic Proofreader: Mohamad Hamdan

Designer: Iain Hector
Arabic Designer: Larry Issa
Publisher: National Pavilion UAE La Biennale di Venezia
Co-Publisher: Kaph Books

Exhibition Production
Graphic Designer: Iain Hector and Larry Issa
Exhibition Designer: Milk Train, Rome
Lighting: iGuzzini illuminazione, Recanati
Exhibition Construction: Tosetto Allestimenti, Venice

National Pavilion United Arab Emirates
Coordinating Director: Laila Binbrek
Communications Manager: Dana Al Sadek
Senior Exhibitions Coordinator: Farah El-Rafei
Internship Coordinator: Rawan Al Ramahi
Office Coordinator: Jay Yambao
Venice Coordinator: Emanuela Semiani

The publisher gratefully acknowledges permission granted to reproduce the copyrighted images in this book, including from the archives of The Flying House, Emirates Fine Arts Society, Sharjah Art Foundation, Tashkeel, Universes in Universe, Lawrie Shabibi, and the personal archives of Fumio Nanjo, Mohammed Kazem, and Mohamed Ahmed Ibrahim. Every effort has been made to contact copyright holders and to obtain their permission for the use of copyrighted images. The publishers apologize for any errors or omissions in the above list and would be grateful if notified of any corrections that should be incorporated in any future reprints or editions of this publication.

Printed in Belgium

ISBN: 978-614-8035-44-9

Distribution in Europe:
Les Presses du Réel
35 rue Colson
21000 Dijon
France
Tel +33 3 80 30 75 23
www.lespressesdureel.com

Idea Books
Nieuwe Hemweg 6R
1013 BG Amsterdam
The Netherlands
Tel +31 20 6226154
Fax +31 20 6209299
www.ideabooks.nl

Distribution in the Middle-East:
CIEL Book Distribution
3rd Interchange, Al Quoz Industrial I
P.O.Box 282005
Dubai, UAE
Tel +97143232170
Mob +971509126932

Distribution in the Americas,
Asia and Australia:
ARTBOOK | D.A.P.
75 Broad Street,
Suite 630
New York, NY 10004
www.artbook.com

Image Scanning and Digitalization Services by al Mawrid Arab Center for the Study of Art, NYU Abu Dhabi

National Pavilion UAE La Biennale di Venezia
P.O. Box 769307, Abu Dhabi, UAE
nationalpavilionuae.org

Front cover
Installation view of *Mohamed Ahmed Ibrahim: Elements* at the Sharjah Art Foundation, 2018

Previous page
Mohamed Ahmed Ibrahim creating his artwork for the *Mohamed Ahmed Ibrahim: Elements* exhibition at the Sharjah Art Foundation, 2018

Back cover
***Falling Stones Garden*, 2020**
Painted fiberglass, 320 pieces, dimensions variable
Site-specific installation at Desert X AlUla, Saudi Arabia

Contents

You find you are no
what you're doing i
like that. I did not u
art could mean for

an] artist and
not art. Simple
erstand what
e until later.

All quotes in this book are
from interviews with the artist
conducted by the editors.

Foreword

**Salama bint Hamdan Al Nahyan Foundation,
Commissioner of the National Pavilion UAE**

We are a product of our circumstances, our particular heritage, culture, and environment, as well as those specific things and nuances that make us, us. Nature and nurture. We are both a part of the society we grow up in as well as an individual in that society, with our own unique life experiences. These are at the same time, both unique to us as well as shared. And, of course, what we see and how we make sense of things is also unique to us and also shared. Artists work by looking very long and hard and then working very long and hard to tell us what they saw. It is in these moments of processing and sharing that we perhaps see new things in the world, from other people's perspectives, cultures, and histories. It is in these moments of sharing that we start to make some form of collective sense.

Mohamed Ahmed Ibrahim's work is a testament to the artist's gaze, how he sees objects, shapes, and colors around him, and how they manifest in his artwork. For the project in the Venice Biennale, it is also an indication of the dialogue that artists have, as with curator and this book's co-editor, Maya Allison, who also brings her unique history and experiences to the process. Ibrahim has had a lifelong fascination with the world around him, the social world as well as the natural world. He has a commitment to his art process, a conversation through objects that brings that dialogue to life.

Every one of our exhibitions includes a thoughtful publication as a key part of the installation, leaving behind a legacy and an indication of context, thought, and process for future generations of artists, scholars, or those with a keen interest in the arts. This publication is a testament to the core and evolution of this artist, and to his deep dialogue with his community, as reflected in the work of Cristiana de Marchi as co-editor of this book, which is a celebration as well as an exposition of the artist's commitment and experimentation. We hope that it will be shared, discussed, and studied for decades to come.

We believe in the power of art, how it can bring cultures together while, at the same time, sharing our different ways of seeing. We believe that art is the product of an intellectual and emotional process, one embedded in deep thought and commitment to practice. Over the years, we have worked hard to ensure that the core values of research, collaboration, creativity, and legacy are all part of our process. This year is no exception, and we are pleased to collaborate with our partners and participants who have made this work possible. In particular, New York University Abu Dhabi has provided support to this project and has become a significant player in the UAE art scene through their sustained study of the region.

As commissioner of the National Pavilion United Arab Emirates at Biennale Arte 2022, we are very proud to support our artists and curators and share their work with the world.

Foreword

**HE Noura bint Mohammed Al Kaabi,
UAE Minister of Culture and Youth**

Over an incredible 10 exhibitions, the UAE has brought some of the best local culture to a global audience. The UAE's representation at the Biennale Arte 2022 is a point of pride for the nation, and every year its exhibitions bring to the world stage diverse aspects of the country's dynamic cultural scene. Through our participation, we show our rich history and dynamic contemporary culture, and the unbridled talent of those who call the UAE home. Since the UAE's first exhibition in Venice in 2009, we have seen a remarkable transformation across the UAE's art and cultural landscape. Today, we are home to global flagship institutions as well as a vibrant grassroots scene where Emirati and international creatives alike find inspiration in our diversity. We have grown into a real creative hub of the region. As we look ahead, the Ministry of Culture and Youth is putting in place a comprehensive plan to ensure that the cultural and creative industries become one of the top contributing sectors in the UAE's economy.

In order to maintain and elevate our position as a true cultural and creative center, the National Pavilion UAE ensures that the groundbreaking research conducted for the exhibitions over the years is documented and made available for future scholars. Through the exhibitions' accompanying publications, we seek to expand access to this knowledge and to incorporate these untold stories of the UAE into the contemporary art world narrative.

This year, we are proud to present an exhibition by leading experimental Emirati artist, Mohamed Ahmed Ibrahim, who is also an influential member of the UAE's historic avant-garde art community. Curated by Maya Allison, executive director of The NYU Abu Dhabi Art Gallery, the exhibition presents biomorphic sculptures that cluster in undulating color and movement—evoking bodies, mutation, and metamorphosis, to highlight the overarching theme of the Biennale, *The Milk of Dreams*. This theme questions the representation of bodies and their metamorphoses, and the connection between bodies and earth.

Our current and previous exhibitions could not have been made possible without the commitment of the Salama bint Hamdan Al Nahyan Foundation, Commissioner of the National Pavilion UAE, whose efforts have brought the UAE's exhibitions to fruition. The Ministry of Culture and Youth is committed to creating opportunities, enhancing support for talented creators, and ensuring the right frameworks for growth are in place at every stage of the creative industries.

Acknowledgments

Maya Allison and Cristiana de Marchi

The editorial team is particularly grateful for the institutional support and work of our colleagues: the Salama bint Hamdan Al Nahyan for the support of this project; the National Pavilion for their steadfast and crucial work telling the UAE's untold stories (Rawan Al Ramahi, Farah El-Rafei, Dana Al Sadek, Emanuela Semiani, Jay Yambao, and fearless leader Laila Binbrek); The Sharjah Art Foundation, for the access to their important archives, and Her Highness Sheikha Hoor Al Qasimi, for the Foundation's contribution of the *Elements* exhibition of 2018, as well as her previous work on the history of the UAE's exhibitions for the National Pavilion UAE at the Venice Biennale 2015; to NYU Abu Dhabi for the support of this project on many fronts, including the dedication of in-kind support from the Al Mawrid Center for the Study of Art, and the partnership with the department of The NYU Abu Dhabi Art Gallery team, with special thanks to Metha Alsaeedi for emergency Arabic proofing; and thanks to David Webb New York for funding NYU Abu Dhabi to sustain the role of curatorial assistant on this project.

Cristiana de Marchi

I would like to express my thankfulness to Mohamed Ahmed and to Maya for inviting me to share with them this part of their path to Venice: it has been a truly rewarding journey, delving in an extraordinarily rich archive of memorable events with the prospect and in anticipation of an exciting addition to it.

I address my personal appreciation and most sincere gratitude to Abdul-Raheem and Mohamed Abdul-Raheem Sharif for their generosity in sharing the archives of The Flying House; to Nasser Abdallah, for his friendly support and assistance in recovering the earliest copies of *Al Tashkeel* magazine; to Iqbal Shamz, from the Lawrie Shabibi gallery team, for his courteous and professional responsiveness; and to Mohammed Kazem, who has been—and always is—a dearly precious interlocutor in the different stages of my research and mental argumentation.

This book would not have been possible without the full commitment, time and energy of Tala Nassar, Alaa Edris, Ban Kattan, and Farah Al Refaei, who constitute a formidable team in accomplishing their respective chores, and reminding us of ours. A special thanks goes to Sonali Shirodkar, for keeping track of our schedules and making possible the seemingly impossible task to organize our remote meetings.

My deepest gratefulness goes to my family, and adoptive clans and tribes, for their uninterrupted encouragement, patient support, and unconditional faith in my capacities; and to my sons Daniel and Jonathan, for illuminating my days with their presence.

Maya Allison

I second all of the thanks that my co-editor gives to our collaborators. I am deeply indebted to Cristiana for the enormous gift of her poetic, precise, and generous intellect to our work on this book. Her knowledge of the world of Mohamed Ahmed Ibrahim runs deep, both in the sense of factual accuracy, and the value and nuance of the art in question.

For my work as curator on this project, my gratitude flows back across decades and continents: to Peter Parshall, Judith Tannenbaum, and Hilary Ballon for their transformative intellectual partnership and mentorship, challenging and entrusting me with opportunities to grow at pivotal points in my career; to Emily Peters, Swethaa Ballakrishnen, and May Al-Dabbagh as my peer travelers in the subsequent journey; to Mariët Westermann, Salwa Mikdadi, Tarek Al-Ghoussein, Fatma Abdullah, Bill Bragin, Linsey Bostwick, Joanna Settle, Lynn Gumpert, Michèle Wong, and Nadia El Cheikh, for embodying the gift of academic and creative community and leadership for the global university where my work on this subject first took root.

My development of this project is possible due to the groundwork laid in previous projects, with crucial thought partners: Bana Kattan and Alaa Edris (co-conspirators on curatorial adventures), Tala Nassar, Munira Al Sayegh, Alia Zaal Lootah, and Aisha Stoby (each fueling the work at key points), including book collaborators, especially Anne Renahan (editor and fellow traveler), Ban Kattan (translator, light-bringer), and the patient and excellent designers Iain Hector and Larry Issa. These projects would not have been possible without the many who have helped make The NYU Abu Dhabi Art Gallery what it is, past and present, of which today's team includes many mentioned elsewhere in these acknowledgments, plus: Laura Latman, Maisoon Mubarak, Sebastian Grube, Melroy D'souza, Marty Ackley, Brian Fitzhugh, and with special thanks for making possible my focus on the Venice project to Sonali Shirodkar's persistent and generous support, to Wafa Jadallah for her energy directing the Gallery's exhibitions, and Hala Saleh for her leadership of the Gallery operations and strategic counsel.

I offer personal thanks to: Ramani Arachchige, Grace Tampus, Nancy Siegel, Smita Prabhakar, Kanchan Chandra, Fiona Kidd, Vasanth Mohan, Elisabeth Anderson, and Andy Tillotson who have each offered refuge and cheer when needed most. And above all, to my family of origin, and of my choosing: John, Valerie, Patrick, and Heidi Allison, plus the extended Kannon Dell family, and, always, to Mark Swislocki, for the sustenance, both intellectual and caloric, and to my son Casimir, for the world.

Thank you, Mohamed Ahmed Ibrahim, for opening your archives, studio, and home, for the long hours of work on this project, and to your wonderful family. And thank you to artists everywhere for inspiring us all.

Introduction

Salwa Mikdadi

A Rhapsody on Reiteration

Mohamed Ahmed expresses ideas of time, movement, and place through leaving trail marks on the surface of the terrain … a kind of romantic mediation that [he] directs to his village people: traces, signs, and behaviors that express an age-old concept … , a manifestation of the ultimate and very distant union between man and nature. The earth is the womb and the first mold for life, where trees, stones and other materials relate to the earth and eventually return to it. These materials are born from the earth and then rot within it. It is the painting of life and death.

—Hassan Sharif on Mohamed Ahmed Ibrahim[1]

1. Hassan Sharif, *Mafhūm al-Fan (The Concept of Art)* (Sharjah: the Department of Culture, 1997). Published on the occasion of the 1995 Sharjah Biennial II (editors' translation).

This collection of essays contributes to the historical and theoretical discourse on art from the Emirates. It is a welcomed addition to an area of study that has long remained under-researched. The seminal essays dedicated to the celebration of the long career of Mohamed Ahmed Ibrahim undertake an analysis of his work and the context for his art practice over a period of four decades.

The first part of the book provides an in-depth study of Ibrahim's practice within the context of the UAE's emerging art scene. A comprehensive essay by Maya Allison examines the characteristics of Ibrahim's practice and oeuvre over the decades, followed by Nada Shabout's essay, which focuses on the circulation of art in the UAE during its formative years from the 1980s and 1990s. Shabout particularly looks at the development of the Emirates Fine Art Society's output of publications and annual exhibitions as well as the Sharjah Biennial. To conclude the first section of the monograph, Venetia Porter's essay reveals the significance of Ibrahim's paper works in relation to both his two-dimensional and three-dimensional pieces, recounting details underlying the very process involved in the creation of the installation presented in Venice.

The second part of the book provides detailed studies of Ibrahim's relationship to artists, poets, writers, and various art groups and institutions in the UAE. Fumio Nanjo provides us with important insights into the informal meetings and gatherings around the leading figure of Hassan Sharif, and shares glimpses of the birth and development of the art institutions in the UAE. Further enriching our understanding of the mutual influences and connections between artists and poets is an essay by Adel Khozam, which highlights Ibrahim's role in these circles in the 1980s and 1990s. While Vivek Vilasini's contribution underlines the central role of ecology in Ibrahim's work and his relationship to the natural landscape, Munira Al Sayegh's study of Ibrahim's working process and material sheds an intimate light on his Land Art works and traces his influence on a generation of UAE artists. Alongside the documentation of Ibrahim's artworks over the decades, Cristiana de Marchi gives us a rare portrait of the artist through an in-depth interview and conversation highlighting the role of friendships and his personal vision of art making.

What comes to the forefront through these essays is that the cycle of life is central to the artistic expression of Mohamed Ahmed Ibrahim, as he draws inspiration from the recurring rhythms of nature. This is reflected in the introductory quote from Hassan Sharif, as he describes that everything returns to the earth, both commencing from it and inevitably disintegrating into the folds of the land. Ibrahim draws his inspiration from deep within the interior of the earth and the surrounding landscape of Khor Fakkan, the Hajar Mountains and the waters of the Gulf of Oman, bringing our attention to the disappearing natural world around us and the immensity of its primordial power. Having worked for several decades with materials from nature, his art speaks to the intimate relationship between humanity, the materiality of the land, and the foreboding estrangement of our contemporary lifestyles—themes that are currently being raised in discourses of art and ecology.

Alongside this intimate choreography between the artist and nature, his resulting work embodies a temporality that comments on fragility and existence. In 1999, the artist burned most of his work, returning it to the earth as ashes and remains. In retrospect, the process can be interpreted as a ritual where he sacrificed his art to create a fire that completes the elements of the cycle of life – earth, fire, water and air. The ritualistic nature of this act connects back to other works where we witness the recomposing of the contemporary with prehistoric and primitive acts, especially in his earlier works that use everyday items. Interpreting the world around him, Ibrahim believes that the role of the artist is "to sort through, to show, to point to what already exists."[2]

The interplay between the present and the past is central to Ibrahim's works, prompting him to explore and examine archaeology using a variety of materials, bridging a conceived divide between contemporary and ancient cultures, while also questioning ideas around iconoclasm. This interaction with archaeology is significant and speaks to traditions in Arab art that have developed over the course of the last century but, for Ibrahim, it is also deeply tied to learning from our ancestors and from nature. The artist grew up in Khor Fakkan, which has a long history of human habitation and speaks to his connection with the land – "I am carrying this place in my genetics."[3] He often spends days in the wilderness where the experience enables him to search for and collect his materials.

The relationship between the individual and nature has been central to life in the Arabian Peninsula. Historically, a feeling of unity or oneness with the desert and other ancient landscapes provides an understanding of our own existence and mortality in the face of the immensity of nature and histories embedded in these landscapes. Lamenting on the demise of this relationship, Ibrahim states that "They make concrete for skyscrapers. They take the mountain[4] and bring it to the city. Maybe the next generation won't have a mountain anymore… What is gone will never come back."[5] His work calls us to engage with the latent energy and mysteries embedded in the landscape. Through the bareness of its materiality, working with stones, earth, and revealing ancient elemental symbols, he creates hypnotic visual experiences.

The signature shapes in Ibrahim's work are reminiscent of musical notations arranged with patterns in a linear order, an inner vision that flows freely across two-dimensional and three-dimensional surfaces. The patterns engulf the viewer like an unrestrained musical rhapsody. One can almost see these repetitive patterns as prose. The poetic rhythms suggest an existential meditation, which echoes and undulates throughout his practice.[6]

This exhibition and seminal publication celebrate a landmark in Mohamed Ahmed Ibrahim's journey, and brings decades of his practice into the spotlight for both UAE and international audiences. It is an important contribution to the art historiography of the United Arab Emirates.

3. Jones, "Where I Work," 3.
4. Materials for concrete are sourced
    from the mountains.
5. Jones, "Where I Work," 4.
6. Ibrahim was influenced by his
    lifelong friend, the poet Ahmed
    Rashid Thani, who was born the
    same year as Ibrahim in Khor
    Fakkan.

Sunrise

Maya Allison

On Not Knowing

<u>Preamble: Unlearning</u>

Shortly after I settled in the UAE, in 2012, I was touring a studio in Dubai, where a number of different artists stored their work. From a distance, a sculpture in the next room captured my attention. It had a dense texture I'd never seen before. As I approached it, the neutral tones gave way to myriad chromatic variations, compressed in millimeter-sized bits of paper and natural material. This raw papier-mâché sculpture was roughly my own height. It both invited and refused figurative interpretation: not animal, not human, not plant, not architecture, but distinctly intentional, organic, awkward— even gangly. It was clearly constructed by hand.

I asked my host, who said it was by an artist who lives out in the mountains, in a remote area, that he makes work that responds to the landscape, and that he is also a land artist. Based on the work in front of me, I wouldn't have been surprised to learn that the artist was recently out of a rigorous MFA program, an emerging star of the art world. This spare biography conjured a kind of radical hermit, someone wise enough to reject the urban centers of art, but not disconnected from art's pressing questions. I imagined someone with a very serious, informed, and advanced practice.

I got the last half right, at least, but I got a lot wrong—at the time, I could not have imagined the artist I've since come to know: a jovial adventurer and bit of a rebel, former president of the local Harley-Davidson chapter, patriarch of a large family (including many grandchildren to whom he is devoted—along with a small village of cats that live in his studio). All this and: one who has spent the better part of four decades developing an intensely experimental and prolific art practice—ever more on the rise—as part of a community of artists who share his unflinching commitment to, and joy from, their work.

It's not surprising that I could not have guessed what sort of artist would have made this sculpture. In 2012, very few people could have guessed it, given the limited circulation of knowledge about the region's art histories, and, in particular, of the last half century of modern and experimental art practice that flourished in small, intense clusters around the Arabian Gulf.

I have spent my time since that encounter learning about the group of artists around Mohamed Ahmed Ibrahim and also unlearning: deconstructing imported frames of reference, using what helps, discarding the rest. How to parse this sculpture into a coherent narrative? How to situate his practice? The graffiti-derived work of Keith Haring might come to mind, but the comparison might obscure more than elucidate Mohamed's cipher drawings —and yet the formal parallels exist.[1] Minimalism and Land Art are also

1. One writer, who clearly admired Mohamed's work, referred to him as "the Keith Haring of the desert"—that formulation, "the X of Y" is meant as an honor, yet can have an unintended effect of causing the reader to tick a box of recognition and dismiss the work as already understood.

relevant formal terms but smuggle in frames of reference that cannot capture a vast range of content and meaning from the work's milieu. The first hurdle is how not to under-interpret the practice of Mohamed Ahmed Ibrahim.

An example: on the one hand, Mohamed is wholly aware of the field of Land Art, and embraces the term for some of his work. On the other, he started making Land Art before having heard there was such a movement[2]—when he did, it was a positive "eureka" moment of discovering his fellow land artists. But comparing his landscape interventions to that of the "canonical" land artists only partially reveals what he is doing. His work derives first from his direct experience of, and dialogue with, the landscape, and often from its archaeology, but also from reflecting on the nature of sacred structures and his readings in psychology and philosophy. He deliberately makes way for his unconscious, working from what he refers to as "the memory drum" of childhood, in particular the pre-language phase.

<u>Situating</u>

First, to un-situate: Mohamed Ahmed Ibrahim both is and is not an "outsider" artist, and is and is not a "self-taught" artist. However, these categories don't translate well into his context.

Strictly speaking, Mohamed does fit the definition of an "outsider" artist: he did not attend formal art school, and—until recently—did not show in institutional contexts recognized by global art centers, institutions that render artists "insiders." And yet, he is the ultimate UAE "insider": working in the vanguard of the UAE's vibrant art scene since the 1980s.

For the first two decades of his career, he showed annually at the Emirates Fine Arts Society in Sharjah, and was in every Sharjah Biennial, where he regularly won awards. He also showed in exhibitions, from Moscow to Havana to Dhaka, with a few appearances in European shows organized around art from the UAE. Then, in the last decade, the UAE's cultural infrastructure grew and became increasingly legible to the biennale-hopping, English-language art world mainstream.[3] Those institutional developments enabled his work to become more visible: now with commercial gallery representation, and substantial exhibitions in the UAE's rising new institutions, his work is collected by multiple museums, here and abroad.

Therefore, I propose to dismiss the term altogether, except to acknowledge that he worked largely "outside" of North American and European art centers until recently. The term "outsider artist" simply isn't built for his context.

2. This sequence—of making and only later naming the activity's outcome as art—turns an art historian's question into something more philosophical: before he discovered the category of Land Art when he was already making interventions in the landscape, what was he doing? He tells me this applies, in fact, to all of his art. He said that he and Hassan Sharif would postulate that none of what they did was art; they weren't artists. "Art" is just a word, "artist" is just a name that allowed them the freedom to pursue whatever it was they were doing, and to identify more of their kindred.

3. For more on the UAE's cultural institutions and their legibility to the non-Gulf art world, see my essay "The Role of an Art Institution: The UAE's Cultural Infrastructure, 1971–2021," in *Art of the Emirates*, Vol. II, ed. Melissa Gronlund (Abu Dhabi: ADMAF, 2022), 140–144.

4. For more on the evolution of this term and this group, see also: Maya Allison, ed., "Introduction," in *But We Cannot See Them: Tracing a UAE Art Community, 1988–2008* (Abu Dhabi: Akkadia Press, 2017), 1–11.

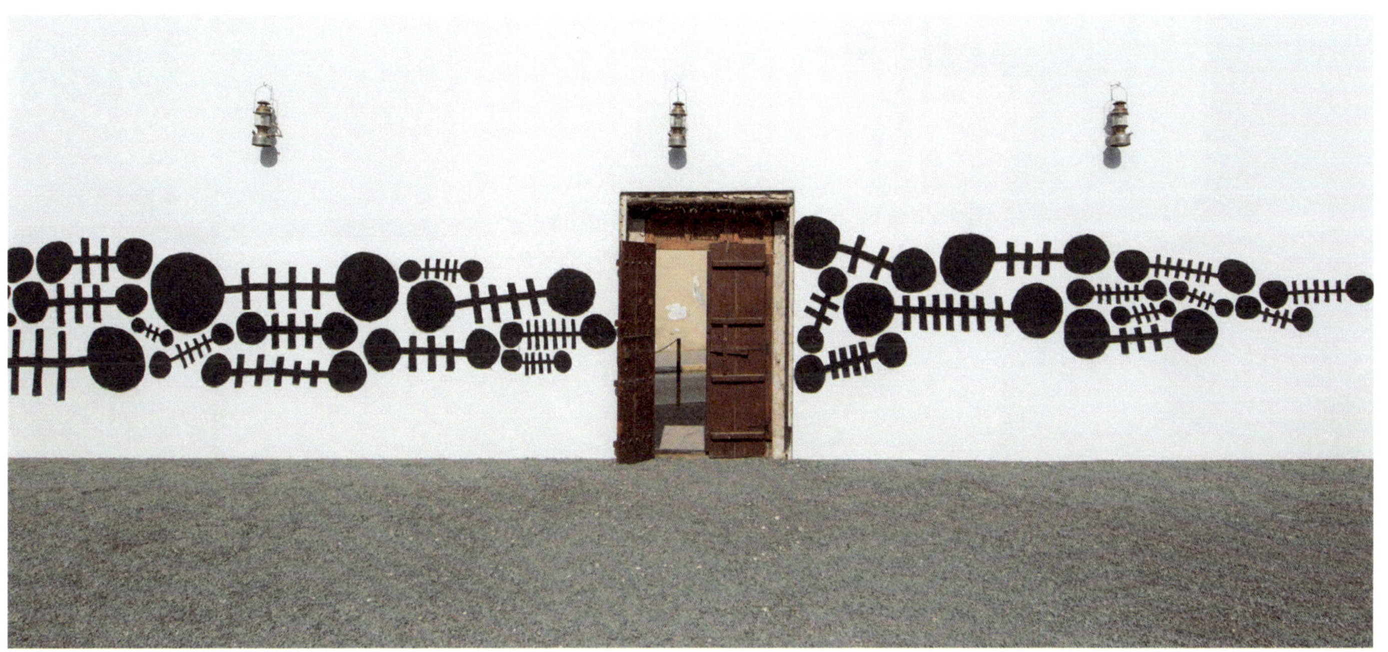

Moving from the term "outsider" to "self-taught": this term is also not wholly accurate. When an entire community of artists bands together around learning, experimentation, and artistic growth, one cannot really call them self-taught. They teach each other. If anything, I am reminded of the spirit of Black Mountain College, an experimental, short-lived college in the United States that espoused a non-hierarchical curriculum, such that educators and students were investigating art and ideas together.

Mohamed is part of a distinct group of artists historically referred to as "the five."[4] The term originated with the 2002 exhibition *5/U.A.E.* at Ludwig Forum für Internationale Kunst (Aachen, Germany). This group is embedded in a tightly knit circle of creative practitioners. Mohamed describes his community as all mentoring one another, and indeed, each brought distinct knowledge to the group. Hassan Sharif had studied art in London and particularly responded to the work of Marcel Duchamp, Joseph Beuys, and Fluxus—and it is through this lens that the work of this community is most frequently interpreted. Hassan's brother Hussain studied theater scenography in Kuwait. Mohammed Kazem studied music and is a proficient *Oud*-player. Abdullah Al Saadi studied English but also spent a year looking at traditional art in Japan. Vivek Vilasini brought knowledge of art from his own community in India, which included then-emerging artist Anish Kapoor. Jos Clevers came from a curatorial role in the Netherlands and was an artist himself, in search of non-European perspectives on art. Mohamed's studies took him from Pakistan where he explored archaeology to Al Ain (UAE) where he studied psychology, and where, in the early 1980s, he started connecting with poets and artists, and his artist journey really began.

It was art that brought this group into contact, the code by which they recognized their fellow travelers, and around which they formed bonds.

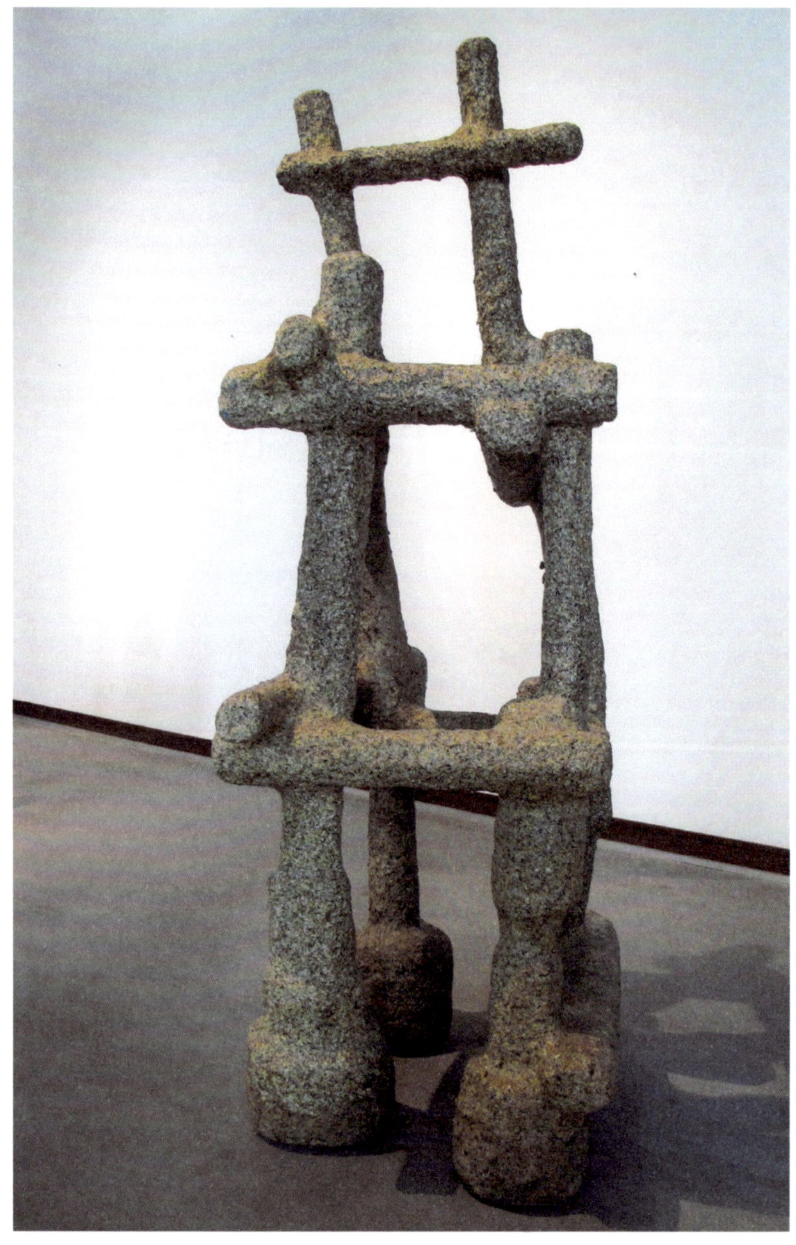

They shared knowledge, ideas, art materials, and books. To give the reader some flavor: Heidegger was important, but also the medieval philosophical text of Ikhwan al-Safa,[5] among numerous other philosophers, art theorists, and poets. Regular exchange and critique were central activities of this community, starting in the 1980s.

Along with "outsider," I propose to dismiss the term "self-taught" as well, and opt for describing his education instead as largely extra-institutional, intensive, non-hierarchical, and ongoing. It is a kind of learning for which we still need a term but is a far cry from the autodidact or naive artist.

5. "The Brethren of Purity" (*Ikhwān Al-Ṣafā*) was a secret society of Muslim philosophers active in Basra, Iraq, in the ninth or tenth century. Their esoteric teachings and philosophy are expounded in the *Encyclopedia of the Brethren of Purity*, a compendium of 52 epistles that would greatly influence later encyclopedias.

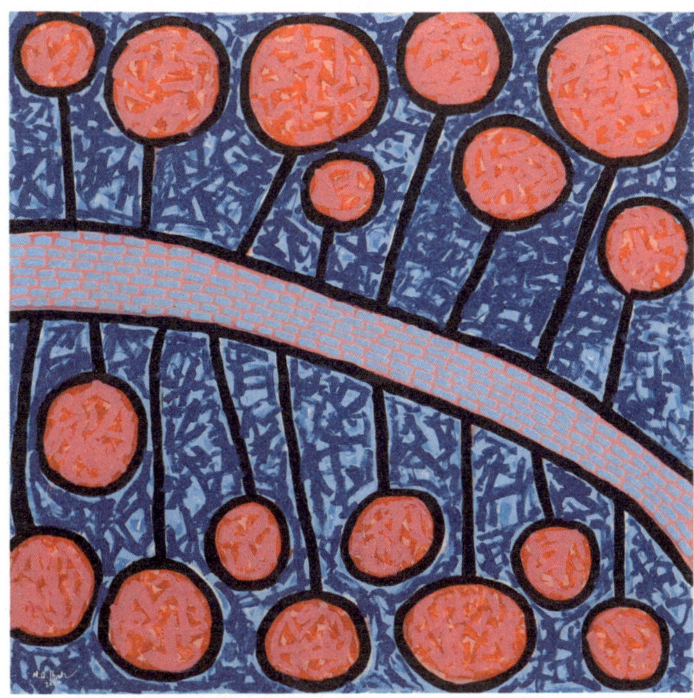

Metamorphosis

The sculpture I encountered in 2012 is titled *Tower* (2012). Mohamed barely titles work, preferring to let the viewer find their own narrative. With that word "tower" the sculpture takes on a resemblance to the *barjeel*—the jutting wind tower that brings cool air down into a traditional house in the region. Like the *barjeel*, Mohamed's tower also has protrusions from each corner, where the branches crisscross, stack, and tie together to make a rough rectangle. At one point, he may have confirmed that the tower referred to a *barjeel*. When asked again about the title, however, he says it refers to the towers along Sheikh Zayed Road—a highway lined with Dubai's famous skyscrapers. A productive reading of this sculpture emerges when both interpretations of "tower" are in play: in the viewer's mind, the scale shifts from human- to skyscraper-scale, but also from traditional clay-and-wood construction to urban engineering, glass, concrete, and steel.

From *barjeel* to skyscraper: that visceral, dizzying metamorphosis in our imagination frequently accompanies sustained viewing of Mohamed's work. A recent painting series includes shapes like close-ups of flower petals and stamen, but that, with a tilt of the head, now looks like city maps with housing developments and cul-de-sacs, looping highways and dotted lines down the road. The branches sprouting from apparent tree sculptures recall one of his earliest paintings of a barren tree (1987, p. 28). Viewed alongside his *Sitting Man* series (2010–2015, pp. 150–151), the fingers of the sitting man might form a visual rhyme with the fingers of the tree, awkwardly extending from round bare trunks.

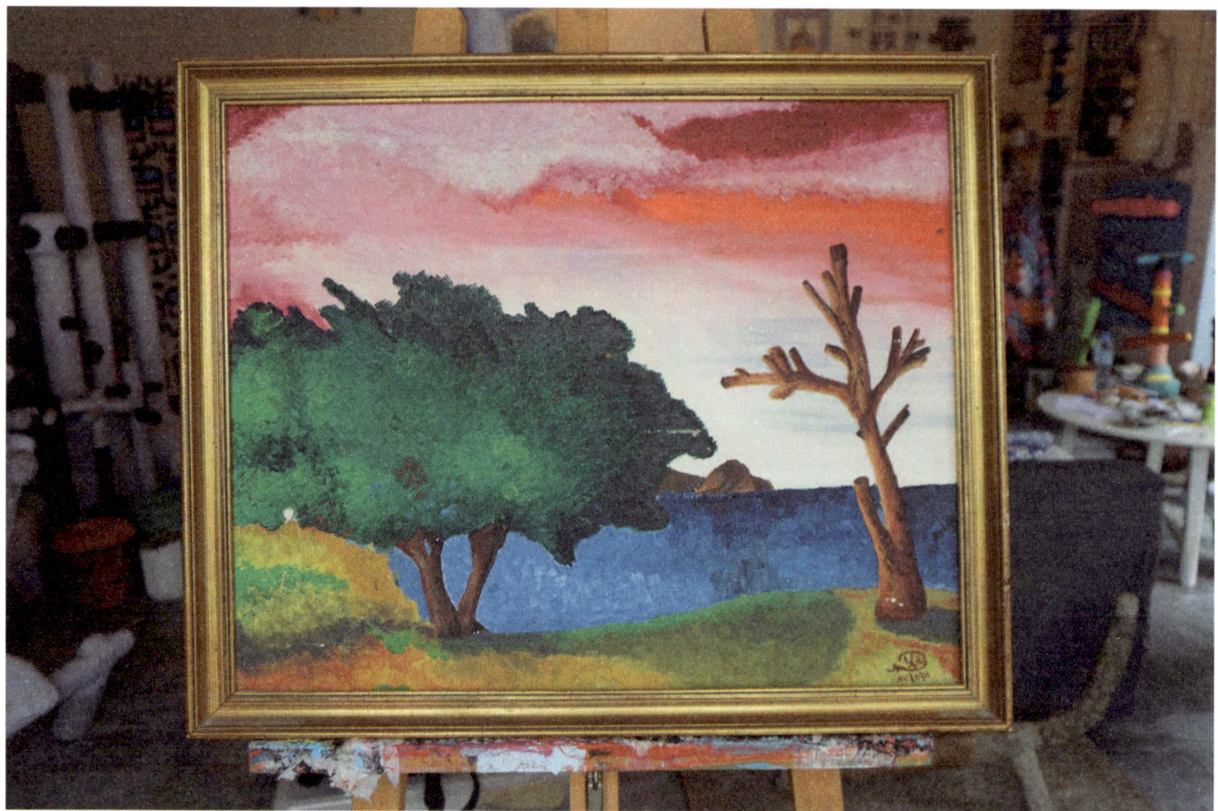

Landscape, 1987
Oil on canvas, 40 x 50 cm

Of course, we might also interpret his work's morphing effect through the lens of his country's transformation. The UAE has undergone a radical metamorphosis in the half century since its formation. It has fast-tracked a mission to develop infrastructure on all fronts, transforming unpaved desert roads to complex, flower-shaped highway systems, with the human infrastructure to match: new educational, medical, legal, financial, and cultural institutions.

The shock of the UAE's single-generation change is perhaps most visible at the level of Mohamed's day-to-day experience: when he was a child, the water delivery person drew tally marks on the wall by the gate of their clay house, indicating how many jugs of water were to be paid for. Mohamed's countless drawings of lines can look like tally marks, echoing those hand-drawn rows of counting, but also abstracted lines of text—bits of pure narrative. Simultaneously, in that way that his work morphs in our mind's scale, his lines can echo rows and rows of windows in a building—and then a city street full of them, windows filling today's urban landscape. Lines for water jugs delivered to the clay house, lines for steel and glass windows—where water is still delivered in bottles but also in plumbing systems.

Throughout the artist's work, one finds this characteristic of expansive elasticity, allowing the viewer to bring their own interpretation from micro to macro and back, but also reflecting the quality of transmutation that suffuses the past half century of the nation, and, with it, the artist's own lived experience.

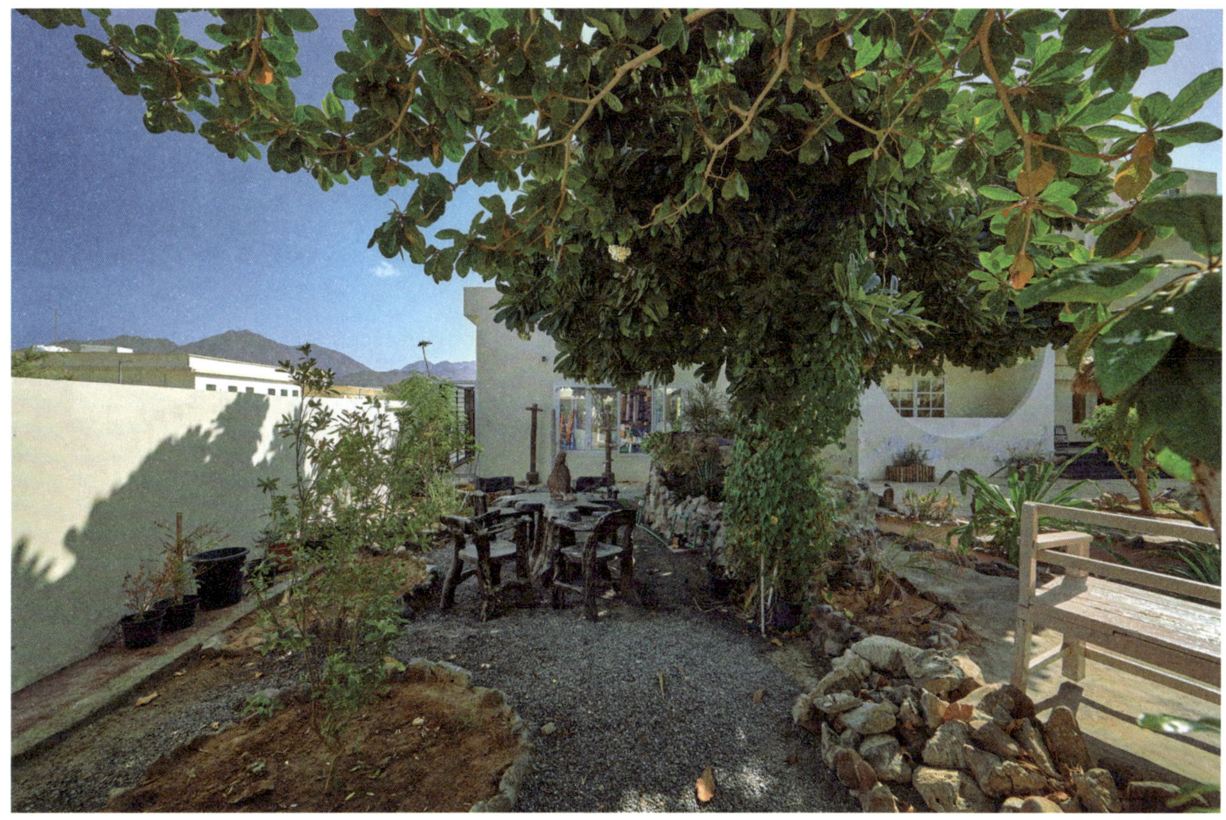

A view of Mohamed's studio
from the garden, 2022

Cultivation

At the core of the *Tower* sculpture, under its layers of papier-mâché, is a skeleton of cardboard, rolled and bound together at the joints. The soft bindings allow the skeleton to shift and adjust to the weight of the papier-mâché that Mohamed applies. This process is the same as that used for the series of sculptures for his Venice installation. These three-dimensional forms are an expression of his hands: he feels his way around the structure, adding material and changing the color of the papier-mâché where it seems good to do so. He never paints the work but instead changes the color of paper he uses to make his medium. The process is one of accretion, building up, adjusting, adding limbs and material until the form comes into its own and feels done. Another, earlier work from the series, *Animal* (2008), leans precariously to the side and seems to defy gravity—surely, it's about to fall. He explains that this piece shifted its weight to the side partway through the making while the papier-mâché was still wet. He collaborates with these shifts as he guides the work, and the work finds its own personality.

This process all happens in his studio—once a tiny garage, now a large dedicated space—on the grounds of his family home. It's a large house surrounded by walls, built in a style that enlarges the traditional regional house structure and gives it a Mediterranean silhouette (today, houses here are almost universally called "villas"). It is home to several generations, the youngest of which plays just beyond the studio windows, periodically riding tricycles through his forests of sculpture and painting.

Also, outside his studio window, a huge tree spreads its shade across a phenomenal garden. These plants—or rather, his relationships to them—are important to his practice on multiple levels. They speak to his bonds with others and his working process.

That tree spreading its umbrella across the garden grew from a clipping given to Mohamed by Hassan Sharif. Inspired by Vivek Vilasini, Hassan had dug up his concrete courtyard and planted a garden, which flourished and filled Hassan's space during the period of Vivek's tenure in the UAE (1990s). The work of gardening connected these artists, alongside the work of art-making, and sometimes it was one and the same: decades later, Mohamed went to work with Vivek on an agricultural art project in India for a period of months.

Under "Hassan's tree" is another plant that thrives in the desert and from which Mohamed has given clippings to many visitors (including to the editors of this book, Cristiana de Marchi and Alaa Edris; the one he gifted me in 2016 now has offspring living with other creatives in my community). Near the edge of the garden is another tree that has a relationship to his mother. Here, every plant has a story.

The garden's personality reflects that of the work in his art studio—joyous, jaunty, poignant, awkward, magnificent. I once asked if his artwork is inspired in part by the plants outside his window, so many of which bear a striking resemblance to his branching sculptures. No. In fact, he also shapes the garden. The word he uses in Arabic is *tahdhib* (translating to grooming, pruning, or cultivating: refine, discipline, correct, polish). Mohamed describes his method of shaping his plants, a process that mirrors that of his art-making: he responds to the plants as they grow, adjusting and changing their form. He describes one that would normally spread out, but "with the passage of the years, I guide the plant to where I want it to go. I wrap it, I guide it— I don't leave it."[6]

At first impression, this act of *tahdhib* might seem to contradict the free-wheeling, direct connection with nature for which Mohamed and his work are known. Over our visits together, I watched him work in his garden, then his studio, then with his cats, his grandchildren, then his garden again. All of it has some *tahdhib* involved, but also, these areas all shape each other—less him dominating nature, more him as part of that continuum, as neighboring trees bend and grow around one another to reach for light.

For the development of his project for Venice, *Between Sunrise and Sunset*, he began with the color palette, moving from color to black and white. Then the forms: he envisioned a cluster of sculptures that would fill the space. But what form should the sculpture take? He worked on the sculptures, a series

6. When the artist is directly quoted in this essay, it comes from an interview conducted over several days in June 2021. It was conducted partly in Arabic, in collaboration with Alaa Edris, and translated here by Ban Kattan.

that initially suggested human forms: hip joints, legs, giant height. He describes how "In the beginning, the figures looked like they were going to be like people. As I started the work, I found that, no, it has become a forest, as the figures were becoming trees." The metamorphosis of vision, of shift in scale, not only occurs in the mind of the viewer, but in the process of the artist in the course of his work. In most cases, he works without a sketch, without a pre-planned structure, and, as he puts it, "without dogma." The interpretation—and the way to install it—transforms and unfolds in its making.

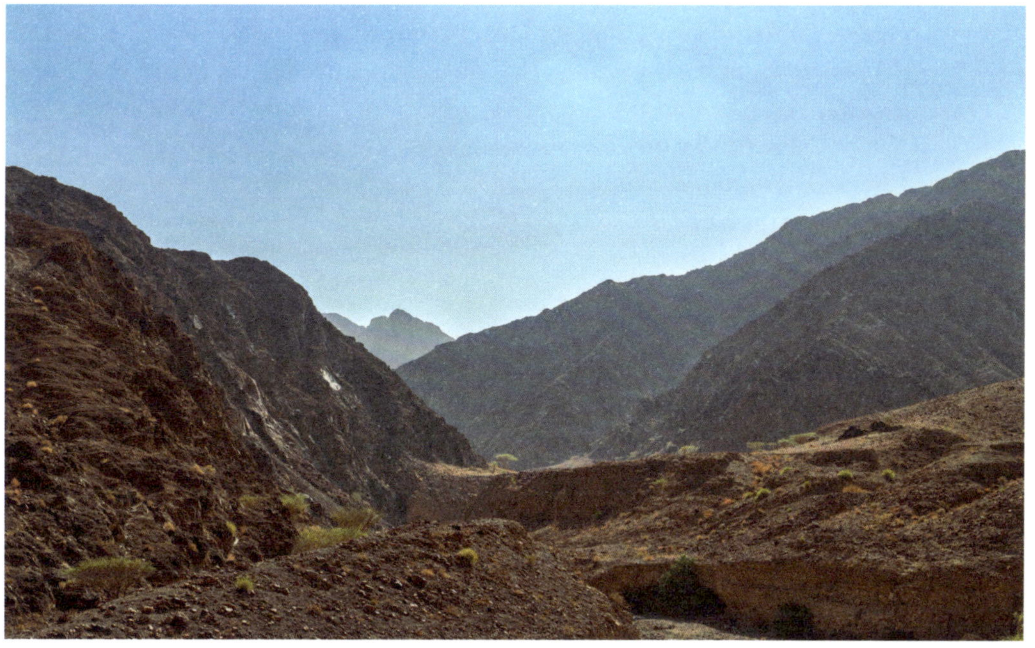

A view of the Al Hajar Mountains

Origins

Beyond the walls of Mohamed's home is the town of Khor Fakkan, which encircles a bay that lets out on the Gulf of Oman. The town is ringed on three sides by the steep and rocky Al Hajar Mountains and their high desert landscape. On the peak of one such mountain is a fort, built to look out to sea, as Mohamed puts it, "watching for the Portuguese," who attempted to control the surrounding Gulf passage during the later 1500s.

Mohamed's family has been here for generations. He spent his early childhood in a traditional house near the mosque on the south end of the waterfront. That house was made from clay and stones, the clay floor whitewashed, halfway up the walls, with a powder from India, the same material used to waterproof boat hulls—called *noura* in Arabic. Electricity arrived partway through his childhood.

His father worked in a seafaring trade. Eventually, as a ship pilot for the British military, he relocated the family across the water to Kuwait for most of Mohamed's grade school years. There, art classes were part of the school curriculum, and Mohamed became skilled at drawing and painting, which, in turn, became part of his social identity, as classmates and teachers asked him to draw maps and illustrations. These were representational, figurative works.

He recalls the return from his childhood in Kuwait, by boat: the mountains made a profound impression on him rising from the sea, imposing, over the port-town of Khor Fakkan. That mountain range figures in his work on multiple fronts and in the title of his project for the UAE Pavilion at the Venice Biennale: *Between Sunrise and Sunset*. The sun rises over the town of Khor Fakkan from the Indian ocean in the Gulf of Oman. By mid-afternoon, the mountains block the sun, and the town remains in shadow until night falls—they never see the color of sunset.

A restless teenager exploring these mountains and Khor Fakkan of the 1970s would have had regular encounters with structures and traces of history and pre-history. The seemingly barren rocky mountain landscape holds dozens of bronze-age petroglyph or rock art[7] clusters in the *wadis*[8] that lead to the Khor Fakkan port—humans have been making art and proto-writing here for millennia. Just north of the town stands the Al Bidya Mosque, once thought to be the oldest in the UAE, estimated to date from the fifteenth century and restored well after Mohamed's teenage years. It was built from rocks, coral, wadi sand, palm leaves, and mudbrick. In the surrounding landscape, remnants of the Portuguese occupation include piles of rocks as well as grooves in the ground outlining the traces of the former fort.

All these elements played a backdrop to his coming of age, only to re-emerge decades later in his work, transformed. The petroglyphs, the mud-walled mosque, the ruins, and their traces all resonate in his symbol-like forms, earthy materials, and construction techniques. Sometimes, as he puts it, he realizes how something is connected to his history only after he's made the work. He acknowledges the connection in a matter-of-fact way as part of his larger dialogue with the world.

7. The petroglyphs in this area are thought to date from the Bronze age. Michele Ziolkowski has conducted sustained study of the petroglyphs in the surrounding mountains and does a close reading of the forms as rock art in her paper, "A study of the petroglyphs from Wadi al-Hayl, Fujairah, United Arab Emirates" in the journal *Arabian Archaeology and Epigraphy*, 1998, https://www.academia.edu/4761924/A_study_of_the_petroglyphs_from_Wadi_al-Hayl_Fujairah_United_Arab_Emirates_1. Recently, studies of the wider Gulf region's petroglyphs have made a case for them as eventually evolving into writing—it's unclear if the Al Hajar Mountain petroglyphs are part of this group: https://www.arabnews.com/node/1997576/art-culture

8. Ravines that are dry except during rainfall.

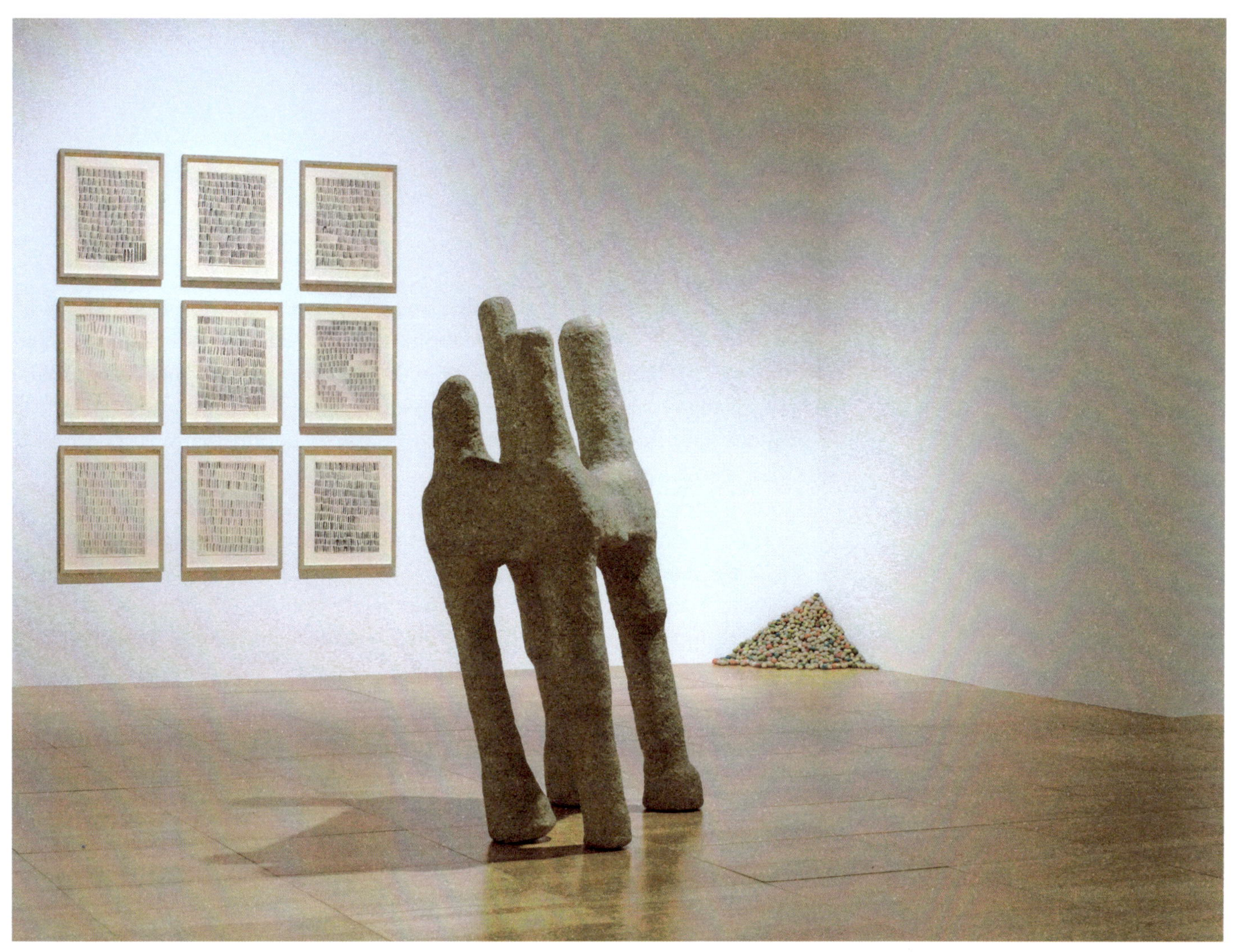

Installation view of *But We Cannot
See Them: Tracing a UAE Art
Community, 1988–2008*, 2017,
at The NYUAD Art Gallery

<u>When the Shapes Come to Life</u>

Over almost four decades, Mohamed's work has matured, characterized
by a deepening trust in his own specific methods, which include his direct
response to his environment. Each time he leaves the *wadis* and petroglyphs
of the Arabian peninsula to spend time in other parts of the world, his work
undergoes a distinct change: it picks up the tones and textures of his new
studio, of the landscape around him, of the streets outside his window, and
of the materials and people he finds there. His work might develop into
performance, installation, collage, conceptual work, land art, or sculpture.
It might become bright and colorful or muted and earthy. It might look
busy and dense, or spare and minimal. All of this adaptation is part of his
practice, which is fueled by a gestural dialogue connecting his materials,
his perception of form, and his surroundings.

His trust in the nature of his practice was an early discovery that paralleled
his emerging identity as an artist. There is a distinct "before" and "after"
in this emergence. As a child in Kuwait, his art-making included figurative
paintings and drawings and, remarkably, a cinema box for which he charged
admission. Then, he abandoned these things as childish until returning to
Khor Fakkan in high school. There, he and three other students who were

identified as talented artists painted and illustrated school projects. They even raised a protest at one point about having to paint the same things year after year. Mohamed tells this story with great verve and humor, as he does with his many tales of adventure as a young artist. The protest took place on a bus, and the school authority to whom it was addressed was speechless with anger. As Mohamed tells it:

> Then he said something I still remember to now, [imitating shouting] "Is the donkey you drew last year the same as the donkey you drew this year?" [laughing] It was a polite way to curse at us, but he really made me think. He made me think, "Oh Mohamed, the donkey you drew last year is really not similar to the donkey you drew this year" [goes back to laughing]. This is a memory I can't forget. These end up accumulating into something else. Through this phrase, a concept subconsciously and involuntarily formed in my head that art indeed had a function. The donkey was indeed different [laughs], so there is indeed a message here.

Then, when the art curriculum ceased, so did his painting. He had been a talented draughtsman, but, looking back on this pre-college period, he felt that in the end, "you find you are not [an] artist and what you're doing is not art. Simple like that. I did not understand what art could mean for me until later."

A few years into college, the longing for art stirred him to read literature and write poetry. Here, he began forming bonds of the kind that would come to nourish his art in the years ahead, beginning with the poet Ali Al Andal, with whom he would discuss philosophy texts they were reading. He describes how, after 1983, "This nostalgic yearning began for the form of art I knew before. So, I started reading books about art: the history of art, books about artists, and so on. I started to develop a cognitive reservoir on art."

As he tells it, in college, his study of psychology also led him forward to art:

> There are many things in psychology that are close to art's rhetoric. In 1984, I started painting. The beginnings were on paper, using coal, etc. I told myself to go back to painting a little… I heard that Yaser Dweik had a workshop through a small classroom he established to teach art techniques. So, I went there to take a few workshops with him: the foundations, the techniques of oil, acrylic, pastel, and so on. I loved the process, selecting materials and experimenting. I started to implement that in Al Ain, I was painting there using oil colors and pastels. At first, I drew figures. I used to draw women's faces, the faces of sad women, happy women, and so on. I imitated paintings as much as I could. I began to notice that I was deviating from the imitations, automatically.

I especially noticed this when I first began using gouache paints, which were only recently available in the early 1980s. Gouache on paper would give me this different type of flow.

When he noticed how the gouache paint distorted the paper, he allowed the process to lead the form away from figurative representation and into abstraction. This pivotal moment instigated the journey to his current practice: he began finding non-representational forms through gesture.[9] From there, he developed his early abstract paintings, where lines swoop through squares and around circles (see p. 148). He describes a distinct difference in that new mental state, making abstract forms, and a particular "desire and joy" when abandoning representation and moving into abstraction:

> Because I am doing this for myself only… So, this shape may be unpopular with the others or become a barrier for them. For example, I used to draw camels. It is known that it is a camel, and people would come and say, "Oh, you made his hump this way, if you could so and so…" But when the viewer stands before a form he does not recognize, this connection is lost because he doesn't know what it is. (And I don't mean the exhibition viewer as there was no exhibition, I mean the viewers that came to visit me). This, however, made me grow closer to myself. Going back to the idea of feeling different than your peers and so on. Going back, this is what I'm doing now. I'm different, it's up to you to like it or not, this is the real question.

He particularly valued the dual mental process that was both psychological and physiological:

> The psychological is where your brain starts creating spontaneous shapes and dissociates what you're drawing from what you're thinking. Then, there is the physiological aspect, which is the space between your eyelid and pupil. This is where these shapes come to life, and this depends on the time of day, the lighting that is around you, how hard you close your eyes or squint.

This shuttling among the visceral experience of the world, his own physical eyes, and the abstract conceptual forces at work in his mind would play out over the course of his work for years to come. The notion of what he has elsewhere called "the space between the eyelid and the eye" does also, of course, overlap with the concept of the Venice project: describing the space between sunrise and sunset. The spaces under the eyelid and between the earth and sky are equally unmeasurable, and his phrasing invites us out of dualities, short-circuiting our standards of measure.

9. He had read about ideas and concepts of abstraction in philosophy, and he had an early, formative encounter with a reproduction of Picasso's *Guernica*, but abstract art was not part of his milieu growing up—nor does he view Islamic design as an influence.

It was also in this period, as a psychology major in college, that he returned to the drawings, or scribbles, from the margins of his high school notebooks. These he began to develop and refine, intentionally, into the forms he now calls *rumouz* in Arabic—usually translated as "symbols" but, here it is closer to "cipher" or "sign." (We have agreed to call them ciphers.) As he developed the cipher forms, he recognized their relationship to the petroglyphs he had grown up with:

> Here, I connected that to psychology. Surely, these shapes are coming from somewhere else? I started to go back in memory to the (petroglyph) etchings we have in Khor Fakkan. Shapes I grew up seeing, and so on… For psychology, working with my cipher forms, the area of thinking that lights up is a different part [of the brain] that has nothing to do with the drawing or the shape. It's not like when I'm drawing a flower. When I draw a flower, my brain would be focused [on representation]. However, when I'm drawing the ciphers, it wouldn't be… The shape is formed involuntarily.

Ultimately, these ciphers are not letters or glyphs of any kind. "I am not trying to invent or produce a language… It's not a language—because of the randomness." At most, he would allow that they are his own spontaneous rendering of a scene, encrypted in its most minimal abstract form, but never intended for decryption:

> When the viewer sees these ciphers (and the viewer is a very important partner), reading them becomes the function of the viewer: seeing a collection of shapes. He has the great freedom to read it as a story or novel or poetry. It can even be used to reach a state of meditation. It's also possible to see it as nothing, like a bunch of scribbles. As a result, this becomes the viewer's relationship to the work, not mine.

On the one hand, Mohamed has liberated his process from requiring the approval of general society. On the other, he experiences deep personal gratification in the work's making and, ultimately, to the connections it makes possible with the viewer and other artists:

> In art, you search for the others who are also different, similar to you. You may find someone like you in the States, another in the UK, another similar to you in Asia, and so on. Ultimately, this becomes your quest; this is what art is. Therefore, you are an artist because you are connecting to—communicating with—artists. What you present is a message that is read within the context of art. The art allows you to find your kind.

By 1986, Mohamed had embarked on what today remains a defining activity of his art career: this spontaneous, non-representational exploration of form, inspired by the psychology and physiology of sight. His college classmate, the poet Ali Al Andal, knew the artist Hassan Sharif, and, after Al Andal saw the paintings Mohamed had started making, he organized a trip to see Hassan's solo show at the Emirates Fine Arts Society. Once Mohamed met Hassan, it was only a matter of time until the full "group of five" had found each other, all working toward individual new visions of what could be possible through art.

As I've explored in other essays,[10] this group was embedded in, and nourished by, a much larger group of writers and poets, theater artists, and musicians, who were profoundly important to the development of one another's practices. By way of example: Khor Fakkan gave rise to two members of the group of five: Mohamed is one, Abdullah Al Saadi is the other. Abdullah's work is completely different from Mohamed's but equally original and profound and in direct dialogue with his surroundings. The poet Ahmed Rashid Thani also lived there and worked in the Khor Fakkan public library. Some compare him to Hassan in terms of his importance to the Gulf's art community and the groundbreaking experimentation in his work. He made possible Mohamed's studio at the library, which was shared with Abdullah. All three of them had friendships with Hassan, a few hours' drive away in Dubai.

This community's exchange was particularly intense in the 1980s and 1990s when the artists were developing quickly, but the opportunities for exhibitions and art events were few. The 1990s is when the now-legendary "Sand Palace" (*Qasr Al-Raml*) came into being. The term Sand Palace referred to a particular sand dune that was the site of gatherings, but also to people who gathered there, forming a creative community—"the Sand Palace Group." One of those was the poet Abdulaziz Aljassim, whom Mohamed credits for naming his fabric-wrapped trees series, in Arabic, as *Ashjar Muqammasha* (translating a sense of "textiled trees").

10. Allison, ed., "Introduction," in *But We Cannot See Them*, 1–11; and Maya Allison, ed., *Artists and the Cultural Foundation: The Early Years* (Abu Dhabi: Department of Culture and Tourism, 2018).

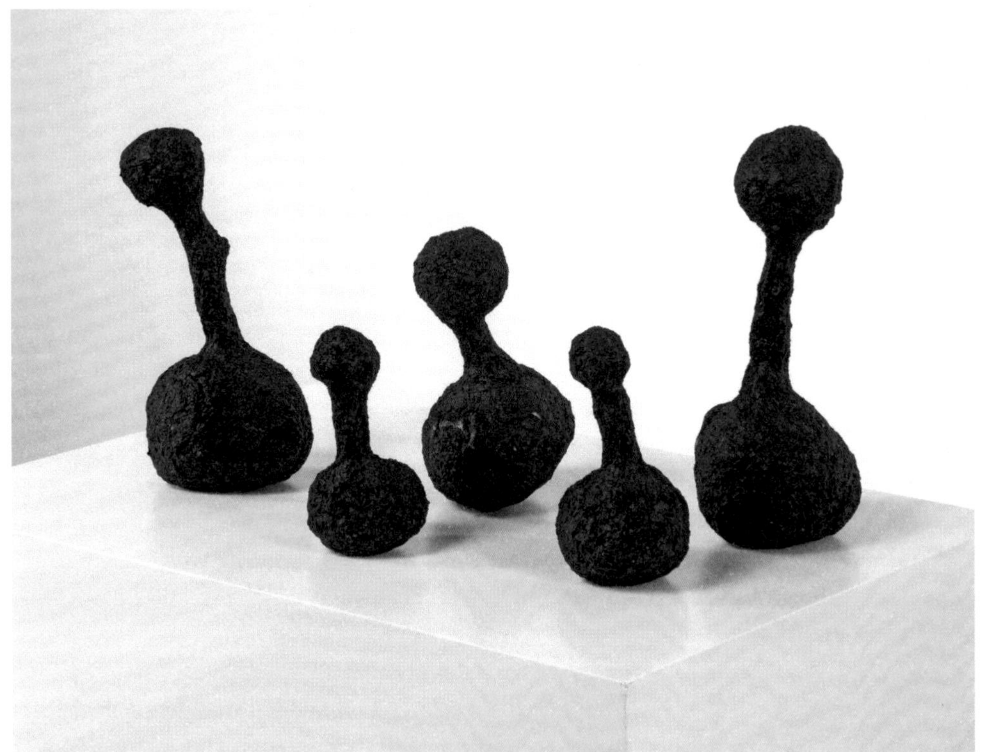

From Point to Plane

Mohamed developed his first intentionally abstract forms out of his experiments with the movement of gouache across the page. Alongside that, he developed his ciphers series from his scribbled, free-form sketching from the pages of his high school notebooks. That 1980s period of discovery and development also saw his growing interest in philosophical art concepts, in particular the relationship between the point and the plane. Mohamed found this concept first in the writings of the Arabic philosophers Ikhwan al-Safa, who develop the idea that a dot begins a line. This image recurs in Arabic philosophy including in the writings of Ibn Sina, who uses it to highlight the role of imagination in human perception.[11] Mohamed also refers to Wassily Kandinsky's book *Point and Line to Plane* (1926), and he's especially fond of Paul Klee's send-up of the idea when Klee writes that "A line is a dot that went for a walk."[12] When Mohamed retells this, he adds his own twist, "The line is coming because the point is going to a picnic!"[13]

Like that dot going to a picnic, from that heady moment when Mohamed began discovering his art process in the mid-1980s, came a stream of developments in his forms and methods. Specific shape typologies recur and evolve throughout the decades that follow: ciphers, circles, flowers, lines, walls—each typology anchors a broad field of artistic experimentation. He develops the shape typologies through strategies of repetition and variation, iteration and discovery, as well as moving across media and context from ink to paint, from rocks to clay, from leaves to papier-mâché. How he engages with his media and strategies shifts with his location, sometimes producing radically different aesthetics. A thumbnail overview might categorize his bodies of work as encompassing Land Art, sculpture and collage, and drawing and painting, as outlined below.

11. My summary of Ikhwan al-Safa and Ibn Sina is taken, with thanks, from discussion with scholar of classical Arabic philosophy, Dr. Taneli Kukkonen.

12. This quote is paraphrased in line with popular usage. For the full quote please see Jürg Spiller, ed. and Ralph Manheim, trans., *Paul Klee Notebooks: The Thinking Eye*, Vol. 1 (London: LH, 1961), 105.

13. Mohamed's appreciation for Paul Klee runs deep. When he first saw his paintings, he felt a jolt of recognition, noticing the cloth Klee was using was the same as that used by Sufis—a kind of jute or burlap fabric Klee would have seen when he traveled to Tunisia and Egypt (as cited on https://www.artic.edu/artworks/134057/exotics, accessed January 17, 2022).

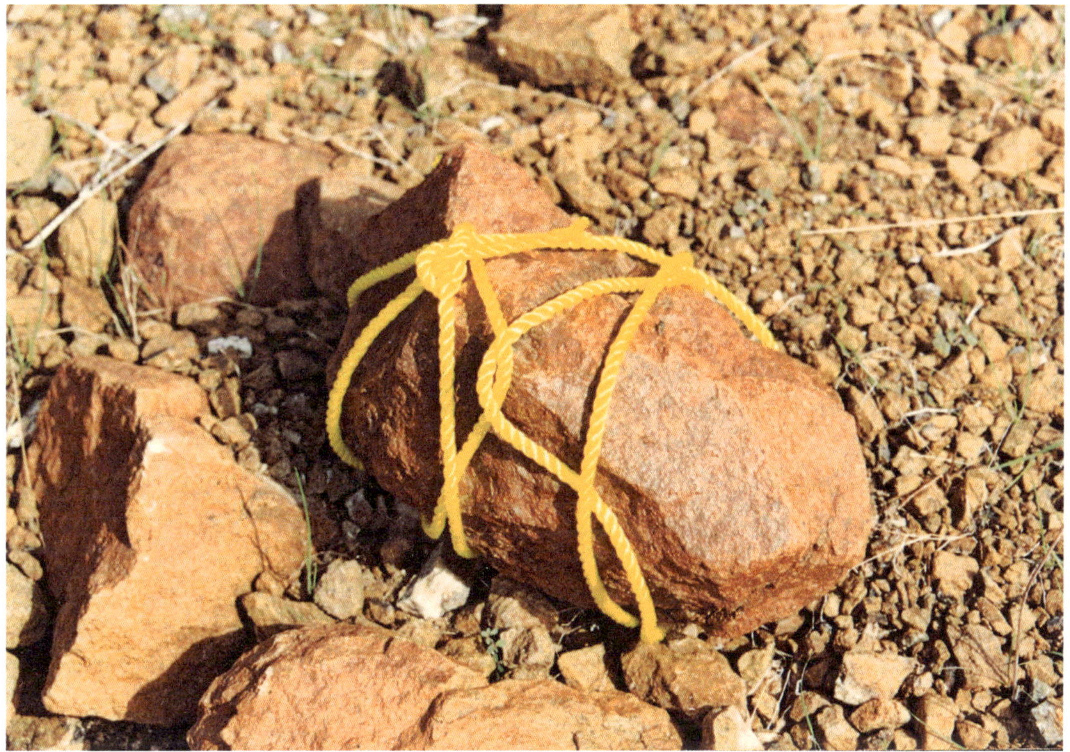

Land Art

Mohamed's earliest moments of Land Art emerged in the 1980s, in parallel with the period of his gouache discovery. While camping in the land around Khor Fakkan, he imagined the rocks he was looking at might never have been touched by human hands: he turned one over. It was light on the other side, the side not burned by the sun. He then went through the landscape, turning rocks over. He describes this gesture as being about ego, man altering land, leaving a mark. This was before he was aware of the term "Land Art"— but where his Land Art began.

In the early 1990s, he took Hassan Sharif to see some of his experiments in the landscape. Hassan exclaimed, "You are making Land Art!" This moment offers a key insight and makes visible an explicit mechanism of discovery and innovation for the group of artists around Mohamed Ahmed Ibrahim and Hassan Sharif. In the moment that Hassan names Mohamed's stone activity as art, he knits him into that art history: suddenly, Mohamed has a new extended family of artist "kin." It was a pivotal revelation for Mohamed, who commenced reading about other land artists. On the other hand, the activity existed before the act of naming, with self-awareness, but without the self-reflexivity. That moment of naming it and the shift into self-reflexivity and intentionality, of course, mark it as "modern" or "contemporary"—as art. However, Mohamed is very clear about this: the impulse that drove that un-named rock-turning was not different from that which drives his other art. Recognizing and dubbing it as "art" simply freed them to do more of it. In turn, it also liberated the word "art" from traditional media.

Two gestures dominate Mohamed's Land Art practice for the first 30 years of his career: displacing and wrapping. The 1980s rock-turning is a gesture of displacing the rocks. Wrapping occurred with both trees and rocks. Early on, he wrapped a series of *Sidr* trees in multi-colored fabric (image pp. 72–73). This gesture reappears through several decades. Then, in 2007, he wrapped hundreds of rocks in copper wire—a metal found naturally in the rocks from Khor Fakkan—and brought the resulting mountain of rocks into the gallery for *Stones Wrapped with Copper Wire* (2007, image pp. 68–69).

Displacing (and re-placing) as a gesture tends to produce circle forms in his Land Art. In 2002, he made a series of circles by displacing rocks across a valley in Khor Fakkan (images pp. 65–67). In 2009, during a visit to Lumière (Brittany, France), he again makes these circles, only this time they are performances, moving rocks and sticks to make a circle, then again by the sea with shells (images p. 221).

Another recurring form resulting from displacing and re-placing is that of a circular rock wall, often held together with clay or mud. In the 1990s, these resembled small fortresses, and sometimes he built them in exhibition venues rather than out in the land. They share a resemblance to what is thought to be an ancient tomb in Khor Fakkan on the top of the Zubara mountain— he is quick to point out that most old rock structures are called tombs, but only because no one knows what they are. Later, he built a monumental series of beehive forms from rocks in that same landscape, *The Qubba Project* (2015, image pp. 78–79). Unlike many of his process-generated works, this one derived from a very intentional course of study of how this shape appears across multiple religions in Asia, particularly India but also on the Arabian Peninsula. This moment in his Land Art development also sheds light on his larger conception of art: he has selected a form with its own history, religious or otherwise, but invites us to see it as pure form, as an artwork— a contemporary motive and reception for the same form. In a sense, at this moment, his Land Art phase ends, as if he has resolved the questions driving it.

After *The Qubba Project*, he did not return to Land Art until 2020 for the *Desert X* exhibition (AlUla, Saudi Arabia), where he installed *Falling Stones Garden*. As he describes it, his feeling toward Land Art had changed: he no longer wanted to disturb the land, so he decided to add to it. He installed a series of 320 imperfect, brightly colored spheres, much like those his hand draws, which joined the fallen stones already at the site (image p. 80).

Next page
Lines, 2014
Paper collage on Kathmandu
paper, 80 x 56 cm

Untitled, 2015
Mixed media on paper, 65 x 50 cm

Sitting Man, 2011
Oil on paper, 47.8 x 35.8 cm

 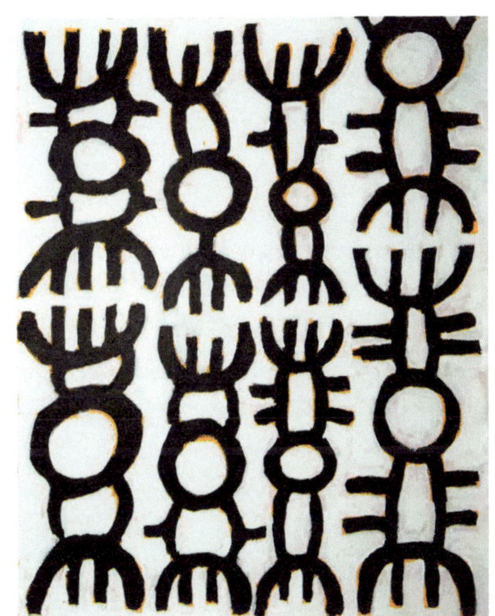 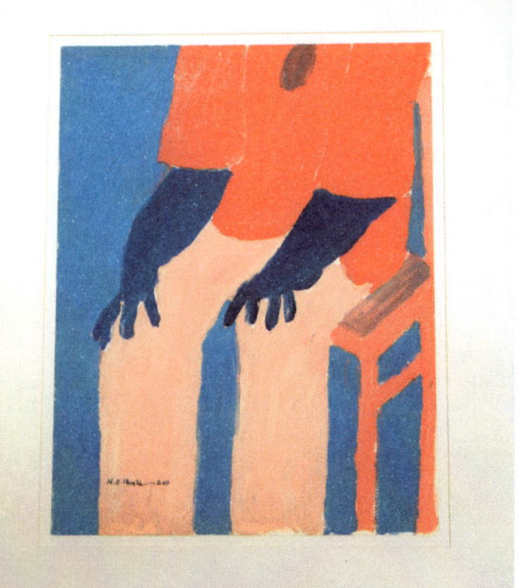

<u>Drawing, Painting: Lines, Ciphers, Sitting Man</u>

In parallel to his Land Art practice, the cipher forms remain a consistent part of Mohamed's work. While working at various office jobs, he filled notebooks with them, in tiny precise script, elaborating the forms in bright, textured paintings, later spreading across large sheets of paper and eventually making their way into sculptural forms. They quickly evolved and became more precise, even within a single notebook (as in the notebook of 1988–89, images pp. 130–131). Some look like a series of male/female symbols; often, they puzzle together in a kind of tessellation, a screen across the entire page. Later, certain ciphers reappear, solo, as large-scale paintings or clusters of just a few. These are not minimalist forms—paint swirls and drips from the brush—but made with extremely reduced, minimal gestures.

Of all of Mohamed's work, only the *Sitting Man* series is figurative (images above and pp. 150–151). It began in 2010 as a result of an accident with a new camera, which produced a photo of Hassan Sharif sitting in a chair, his head cropped out. Hassan and Mohamed had a good laugh. Then, Mohamed made a painting from the photo, copied that painting, and then made dozens, perhaps hundreds, of copies, each copying the last, eventually working from memory. In addition to being color and pattern studies—the color combinations seem endless—the figure of the sitting Hassan becomes increasingly like one of the cipher forms. In later iterations of this painting, the fingers of the hands sprout, bend, and bow very much like the branches of his tree form sculptures.[14]

Alongside the cipher series, the *Lines* series is Mohamed's most sustained "trademark" gesture: line after line, filling page after page of his sketchbooks. Similarly, these also develop into paintings and eventually three-dimensional sculptural form. In Sittard, the Netherlands, where his group has their first

14. The *Sitting Man* series stops exactly in 2015: on December 31, 2015, Mohamed was in Dubai in Hassan's house, painting another *Sitting Man* work. It was midnight: he heard the fireworks and celebrations, and he decided that this *Sitting Man* painting was the last one he would make. He stopped painting at exactly midnight.

exhibition in Europe in 1995, he created an immersive installation, filling the entire room, floor-to-ceiling, with lines of all sizes. Sheets of lines slide and unfurl onto the floor, and black cubes in the center of the room suggest the lines are pushing up three-dimensionally from the floor (image pp. 122–123). The dot and line have become plane and volume.

As mentioned early in this essay, when Mohamed was a child, the water delivery man would leave tally marks on their gate walls, lines drawn with charcoal, indicating the number of water deliveries made. This tally was used to calculate the debt to be paid at the end of the month. Mohamed was captivated by these lines and one day found a piece of charcoal and added lines to the wall, continuing the series already there. Naturally, he got in quite a bit of trouble for multiplying the water bill. One can imagine the frisson, therefore, that drawing lines might carry for him. Even without knowing this anecdote, the electricity of Mohamed's lines comes through, registering the movement of his breath through the movement of his hand. These marks invite rich interpretation. Like text, they come in rows, they fill the page, they are clearly marked by hand. Other times, the effect is closer to that of a stop-motion series of images, shifting from lighter to darker, rippling as your eye "reads" them (image p. 121).

Perhaps the most striking effect of the lines series is how much narrative they suggest: counting, measuring, connecting, and dividing. Sometimes an undulating page of text, sometimes a bank of windows in a high-rise building. And in each window, an imagined story of its residents. The lines, at their root, might best denote civilization: writing and building, reduced into abstraction. If there were a glyph for human civilization, a page of lines just might be it.

One version of the lines comes in palm-sized packets, wrapped with string, hung from sculptures, about the thickness of a pack of cards (as seen hanging from the sculpture in the image at left). It's clear that each small sheet of paper that makes up the pack is filled with lines, but that they can never be seen due to the string binding. Mohamed described the method for making the packets of lines as one that arose out of necessity: he cannot stop working, so if he goes alone to a café, first he cuts up sheets of paper into very small rectangles, which allows him to work at the café without being bothered by people wanting to talk about what he is doing. He thinks of these decks as small books. He eventually realized that they remind him of the small leather-wrapped Quran that his parents attached to him as a child.

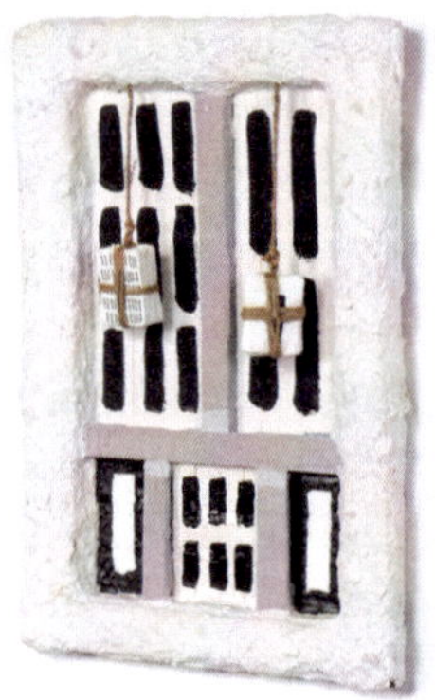

Window, 2016
Mixed media, 46 x 32 x 2 cm

Next page
Khor Fakkan (detail), 2002
Leaf, glue, and clay, dimensions variable

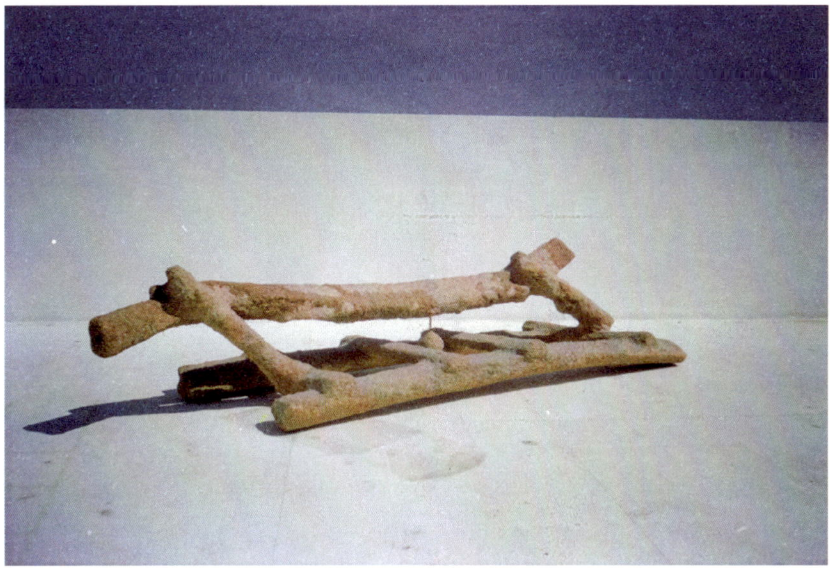

Sculpture

Before *Tower*, Mohamed made a number of sculptures using the building technique seen in *Tower* but with clay instead of papier-mâché, beginning in the early 1990s. He describes feeling close to the materials of clay and leaves. Among the best-known of his works in clay is *Khorfakkan* (2002), made of clay, leaves, grass, paper, and glue.[15] He originally composed it as a three-part sculpture, though the three have since been separated and titles appended of *I, II,* and *III*. Using the most basic building blocks of a structure, as he would later develop with *Animal* and *Tower*, he ties the cylinders across one another to create joints. From the beam of each sculpture is suspended one or two balls of clay, hanging from a string—dipping down almost to the foundation—one might imagine a spit over a fire or a resting ladder. A particularly evocative photograph captures a close-up of one of the joints in the *Khorfakkan* sculpture. Bits of grass and leaves are embedded in the dark orange clay, pressed around a joint that feels as human-animal as it does architectural.

Then, in 2005 there is a dramatic development in Mohamed's work: his earth-based sculptural constructions converge with the bright colors of his paintings and the typology of his geometric cipher series. The installation is also titled *Khorfakkan* (he tells me the name is simply to identify where it was made, while other publications identify it as "Khorfakkan number-2," image pp. 138–139). It is wholly different from the 2002 *Khorfakkan*. Instead of the earlier earthy architectural references to his landscape, here brightly colored geometric shapes interlock across the floor. The cipher forms of his drawings and bright colors from his paintings are now realized in three dimensions. Instead of using clay, he shreds batches of colored paper to produce the desired spectrum for the papier-mâché.

This piece marks the beginning of a sustained sculptural practice and a significant new phase in his work, the precursor of the work presented in his Venice project. A third work, titled *Khorfakkan 2*, appears in 2018: again, the interlocking forms of a square and two circles are joined by a line, but this time, it is in black and white.

15. This work was perhaps his best-known due to its international travel: it premiered in the 2002 seminal exhibition, *5 UAE*, at Ludwig Forum für Internationale Kunst (Aachen, Germany)—the same exhibition that was the source for the name of his group of artists, "the five." The sculptures then appeared in the UAE for the 2003 Sharjah Biennial, and then back to Europe for the 2005 exhibition *Languages of the Desert*, at the Kunstmuseum Bonn (Bonn, Germany), after which the show traveled to Institut du Monde Arabe (Paris, France).

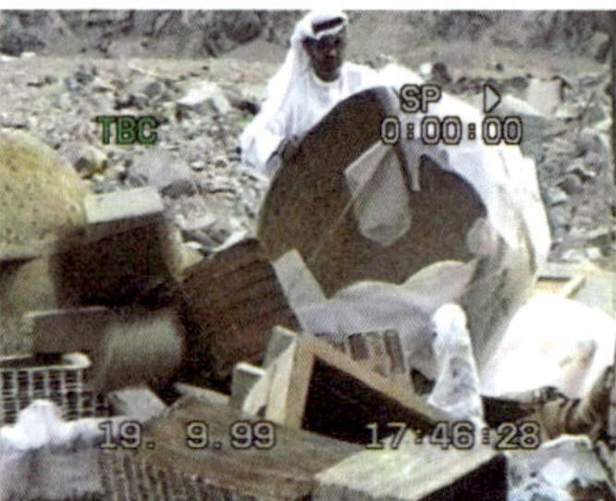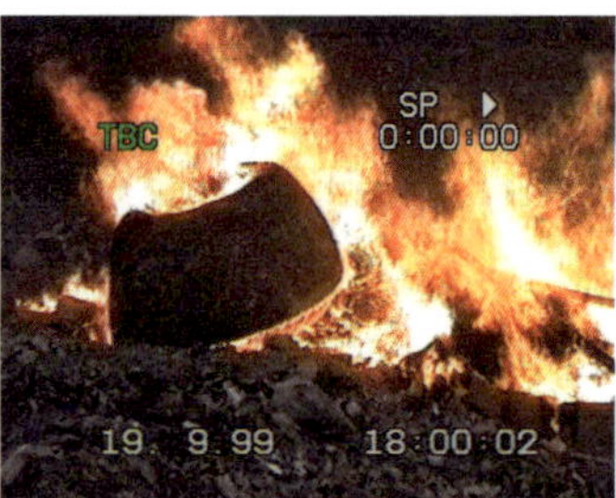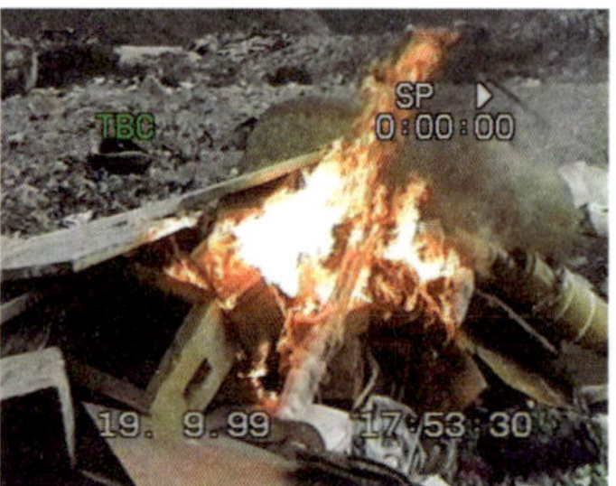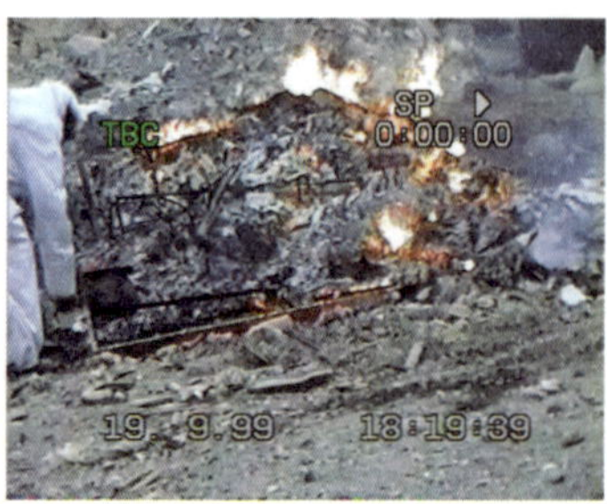

Context

As these techniques and bodies of work developed, Mohamed's community deepened and expanded, and his experience of his practice evolved. In the course of the last 35 years, there were pivotal moments each decade when his art practice went through a sudden growth.

A particularly dramatic pivotal moment occurred in 1999 when he burned most of his artwork. Vivek had recently gone back to India, and Jos to the Netherlands. His job at the local art center had ended, and suddenly he had no storage for his art. Driving two trucks around Khor Fakkan, considering where to put 15 years' worth of art, Mohamed decided to use it for a bonfire in the mountains. The video shows him in a *Kandura*, speaking to the camera with the mountains of his Land Art projects in the background. He douses his work in gasoline, and the video records the burning of the work—much of which can be recognized in the pages of this book.

After 15 years of work had burned, instead of abandoning art, he describes a sense of lightness, positive emptiness, and discovering that he is free to move forward: he made a new painting 30 minutes later. Soon after that, his work took a clear turn in the direction that we know today. In the decade that followed, the emergence of The Flying House venue further invigorated his practice. Then: Hassan Sharif passed away in the fall of 2016, while Mohamed was at a residency in Kochi, India. This period was a moment of reckoning for the art community of the region, among whom Hassan played a vital role. Mohamed's practice became even more intense and focused—in part derived from his extended stay in India, where it flourished, and in part, perhaps, from the reminder of mortality—he noted a sense of urgency, the need to work as fast as he can.

It is important to remember that most of his career developed while he was employed full time. He only finally took early retirement in 2017 and dedicated himself to his art practice full time. In 2018, at last, his sculptures, paintings, forms, and techniques re-converged in his first institutional survey exhibition, *Elements* at the Sharjah Art Foundation. For many audiences, this was the first time the expanse and depth of his work became visible. Since that moment, the recognition of his work has blossomed across multiple continents.

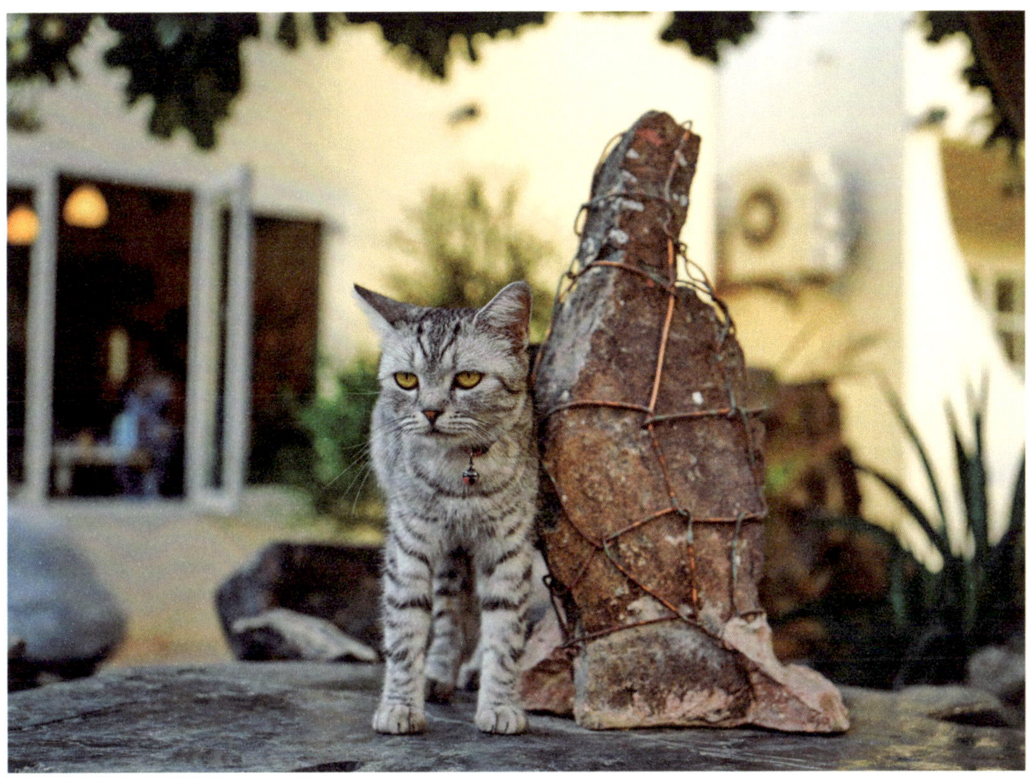

Between Sunrise and Sunset: in Conclusion

The course of this essay mirrors the course of my own navigation as a curator, as I've learned about Mohamed's practice and about his milieu. Walking a razor's edge of interpretation, I am mindful of twin pitfalls: to my left, comparison through a "Western" lens, to my right, a kind of segregation fantasy in which the work is read in an exclusively regional cultural frame.

To my left: by way of example, early on, I saw Mohamed's work and that of his group as functioning much like an "underground art scene" of sorts. Structurally, this is tempting if you look at how the artists supported and reinforced one another despite a lack of institutional validation. But, of course, there is no "underground" without a "mainstream"—and when the artists themselves are not choosing that position: they showed in every institutional context available to them.

To my right: the pitfall of a sophomoric application of anthropology, one that interprets only through the frame of the immediate society's cultural context. This approach is particularly tempting when Mohamed's context is so rich with archaeological material, with his childhood in a clay and mud house with minimal modern amenities in a traditional Arab Gulf port town, framed by petroglyphs and Portuguese ruins.

To make either of these interpretive mistakes misses the watershed characteristic of Mohamed's milieu: the petroglyphs and centuries-old mosque and ancient tombs are as important and influential as the version of Kandinsky's and Ikhwan al-Safa's philosophies that made its way into his circle. Mohamed is in simultaneous dialogue with archaeology, sacred forms, Paul Klee, Islam, etc., fed from across multiple cultures and modernities.

I am watching this book come together with anticipation: it marks the first sustained, monographic study of Mohamed Ahmed Ibrahim's work. This essay begins the process of asking questions that I hope will eventually lead to a more robust interpretive framework[16]—working from the actual context in which artwork is made. What lenses are possible for better understanding, framing, and presenting the work in the fullness of its resonance? As a curator, I find myself asking what art is—really, what do we mean when we say "art?"

That moment when Hassan names what Mohamed is doing as "Land Art" is at once liberating and delimiting. By naming it, the activity is given explicit permission to exist within the boundaries of art vocabularies. Perhaps this is why he doesn't name the work he does in his garden as art.

When I got home from my first visit to Mohamed's studio in 2016, I put two finger-sized plant clippings that he gave me into soil. Today they have become small trees, roots entangled in a large pot. The plant is as tall as me. It juts out in strange directions, jaunty, angular, awkward, and magnificent. I still don't know what the name of this plant is, and yet it grows and thrives.

16. Thanks to sociologist May Al-Dabbagh whose work on "theorizing up" has helped complicate and enrich my thinking on these questions. For more, see her essay "Moving Bodies/ Theorizing Up" in *Arrival: Farah Al Qasimi* (Dubai: Publitas, 2019). Exhibition catalog.

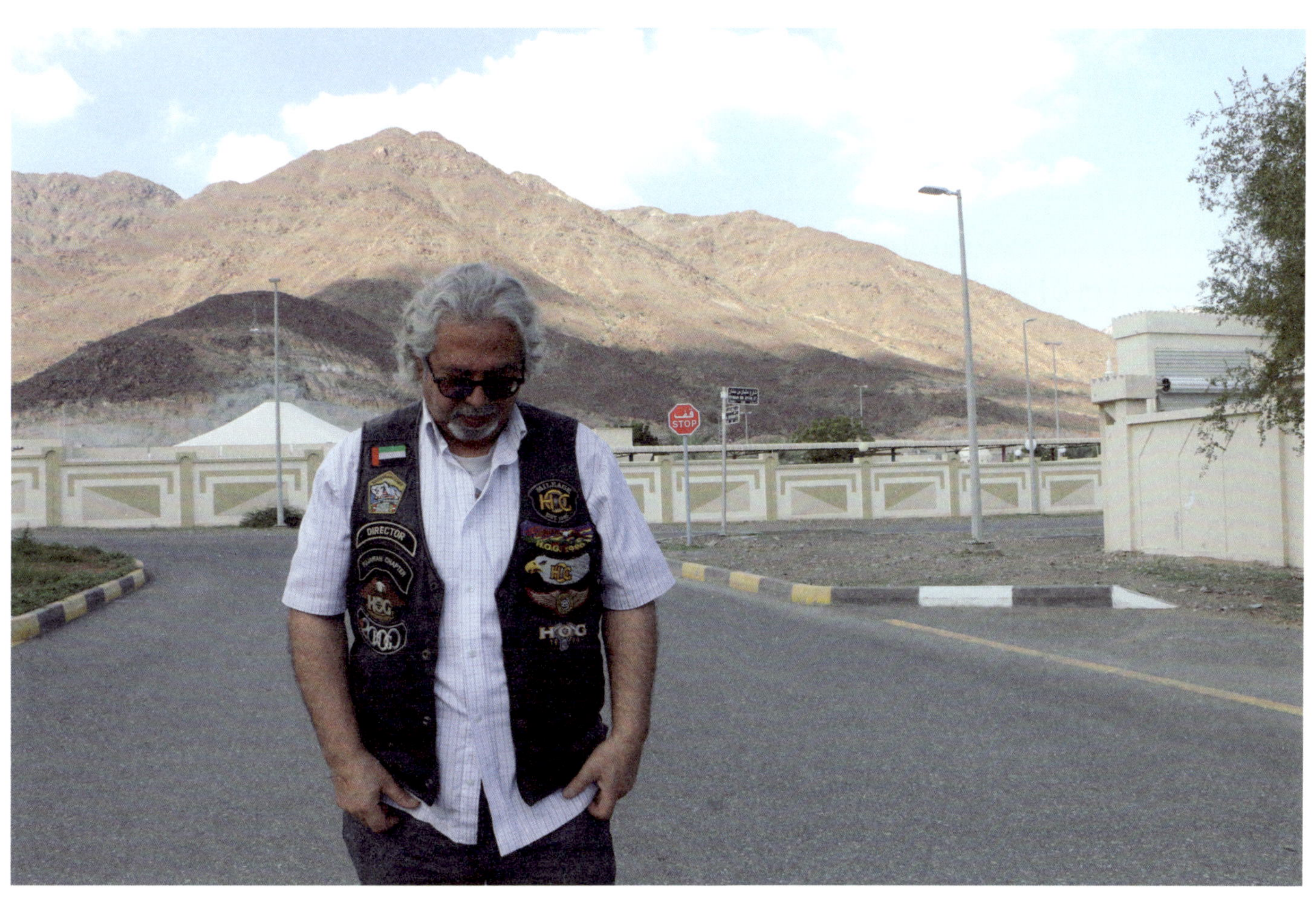

Mohamed on the street outside
of his home, January 2022

Nada Shabout

To Point to the Stars[1]

1. Al Lajna al-Thaqāfiyya, "An
    Nata'ammal Ya'ni An Nu'assas," *Al
    Tashkeel*, no. 3 (1985): 3. A version
    of this essay translated by Yazan
    Doughan appears in *Modern
    Art in the Arab World: Primary
    Documents*, eds. Anneka Lenssen,
    Sarah Rogers, and Nada Shabout
    (New York: The Museum of Modern
    Art, 2018), 443–444.

In July 1971, efforts by a number of artists in the Arab world culminated in the forming of the Union of Arab Plastic Artists (*al-Ittihad al-'amm li-l-fannanin at-tashkiliyin al-'arab*).[2] Among many objectives, their main hope was for regional unity and interaction. The colonial heritage and preceding politico-cultural tensions under Ottoman rule had resulted in much fragmentation in the lands that became known as the Arab World. Each new country in the region was occupied with its own struggles to achieve independence and then a national existence. Alongside this, generations known as the pioneers (first generation or *al-Ruwwad*) in each country were internally trying to assert a specific national identity through the visual.

Part of the postcolonial consciousness was to construct a visual language capable of communicating their national and transregional aspirations through modern aesthetics and to find their place within the larger art dialogue. It was only after some self-assessment and experimentation that they explored shared forums of connection and intersections. The Union's mobilization would lead to the first Arab Biennale, which registered the Arab artists' position and the strong need for a shared forum.[3] The awareness of their fragmented existence within what has been argued throughout most of the twentieth century as a transnational collective strength in the form of pan-Arabism was manifest in their need for better representation. As their contact with each other increased through robust print media and scholarship programs, their desires for a stronger presence in the art scene equally intensified.

The short-lived Arab Biennale (first in Baghdad, Iraq in 1974, second in Rabat, Morocco in 1976, and third in Tripoli, Libya in 1980) allowed for many artists in the Arab World to meet, exhibit together, and hold discussions about their similar and shared concerns. It was, however, the political dynamics of the 1970s that led to its early demise. Other forums more independent yet global in their reach, like the Cultural Moussem of Asilah (Asilah Arts Festival) in Morocco that was started by the artists Mohammed Melehi and Mohamed Benaïssa in 1978, would endure longer and result in rich interactions.

While that first meeting of the Union of Arab Plastic Artists in 1971 included the State of Kuwait from the Gulf region, the United Arab Emirates had not yet emerged as a modern state. Nevertheless, less than a decade after, Emirati visual art entered new creative territory as a generation of young artists gathered their energies, forming the Emirates Fine Arts Society (EFAS) in Sharjah in 1980 by a decree from the Ministry of Labour and Social Affairs, and launching the journal *Al Tashkeel* in September 1984. Under the banner of "Consciousness, Art, Life," the Society struggled. This struggle paralleled that of the Union of Arab Plastic Artists to understand and digest their new realities as they negotiated their future. The formative 1980s and 1990s in the UAE, in connection to wider regional aspirations, presented a missing link in

2. For full text see "Arab Art in Federation," in *Modern Art in the Arab World*, 335–43.

3. For details see Nada Shabout, "Transregional Solidarity: The Arab Biennial in Retrospect," Refractives of *Socialist Solidarity, Mezosfera* magazine's fifth thematic issue, May, 2018, http://mezosfera.org/transregional-solidarity/.

the rich negotiation of modernism as understood and developed globally. A young aspiring artist, Mohamed Ahmed Ibrahim, would become a vital part of this development and a member of EFAS in 1986.

As the orator of the Society, the print publication *Al Tashkeel* became an essential vehicle to promote and articulate the artists' ideas and experiments as well as connect them with other creative individuals in and outside of the UAE. Their trials and conversations would set the path forward but more importantly, provide a nuanced engagement with modernism, addressing and overcoming some of the specific issues that occupied the wider region in the previous decades. As a space of discourse, research, and documentation, *Al Tashkeel* was remarkable from its inception: one of equity and diversity where gender, nationality, style, and beliefs were equally accepted and represented within a global context. They believed that art was the ultimate unity.

Given the lack of an art infrastructure in the country at the time, *Al Tashkeel* played an even more significant role. "To aspire means to construct" was the title of the foreword by the Cultural Committee of EFAS in their third issue.[4] Unlike the previous short and celebratory notes of the earlier two issues, here and in the following issues, the Society would outline their objectives to build stronger art consciousness and ambitions that grew further in every new issue. In its early life, the journal was not able to maintain a regular production schedule (and identified as non-periodic) but took full advantage of its pages when possible. The activities of the Society aimed to establish and grow roots locally, regionally, and internationally. They intended to engage in a dialectical conversation with the other in order to belong and understand the self.

The journal thus acted as a space to connect artists as well as educate them and the larger society. The editorial board was aware of the need for, and thus provided, art criticism and art education. Every issue introduced chapters from the global history of art as well as local experiments. Most significantly, while the successive issues delved into European art history, styles, theories, and techniques, it equally dedicated ample space for art and theories of the global south. Moreover, *Al Tashkeel* contextualized many regional artists and introduced work by pivotal Arab practitioners while giving voice to the specific concerns of the conceptually aware group of local artists, regularly gathering at the Emirates Fine Arts Society. Toward this aim, a number of established Arab artists were also regularly invited to write their opinions and discuss their work. Founding members of the Union of Arab Plastic Artists, such as the Syrians Mahmoud Hammad and Fateh al-Moudarres, contributed to several issues, and the Palestinian artist Ismail Shammout, who served as the first Secretary General of the Union, and his wife Tamam al-Akhal, had generous representations of their lives, struggles, and work in another issue. Other noted Arab artists, like Yaser Dweik, Asaad Arabi, and Abdul Latif Al-Smoudi,

4. Al Lajna al-Thaqāfiyya, "An Nata'ammal Ya'ni An Nu'assas," *Al Tashkeel*, no. 3 (1985): 3.

5. *Al Tashkeel*, no. 6 (1989): 2.

6. *Al Tashkeel*, no. 5 (1987): 20-6.

7. *Al Tashkeel*, no. 12-13 (2003): 28-33.

8. *Al Tashkeel*, no. 16 (2004): 4.

9. Mohamed Aljazairi, "Khatim al-Law ah (The Seal of the Painting)," *Al Tashkeel*, no. 16 (2004): 5 (my translation).

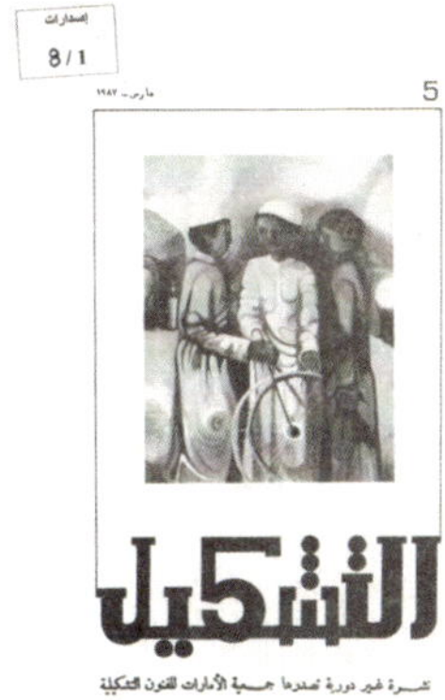

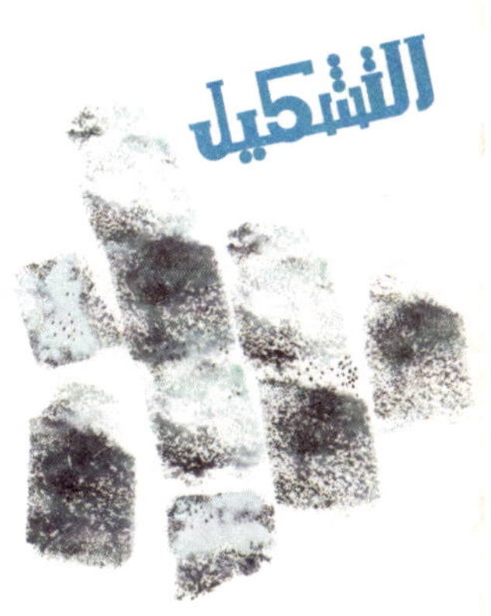

regularly contributed to the editorial contents for several years while also actively engaging with the local artists in the field of art education. Finally, a considerable role in the conversation was played by Abdul Karim Al Sayed and Yousef Aidabi, with their frequent critical contributions and reflections on the UAE art scene, which they witnessed at different stages of its evolution.

Furthermore, pronouncedly aware of the limitation that art's reach and recognition had in the UAE, the Cultural Committee of EFAS identified that limitation as a barrier between artists and their audience in their sixth issue.[5] In their previous issue 5, the vivid coverage of the 1987 Baghdad Festival for Art, a forty-day event that started on October 26, specifically anticipated this concern.[6] The detailed accounts had a specific focus on the public response. They highlighted the audience's dynamic engagement and the increasing number of visitors as the days passed. They listed the daily media coverage as precisely playing a large role in art's promotion.

The role of media promotion would manifest in the journal through various introductions to individual local artists beyond the regular exhibition review. For example, in the journal's eighth issue, the editor dedicated pages to the work of Mohamed Ahmed Ibrahim and Hussain Sharif (who was a member of the editorial board), announcing their new exhibitions and listing their accomplishments. The double issue 12–13 covered the celebrated exhibition of "the Five," (*5/U.A.E.*) that took place at the Ludwig Forum for International Art, in Aachen, Germany, and presented the work of artists Mohamed Ahmed Ibrahim, Hassan Sharif, Abdullah Al Saadi, Hussain Sharif, and Mohammed Kazem. It was fully contextualized within the history of the UAE's development as well as the unique experiments of the individual artists.[7] It was specifically interesting that the work of these five artists, who would become known for their experiments as foundational in the UAE, was discussed as individual experimentation that negotiated "new art" and not as a representation of a national collective memory.

In 2004, Mohamed Ahmed Ibrahim, who was the president of the Society then, became the chief editor of *Al Tashkeel*. In the foreword for issue 16, his colleague, Mohamed Aljazairi, argued for a focus on the art as an object and discussed the multiple hidden dimensions to be found in any work of art. He wrote that the artist is essentially his or her work, regardless of styles, material, or techniques.[8] He particularly championed the "new art," conceptual art. He wrote: "As do many UAE artists who believed in conceptual art (the new art), they formulated their works according to a mixture that contained both: materials derived from nature, and the prevailing and contemporary culture. In this manner, the meaning of the artworks was imbued in their semantic dimension, the messages they carry, and their orientation toward the depth of reception rather than the hasty, superficial, examination."[9]

Front cover from *Al Tashkeel* magazine, Issue 5 (1987). Published by the Emirates Fine Arts Society

Front cover from *Al Tashkeel* magazine, Issue 6 (1989). Published by the Emirates Fine Arts Society

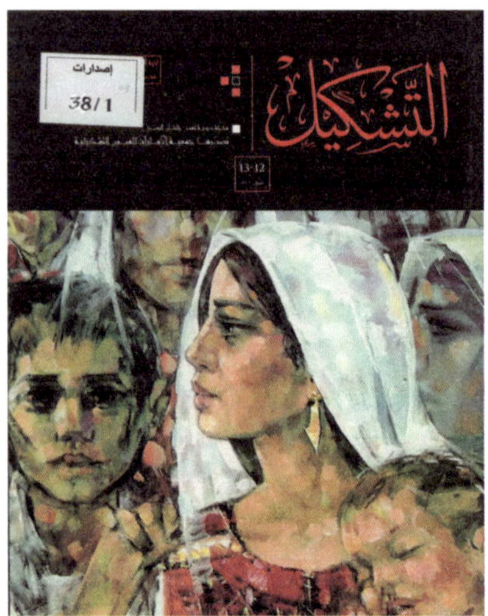

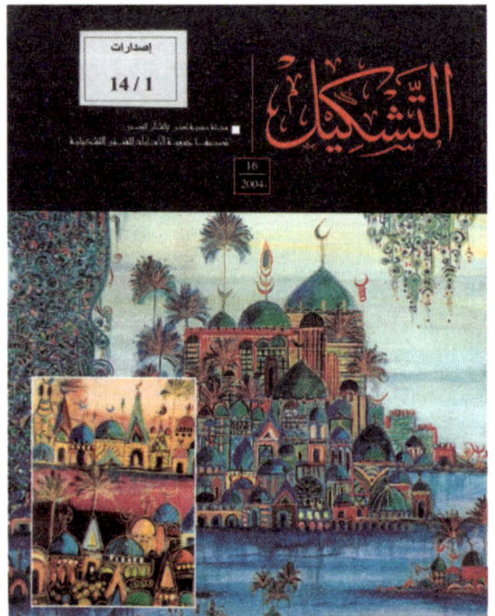

Ibrahim's interest in new techniques, while encouraging change, was further manifest in his foreword to issue 17, in his call for the journal to adopt deeper experimentation as a project, spirit, and significance.[10] In fact, he argued for "re-experimenting with experimentation" as the most important creative project. He also purposely asserted the independence and role of *Al Tashkeel* as a progressive space to document and witness creativity and history. He further renewed the invitation to all artists to participate in enriching the journal. His tenure ended with issue 18, leaving one to wonder what would have been the impact of his direction been in the long run. Nevertheless, the rotation of approaches through the succession of chief editors endowed the journal with multivalent voices and effects.

In parallel to *Al Tashkeel*'s mission and vision, the Society's annual exhibitions, and later the launching of the Sharjah Biennial in 1993, organized by the Sharjah Department of Culture and Information, and their subsequent longevity, would not only ensure local circulation of art but would essentially accomplish much of what the Union of Arab Plastic Artists had hoped to do through the Arab Biennale. Like the annual exhibitions by the Society, Sharjah Biennial's earlier iterations were decidedly regionally focused, which allowed for a wider Arab engagement. It further situated Sharjah (and accordingly the UAE) as a regional focal node, and it was designated by UNESCO as the Cultural Capital of the Arab World in 1998.

Occupied by questions around the national, regional, and global as well as endless contemplations of "what is Arab art," the archive of *Al Tashkeel* is an astonishing documentation of the struggles and progress of the arts in the UAE. The earlier issues, with less funding and support than the journal would garner later, were a true labor of love by the generation of pioneer artists from the UAE. Among many voices, Hassan Sharif, Hussain Sharif, Ahmed Rashid Thani, Mohamed Ahmed Ibrahim, and Nujoom Alghanem, are of specific significance for their courage, candor, and concerns. Their vision was transregional; the national construction, for example, was not seen as a separate or isolated project. The importance of their national consciousness was disclosed insofar that the local was part of the Arab and international scene. Art for them was a uniter as well as a connector, both geographically and temporally.

10. *Al Tashkeel*, no. 17 (2004): 2.

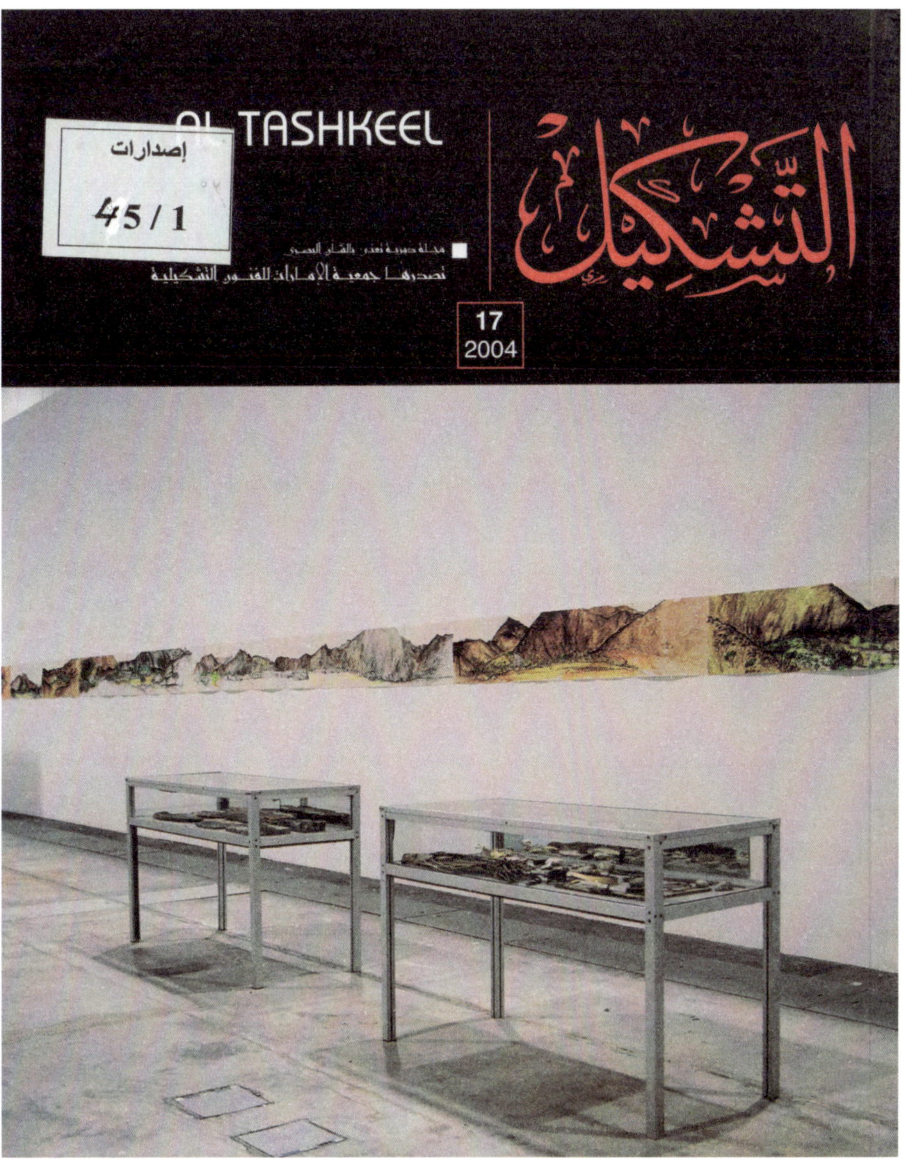

Left
Front cover from *Al Tashkeel* magazine, Issue 12–13 (2003). Published by the Emirates Fine Arts Society

Front cover from *Al Tashkeel* magazine, Issue 16 (2004). Published by the Emirates Fine Arts Society

This page
Front cover from *Al Tashkeel* magazine, Issue 17 (2004). Published by the Emirates Fine Arts Society

Venetia Porter

Signs and Symbols:
Mohamed Ahmed Ibrahim's Works on Paper

Note Book No 01, 1988–89
India ink on paper, 18 x 25 cm

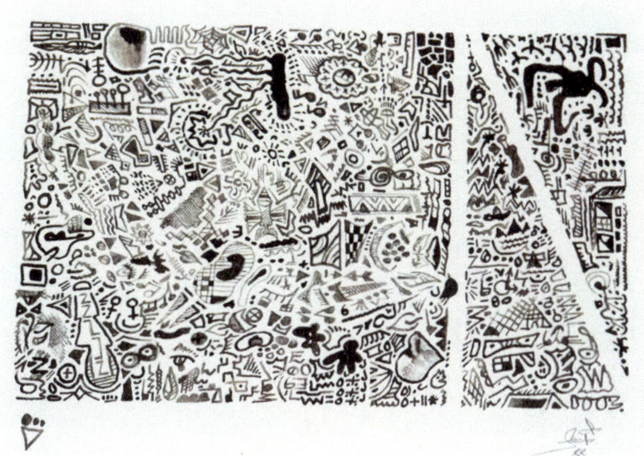

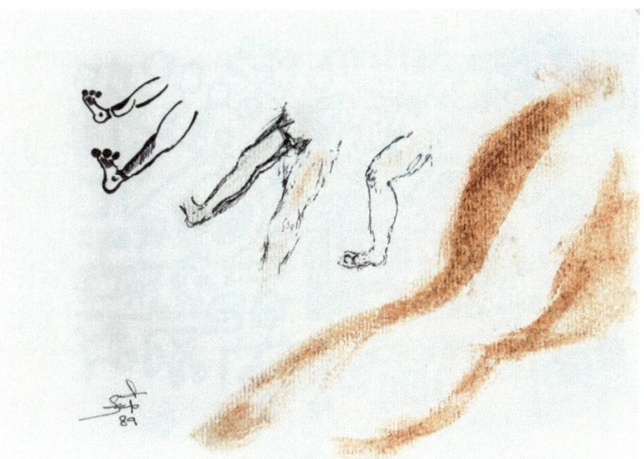

"I found them in one of my high school books."[1] It was 1979; Mohamed Ahmed Ibrahim was bored in class and he began to draw what would become a defining feature of his signature style: symbols and shapes, single or in clusters, that would eventually appear on paper, on rock, across buildings, or turned into sculpture. From random marks on desks and cigarette lighters, the evolution of these early "doodles" can be traced through three notebooks that he kept between 1989 and 1991. Tasked with exploring the nature of Mohamed Ahmed Ibrahim's work with paper, I discovered that these precious documents held the key to a "vocabulary," but this was only the beginning. As our conversation unfolded, I would be led into a world rooted in a sense of place, as instinctive as it was personal.

Notebook 1989

"You can start to read some things but it is not a language," says Ibrahim. In the notebook from 1989, there are dense patterns through which can be discerned little figures, flowers, and butterflies in shades of black and grey. Illusory forms that could be words or letters emerge, and on some pages, the motifs are corralled into shapes bordered by clean white lines. "I didn't mean to make a story but now looking back they look like city maps, with roads and houses," he says. Toward the end of the notebook are surprise drawings of legs as though on a swing or seated, which turn out to be studies for figural works. These connect to another body of work entirely, taking us back to the beginning of his artistic journey before his Land Art works, when he was painting landscapes and portraits at the Emirates Fine Arts Society, with the Palestinian painter Yaser Dweik. A formative influence for him, Ibrahim recalls that "he [Dweik] taught me drawing techniques … how to make the basic paint layer and how to tighten the canvas."[2]

1. This essay is based on a conversation with Mohamed Ahmed Ibrahim in August 2021. I am also grateful to Cristiana de Marchi and to Maya Allison for all their helpful advice.
2. Allison, ed., *But We Cannot See Them*, 116–17. For *Sitting Man* images, see pages 150–151.

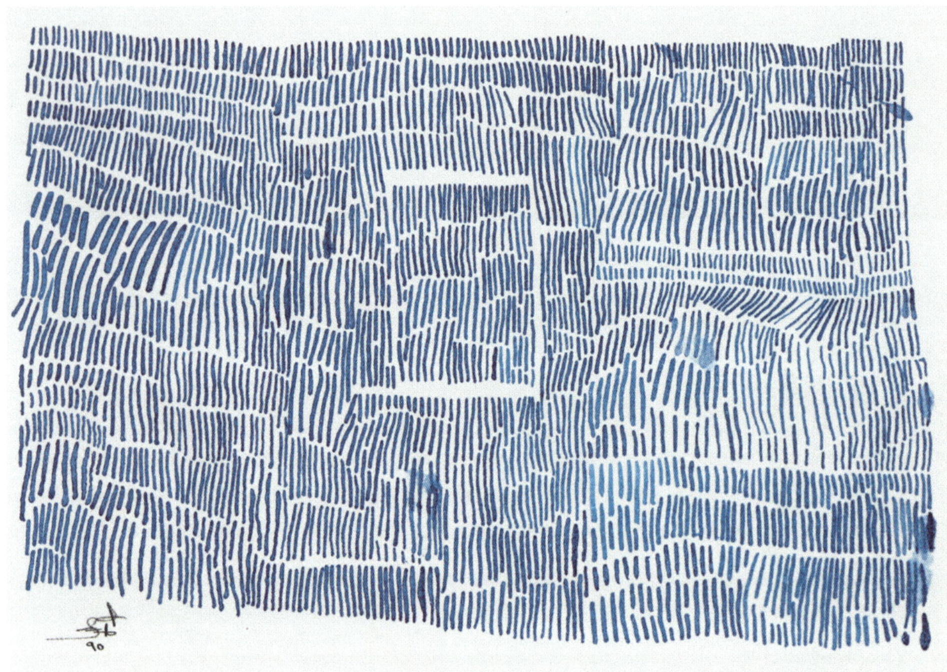

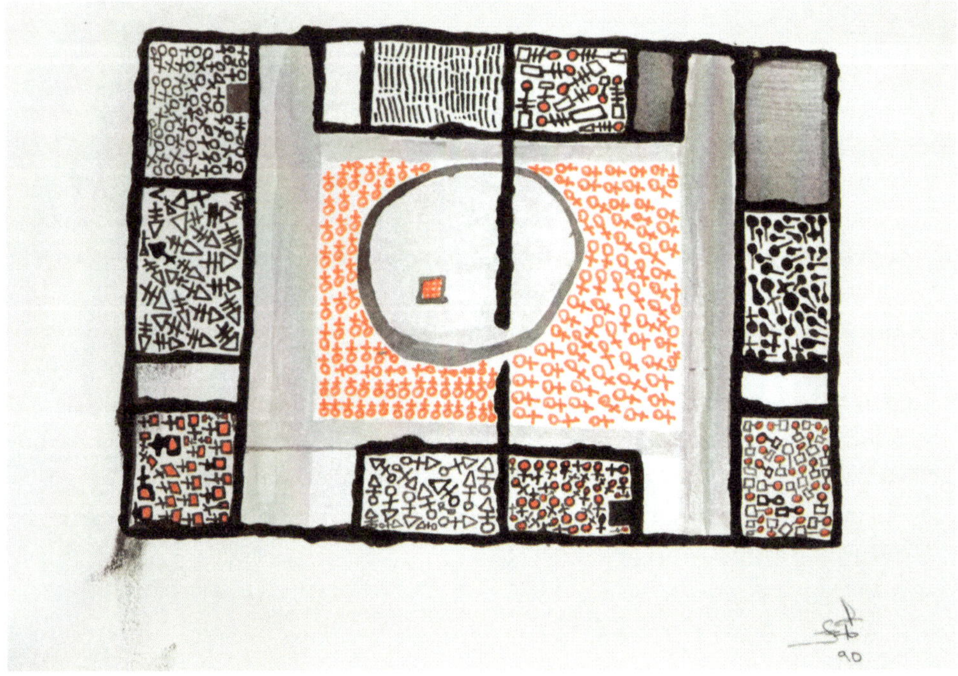

Notebook 1990

The multiplicity of shapes that appear in the 1989 notebook has been reduced, a year later, to only a few forms. Sometimes they are confined to a grid as though echoing the formality of a garden design or a map, but this time it's "off-road," as Ibrahim commented.

Notebook 1991

Single elements are repeated, and there are layers, delicate colors in Chinese ink, and vertical lines. In the notebook of 1991, the color has now gone, and

Both above
Note Book No 02, 1990
India ink on paper, 25 x 18 cm

Both at right
Note Book No 02, 1991
India ink on paper, 25 x 18 cm

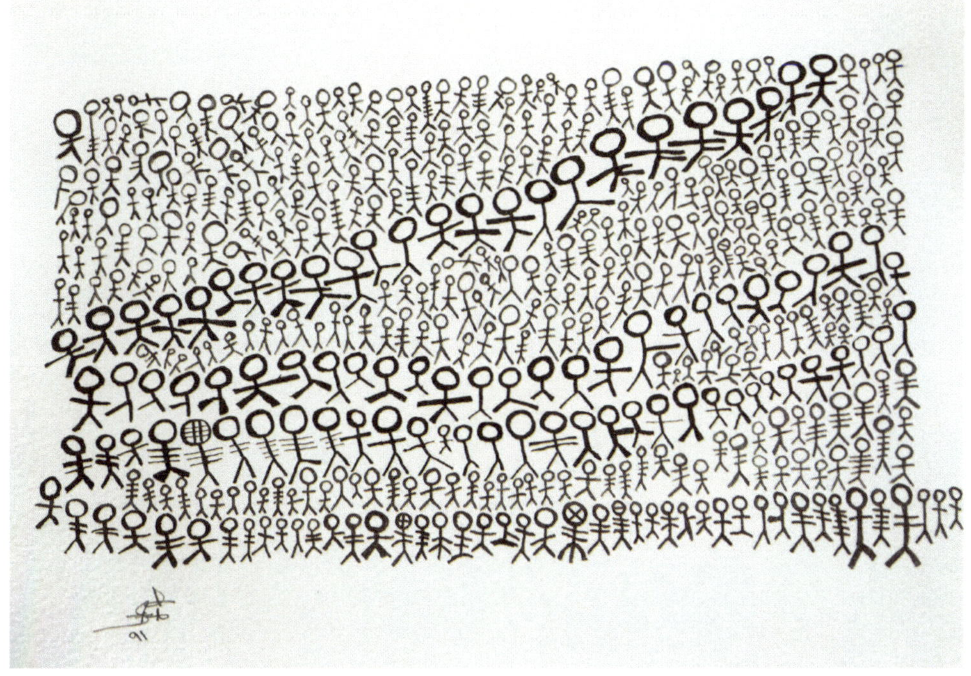

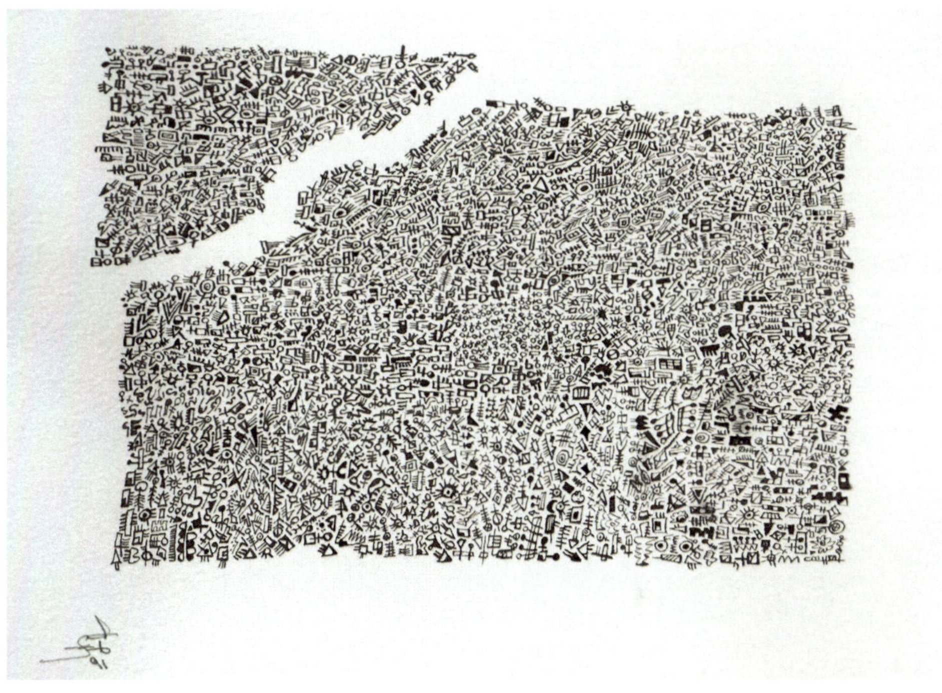

there are experiments with different compositions—stick-like figures march across one page; in another, there is a tear. It is as though a landmass has been pulled apart.

By the early 1990s, Ibrahim was developing his "Land Art." These same drawings were appearing on rocks within the landscape of Khor Fakkan— painted in water-based emulsion, which would disappear after the first rains.[3] "There was no difference in medium, I was jumping from stones to paper," he recalls. With paper still at the heart of his practice, lines and symbols could now also extend across larger surfaces. He began buying 10-meter-long rolls of good quality watercolor paper, cut to his chosen size. With India ink and a dip pen with a metal nib, in an unconscious echo of the *qalam*[4] used

3. Ismail Al Rifai and Patricia Millns, eds., *Window 2006: 16 UAE Artists* (Dubai: Total Arts, 2006). Exhibition catalog.

4. A *qalam* is a type of pen made from a cut, dried reed and used for Islamic calligraphy.

Untitled 4, 2008
India ink on paper, 115 x 115 cm

Both right
Dijon, 2009
Ink and pastel on paper, 22 x 16 cm

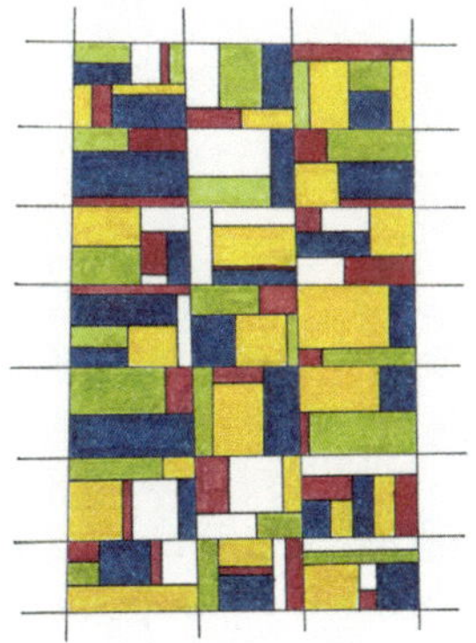

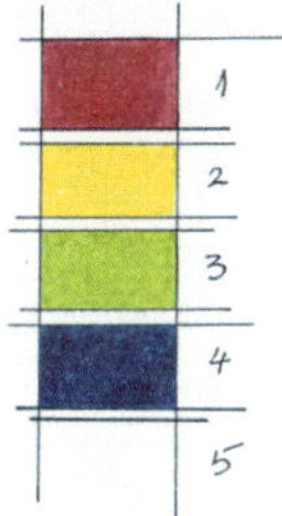

by calligraphers of old, the composition developed organically without pre-planning. Now in the collection of the British Museum,[5] *Untitled II* was made in 2008 while Ibrahim was at The Flying House. It is the first of these compositions into which he introduced patches of earthy color. He recalls how, in this work, he started at the top left corner but then continued as the mood took him across the paper. The symbols now consist of four or five shapes, and when looked at from a distance, the individual elements merge, creating swirls of movement punctuated by black squares or triangles. Up close, the feeling is of being in an ancient place, the symbols a key to a mystic alphabet.

While seeking to understand those early symbols within the wider context of Ibrahim's work as a whole, a more complex picture of his practice emerges. Continuing to change and develop, they become increasingly abstracted in some cases or can crystallize into a single element. For the most part, the works are untitled, but others have names, such as *Salalah Landscape* (2015) or *Forms in Al-Reef* (2017); clear allusions to the importance that Ibrahim places on the land he inhabits that provides him with so much of his inspiration.

Works in different styles and subject matter also emerge: landscapes harking back to an earlier period, on canvas as well as on paper, including an unidenti-fied hospital building in a rural scene in Germany from 1998; experimentation with forms similar to abstract expressionism in 2002, and delicate pencil drawings of maquettes for sculptures in 2007. Figuration is seen in the form of the recurring *Sitting Man*, who first emerges in 2010, an enigmatic figure —and possible self-portrait. The man is always the same—torso and lower body visible, hands on knees—with only the backgrounds, the garments, and skin tones changing from one iteration to the next. Although Ibrahim mostly painted these figures on canvas, in 2011, they appear on paper, even newspaper.

In 2009, Ibrahim undertook a six-month residency in Dijon, and from this period, there is another notebook full of geometric compositions and a series of collages.

Notebook 2009

Returning exhausted at the end of each day from experiencing the city, he described how he would wind down by creating these precise Mondrian-like grids before going to bed. On one page, he even drew the key for the four colors, with the fifth remaining blank. At this time, he also created collages from pamphlets for various events that had been left on his doorstep. In a witty intervention, he wiped out the text, replacing the words with clusters of the now-familiar vertical lines.

5. Venetia Porter et al., *Reflections: Contemporary Art of the Middle East and North Africa* (London: British Museum Press, 2020), 92–3.

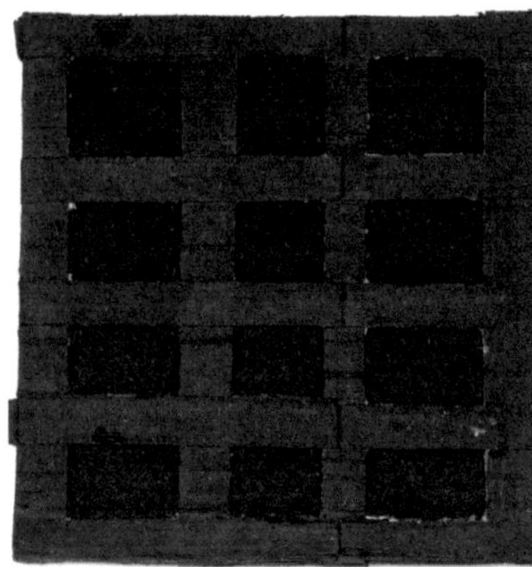

<u>Collages 2010</u>

It was in the 2000s that he began to fully explore the possibilities of taking the drawings from their two-dimensional form to sculpture—this idea was encapsulated in a glorious installation in which single sheets of paper painted with black and white lines were bundled up and tied with ropes. It was during this period that he also turned to papier-maché to begin creating a myriad of shapes that suggest trees, fruit baskets, and what look like children's toys. Large-scale installations of these works, such as *Khorfakkan number-2* (2007, see pp. 138–139), were made in 2006–7, and the present one is being undertaken for the Venice Biennale of 2022.

The process starts with the purchase of sheets of colored A4 paper, which are placed in a shredder. The resulting mass is then soaked in water and mixed with glue. He loves to work with his bare hands, "it gives me pleasure to feel the material." As with the drawings, there is no preliminary sketch, "ideas come while working." As long as the papier-maché keeps soft, he can continue to mold it, so he typically works on several pieces all at once. "When it is dry, it is like wood" and can last even outside—some pieces have been in his yard for over 15 years. Experimenting further, Ibrahim is now creating what he terms "assemblages"—wall pieces of different sizes that are part painting and part sculpture, made from a mix of fabric with paper or cardboard, whatever feels appropriate.

As Ibrahim's work continues to change and evolve in even more inventive and striking ways, the symbols that started as random marks in an exercise book remain an intrinsic part of his practice. He compares them to an addiction: "They have become part of my personality, a habit, like smoking, I just can't stop drawing them."

Untitled, 2016
Paper assemblage, 42.7 x 40.5 cm

Right
Installation view of *Residuals and the Anthology of Narcissism*, 2016 at the Mandalay Hall, Kochi, India

Installation view of *The Space Between the Eyelid and the Eyeball*, 2019 at Lawrie Shabibi, Dubai, UAE

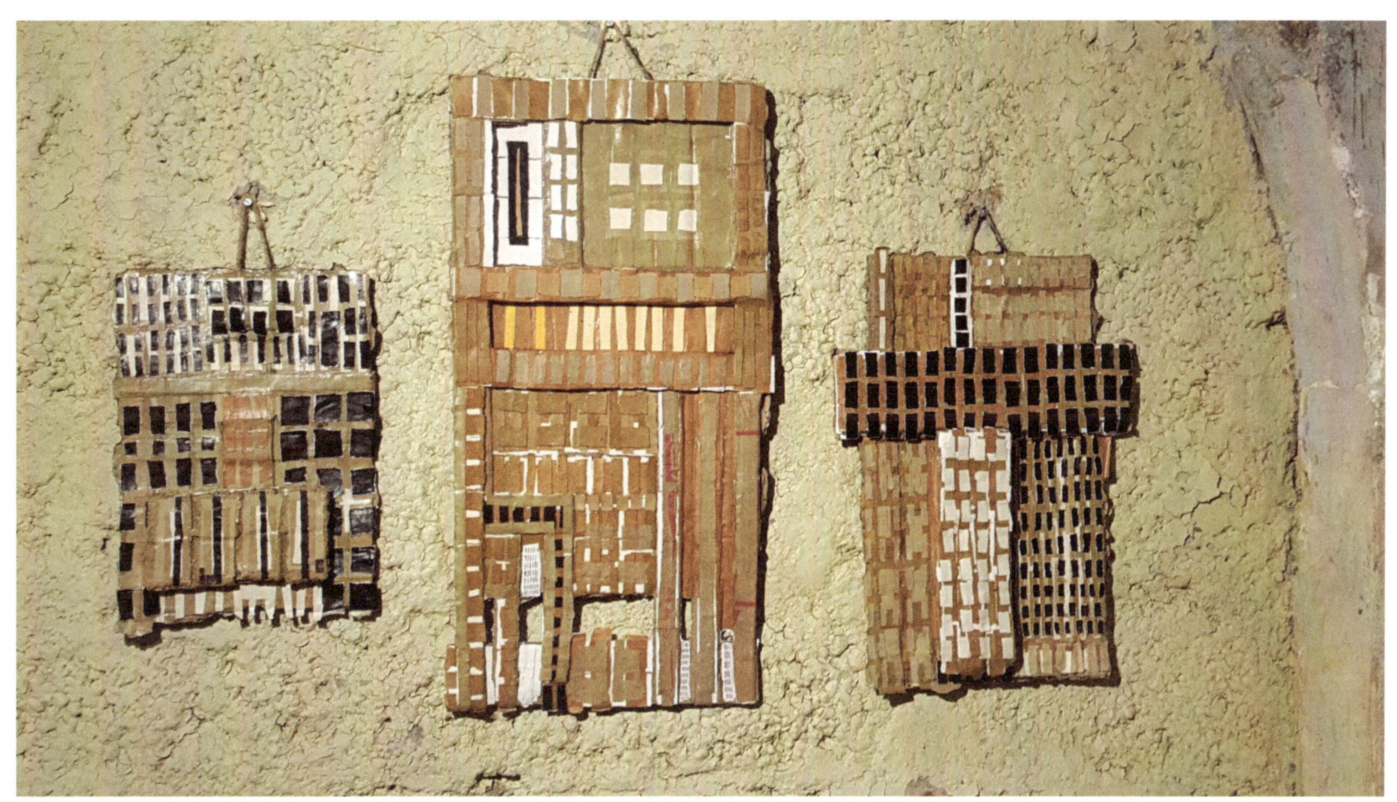

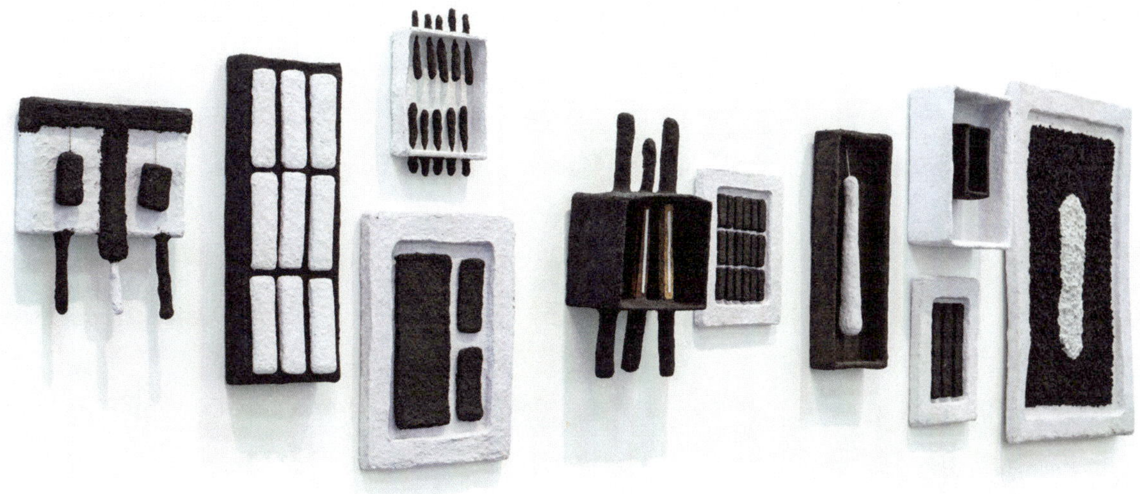

The psychological i
brain starts creatin
shapes and dissoci
drawing from what
Then, there is the p
aspect, which is the
your eyelid and pup
these shapes come
depends on the tim
lighting that is arou
hard you close your

where your
spontaneous
es what you're
ou're thinking.
siological
pace between
This is where
o life, and this
of day, the
d you, how
yes or squint.

Selected Works

Play in the Clay

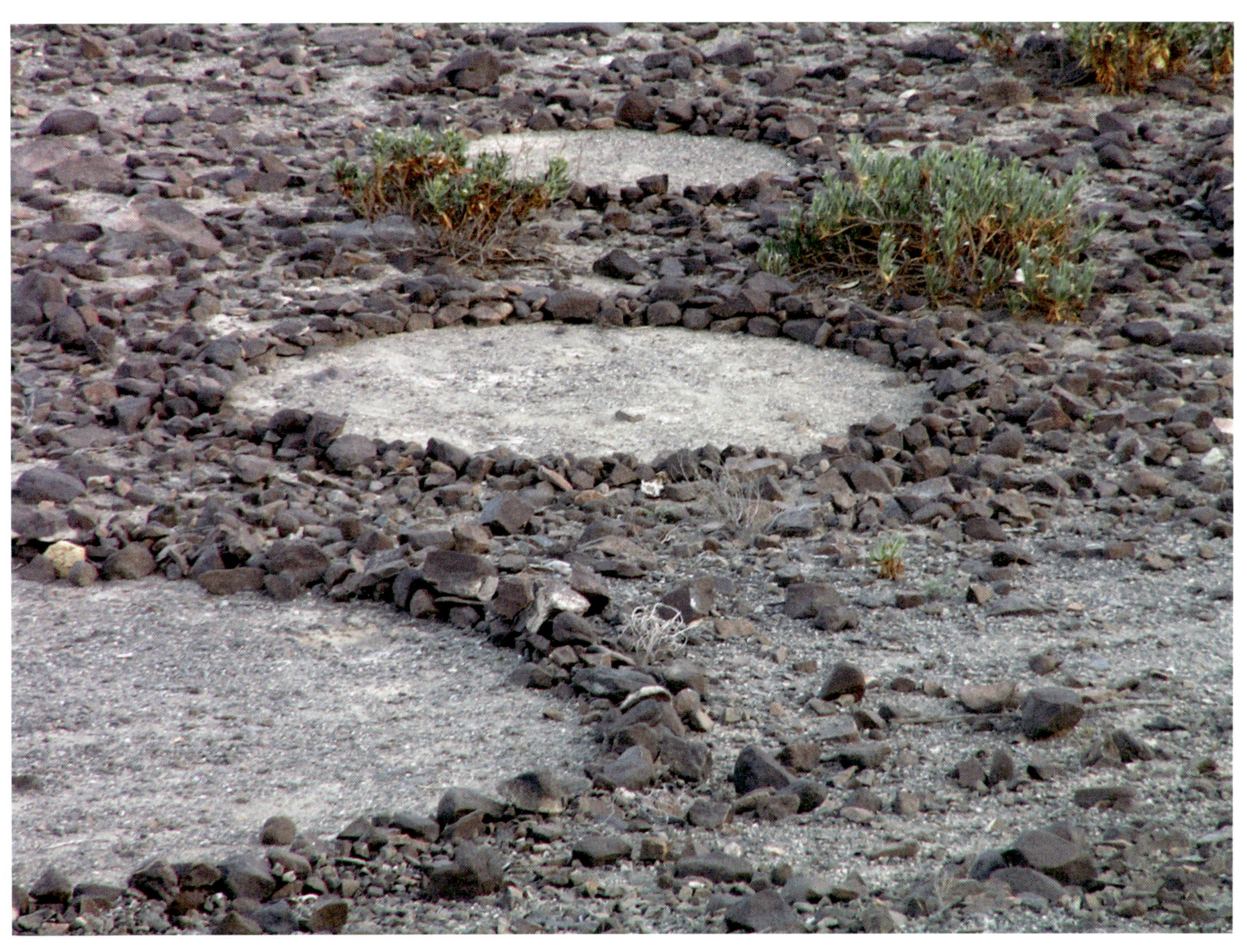

This page and next
Khorfakkan Circles (detail), 2004
Alwasat Valley, Khor Fakkan,
Sharjah

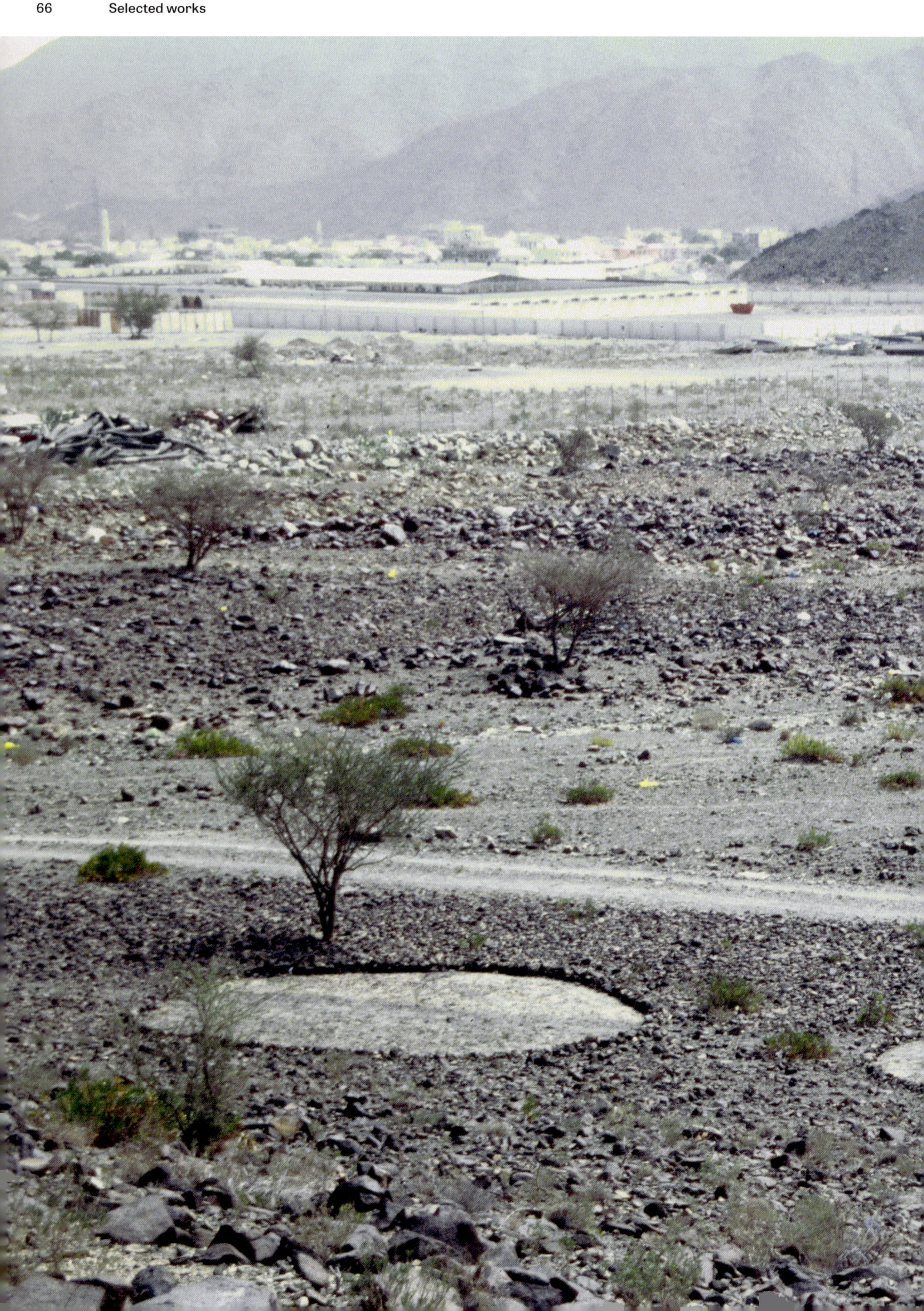

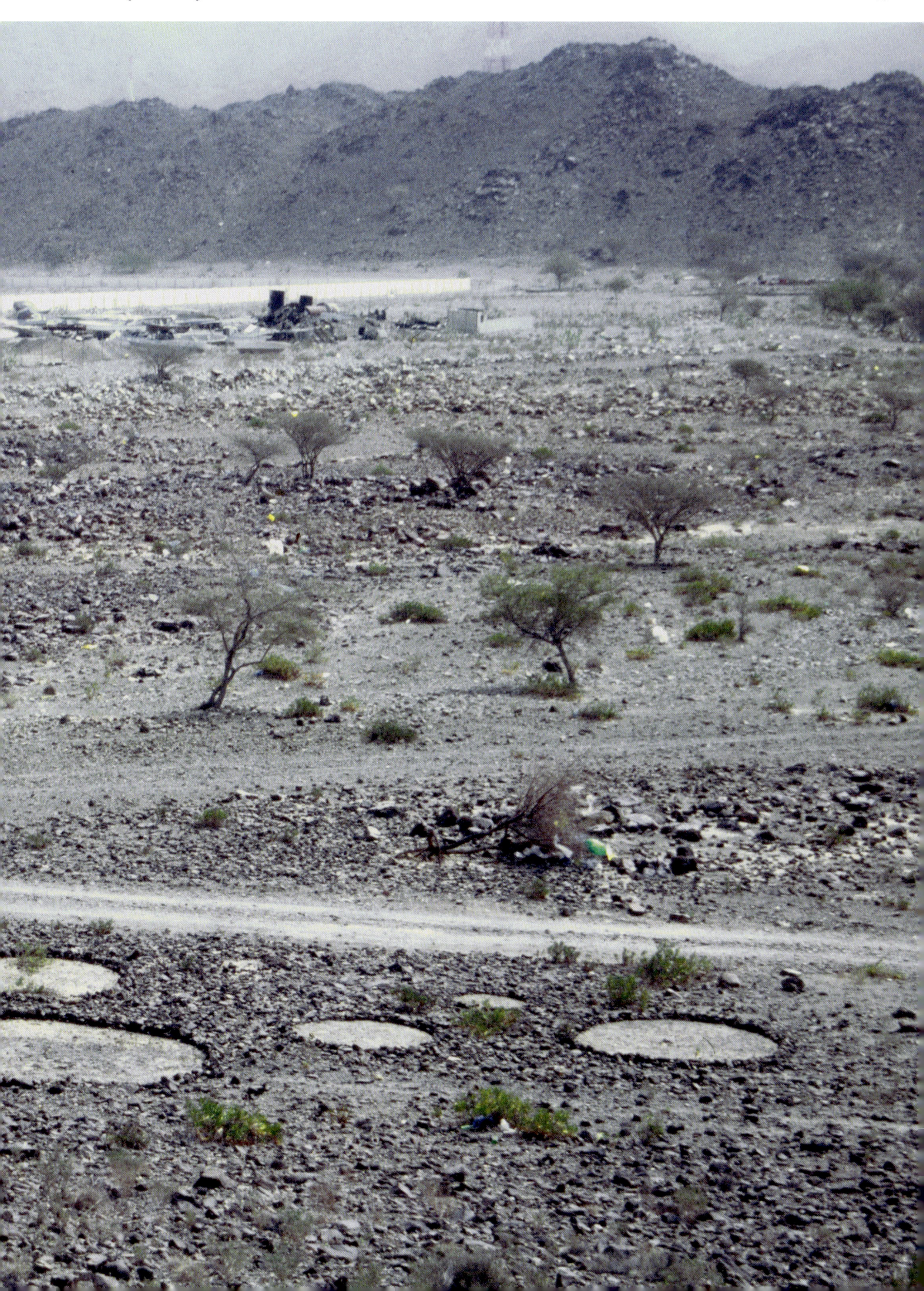

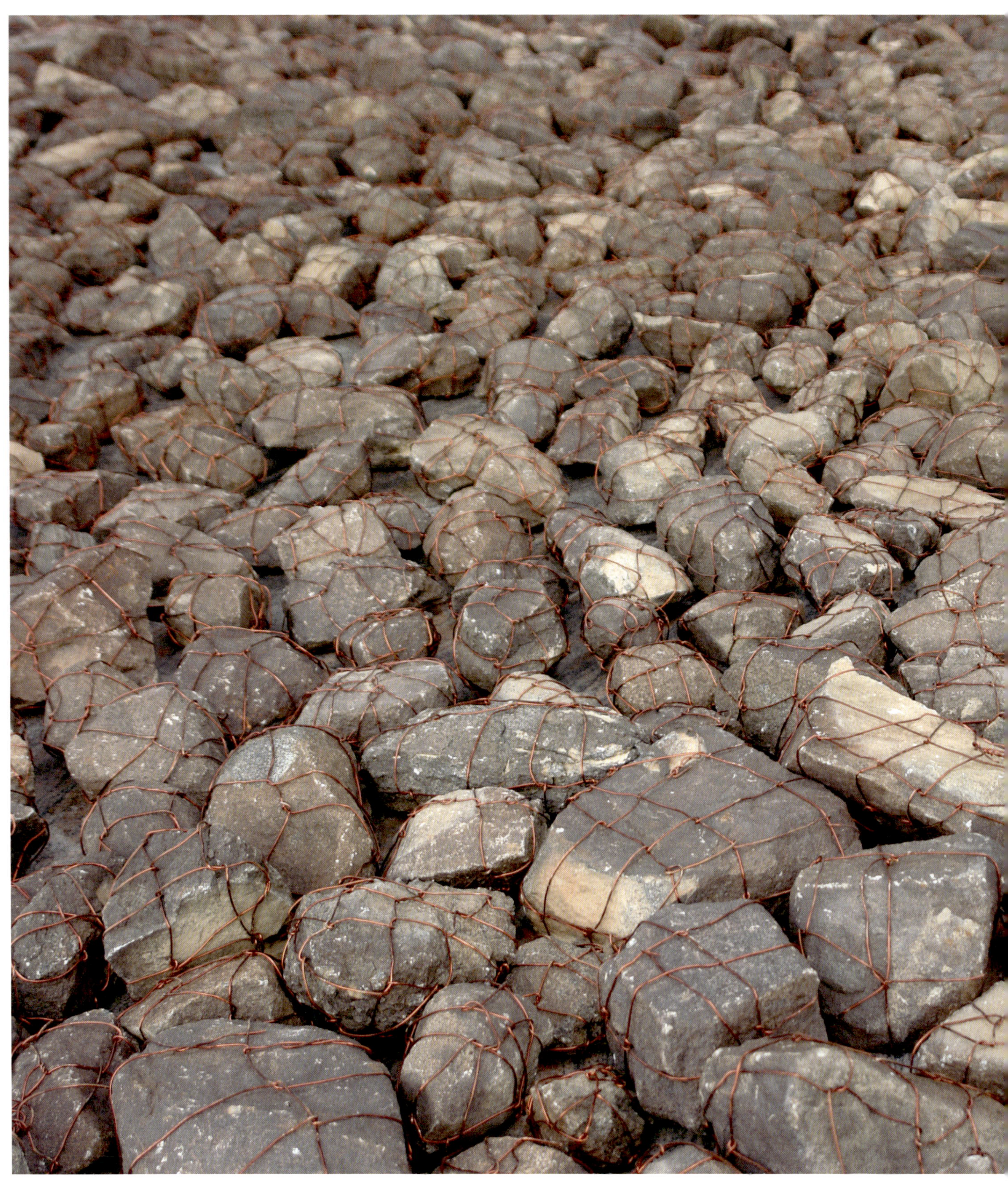

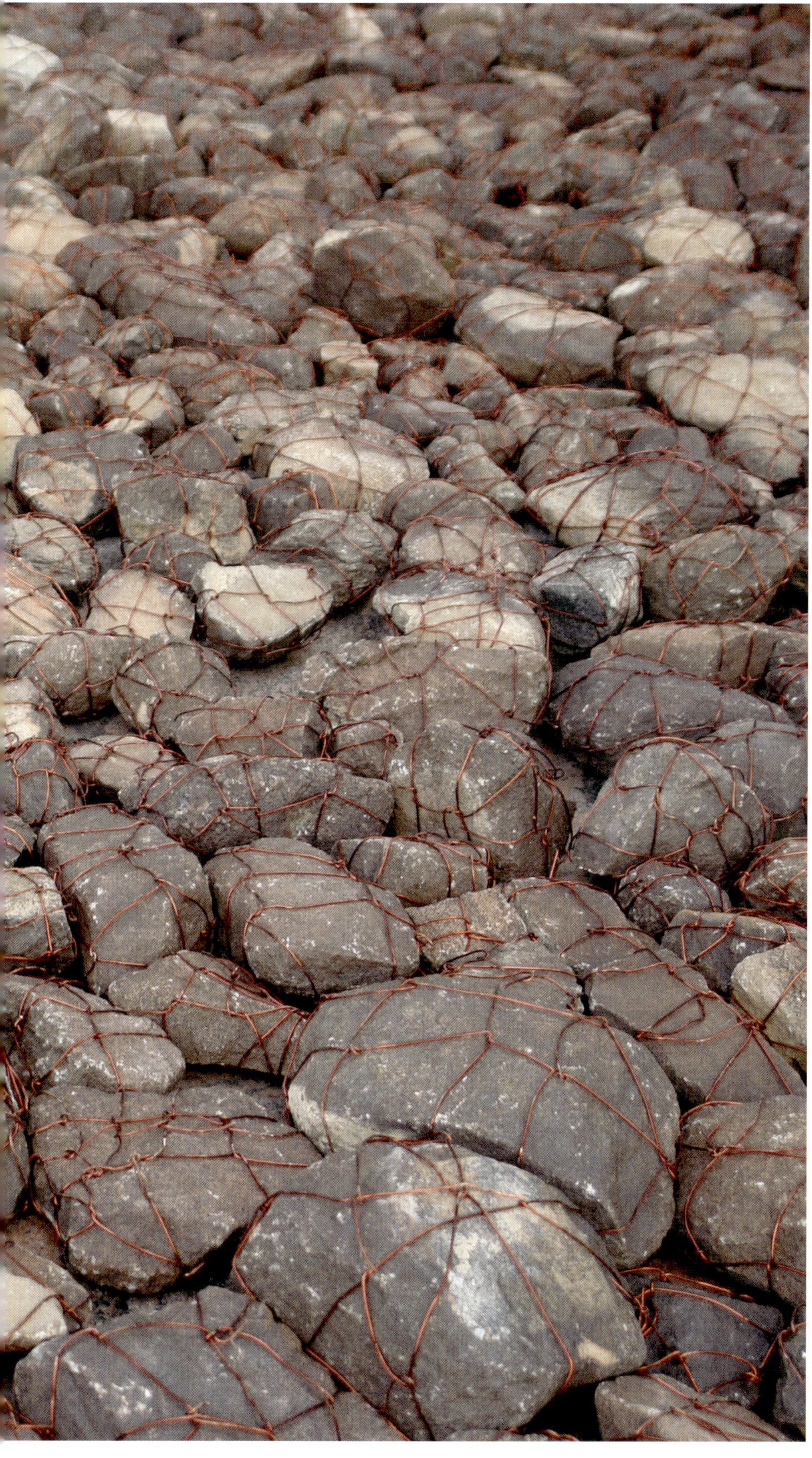

Stones Wrapped in Copper
(detail), 2007
Stones, copper, dimensions
variable

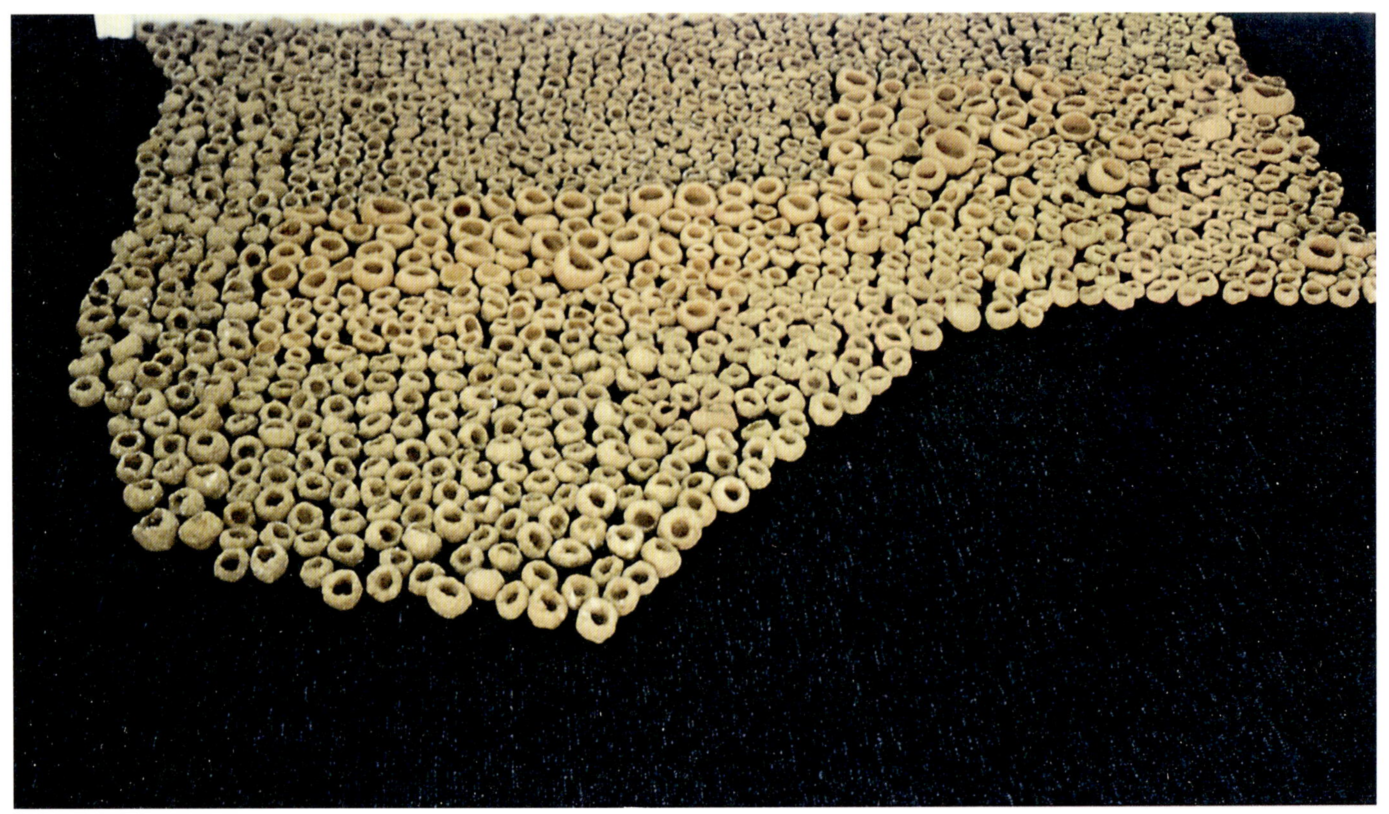

Clay, 1995
Clay, dimensions variable

Installation view of *Mohamed Ahmed Ibrahim: Elements* at the Sharjah Art Foundation, 2018

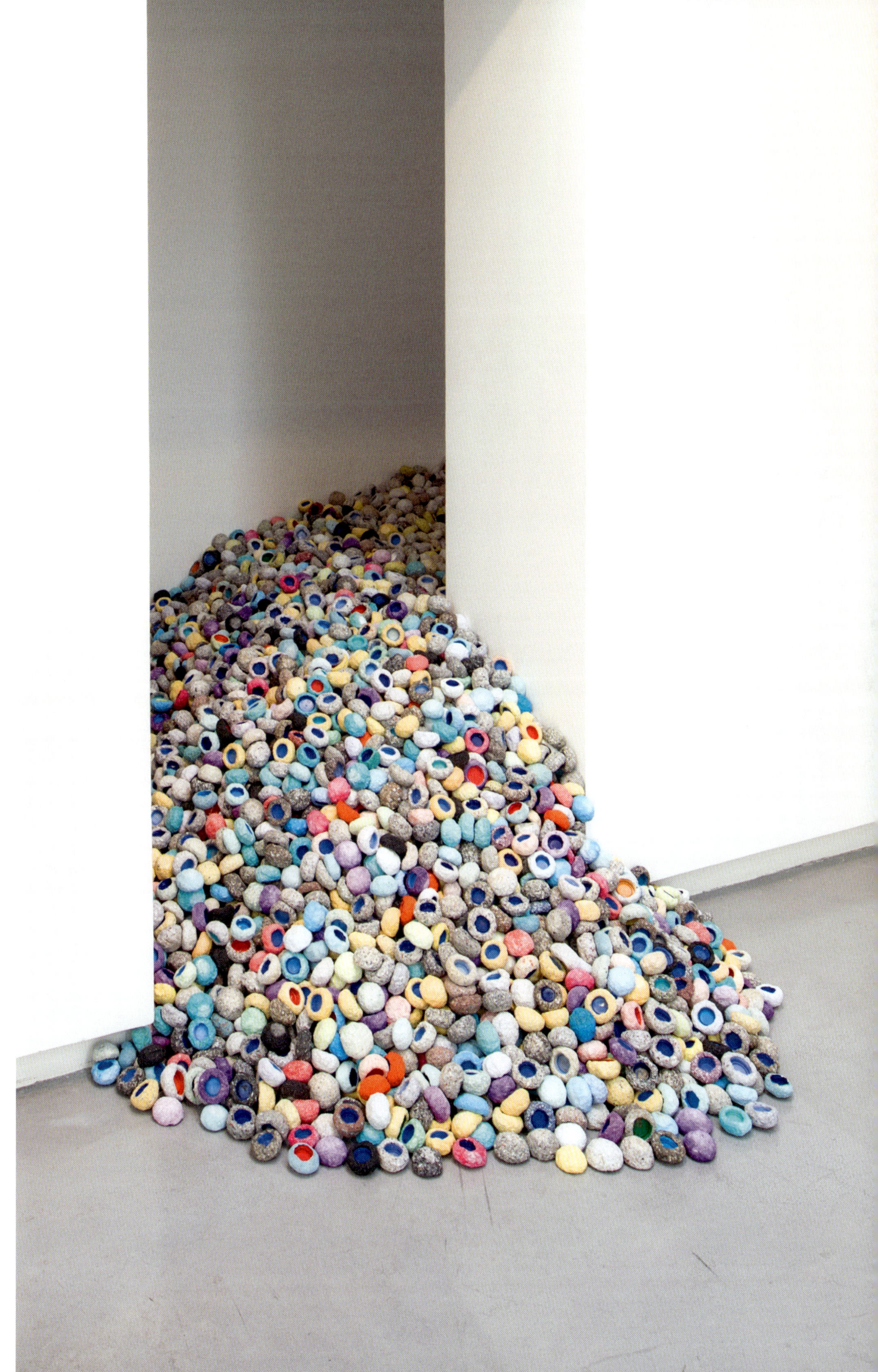

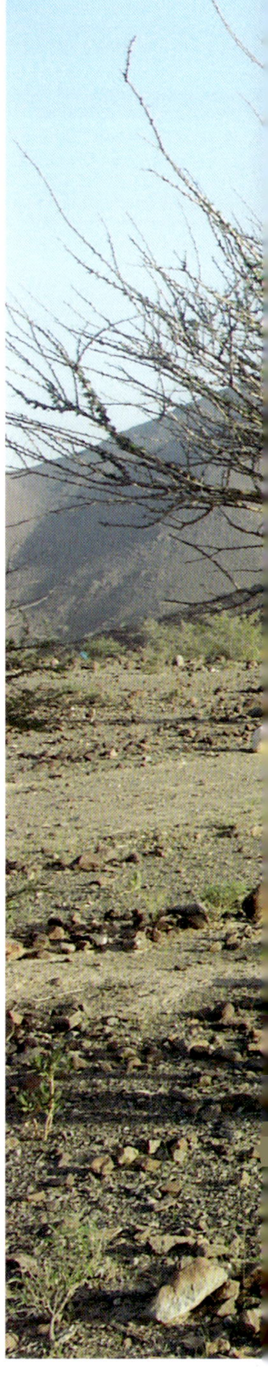

Draped Trees (Ashjar Muqammasha), 1996
Textiles, dimensions variable

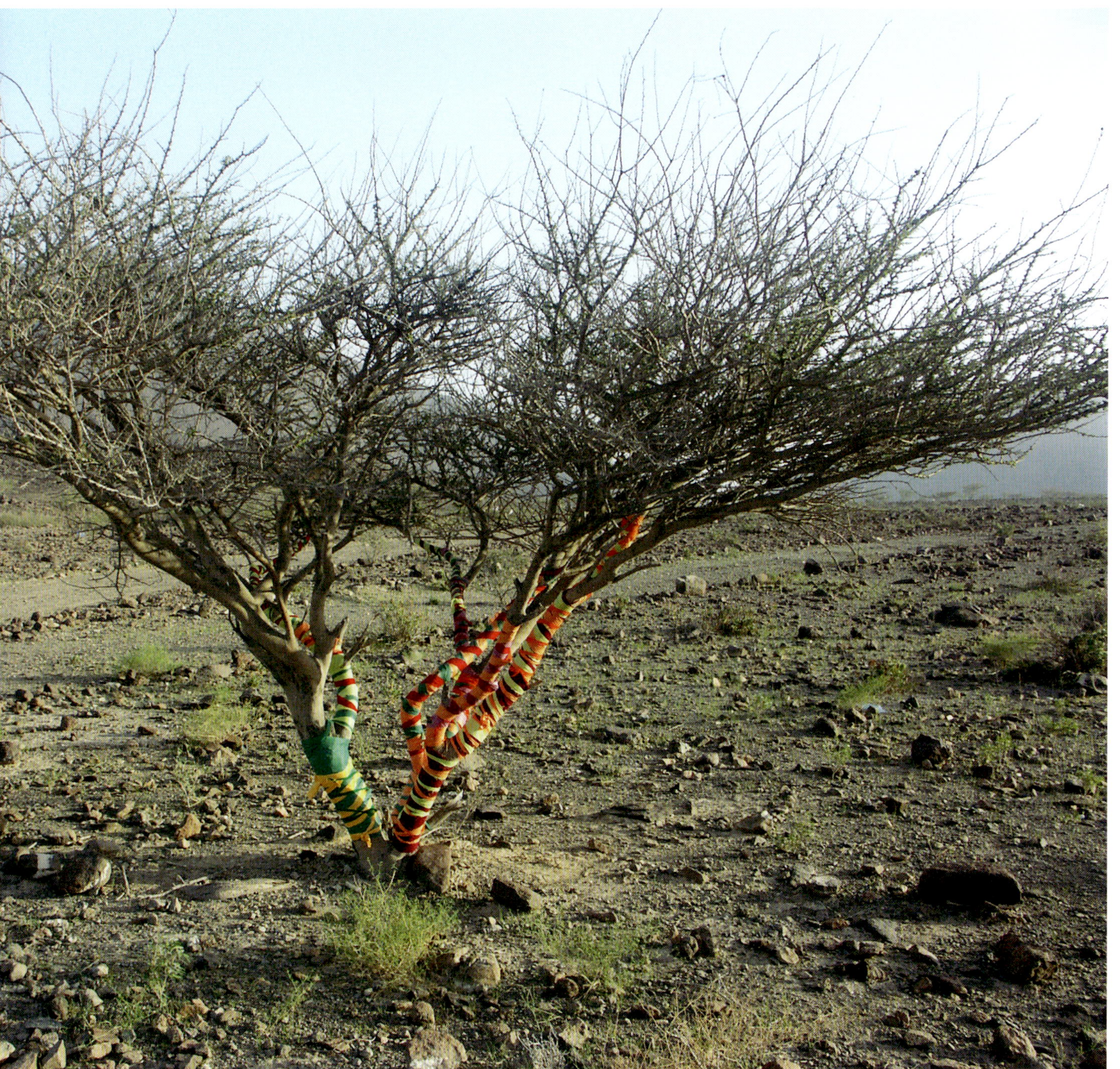

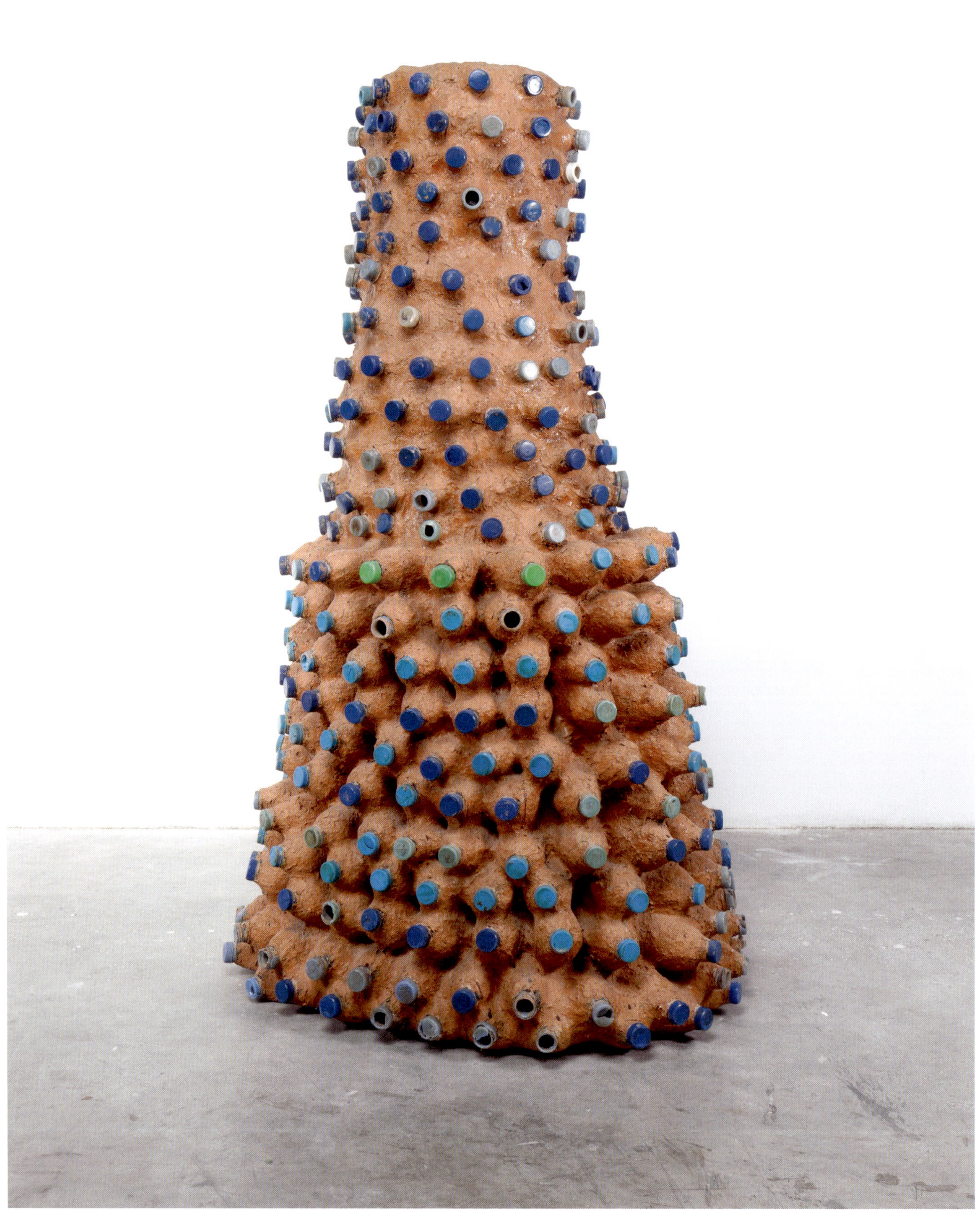

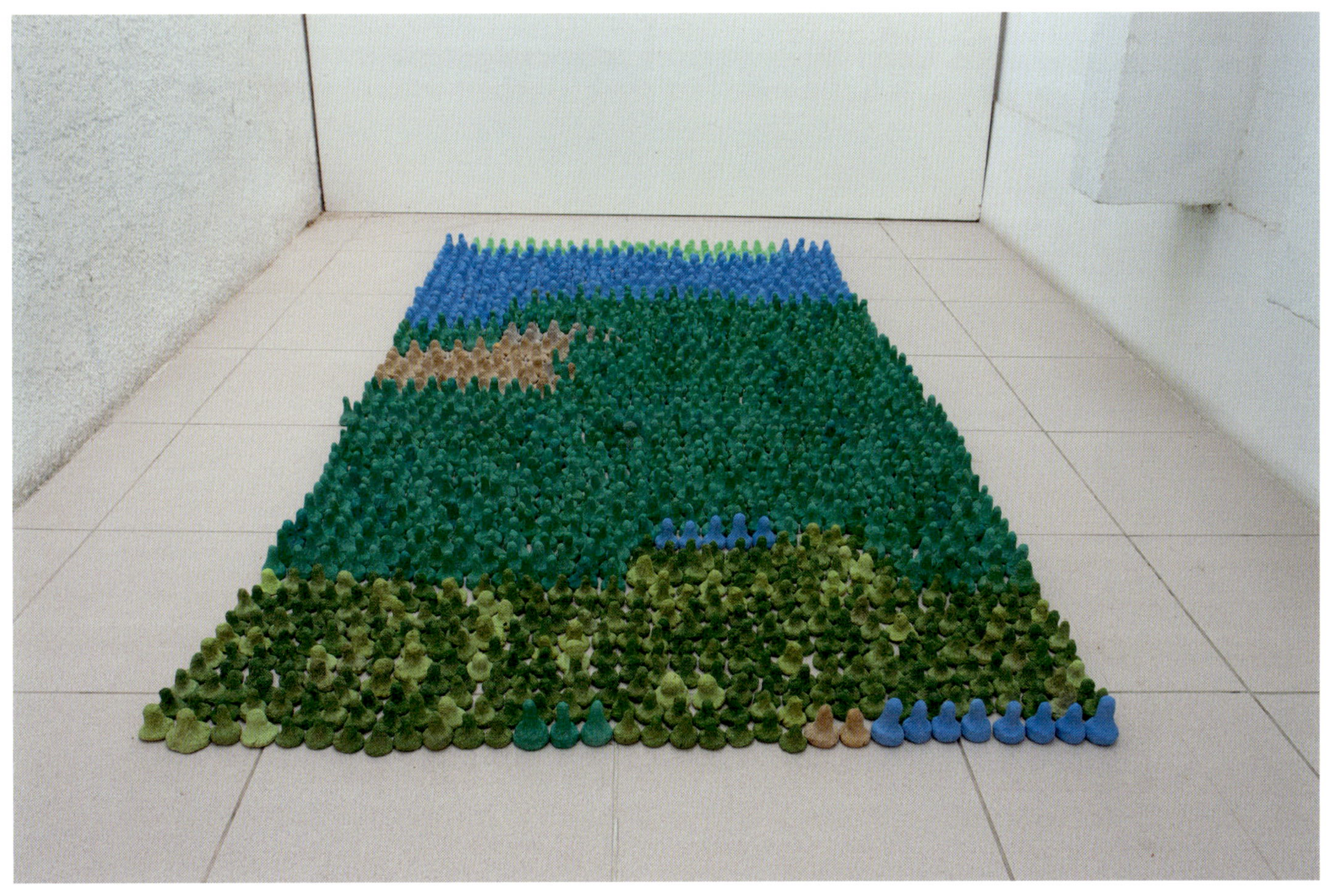

Horn, 2014
Plastic bottles, paper, clay, glue,
145 x 85 x 85 cm

Carpet, 1997
Paper and glue, 300 x 150 cm

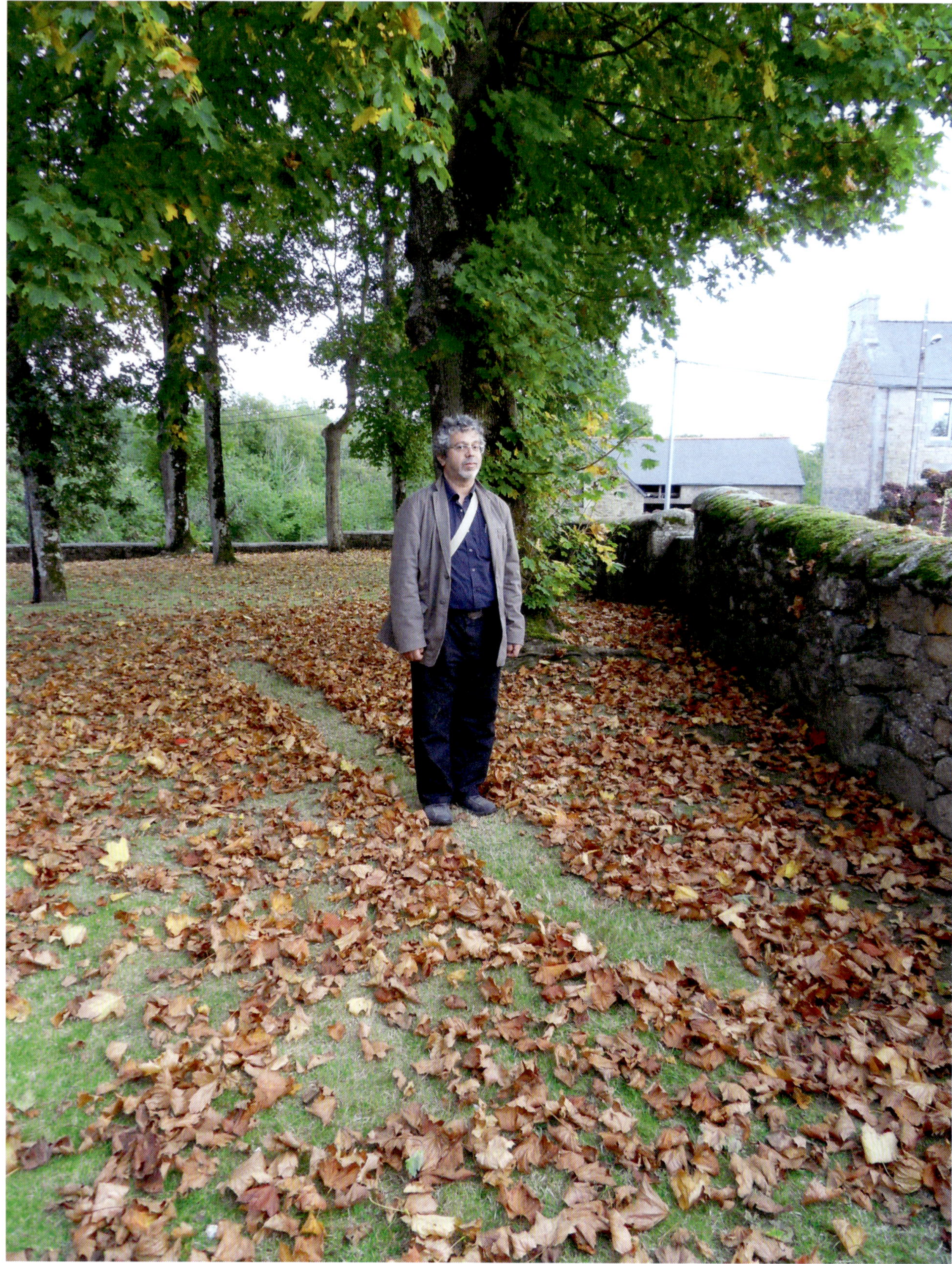

Going and Coming, 2009
Documentation of the
performance in Brittany, France

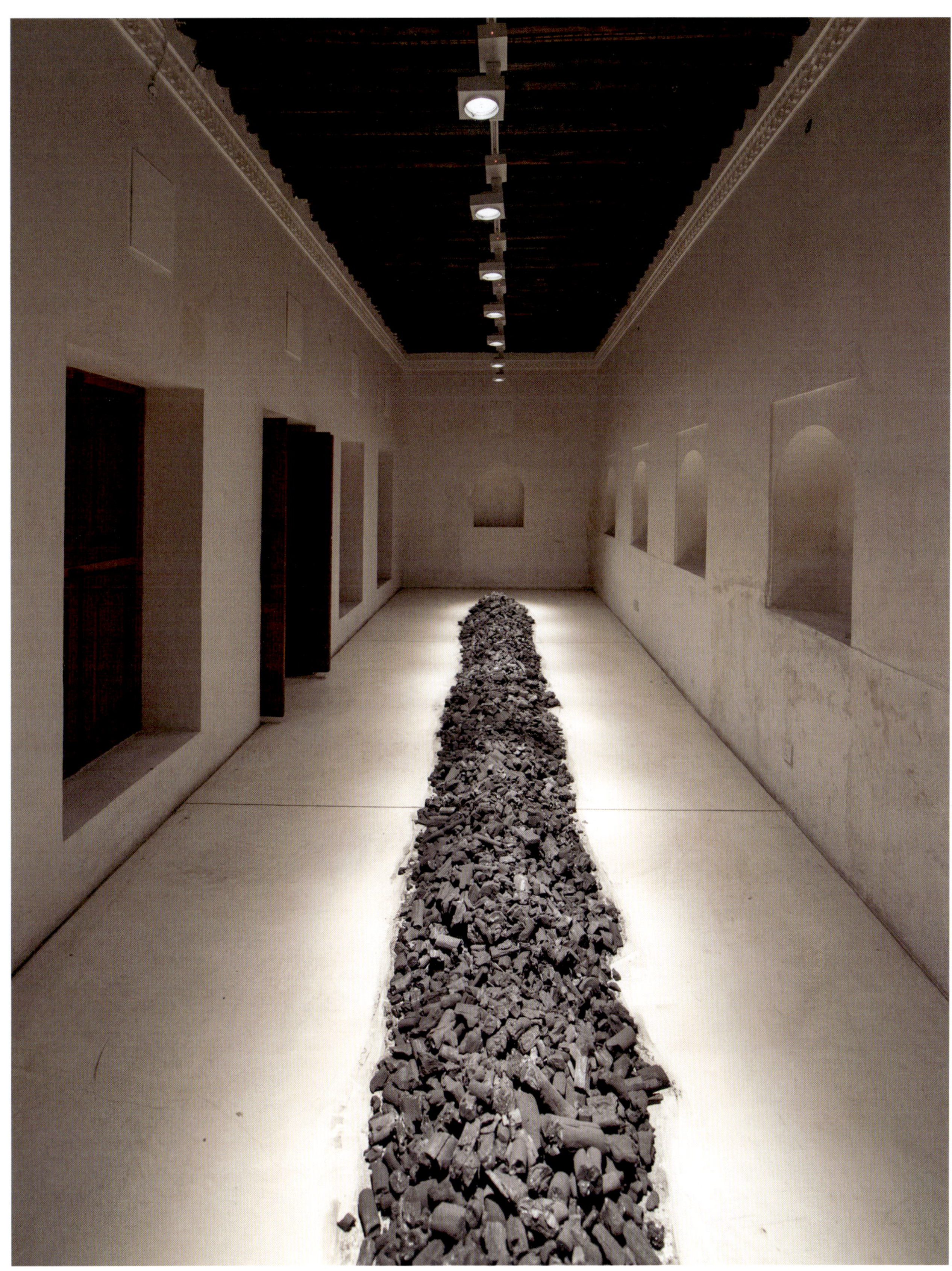

Installation view of *Mohamed Ahmed Ibrahim: Elements* at the Sharjah Art Foundation, 2018

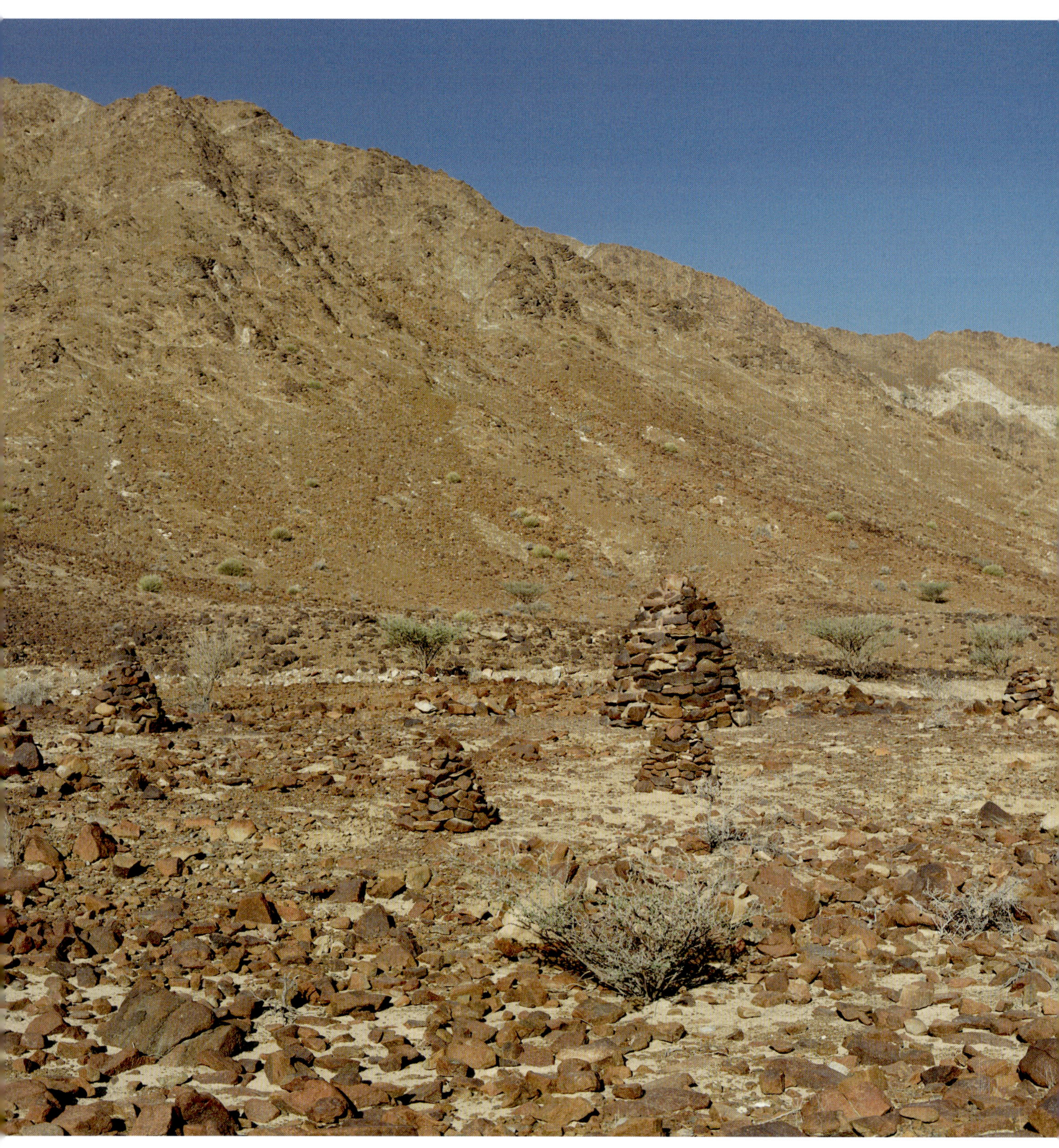

The Qubba Project, 2015
Al Hajar mountain rocks,
landscape, dimensions variable
Later presented as five C-print
photographs and film as an Abu
Dhabi Festival 2016 commission

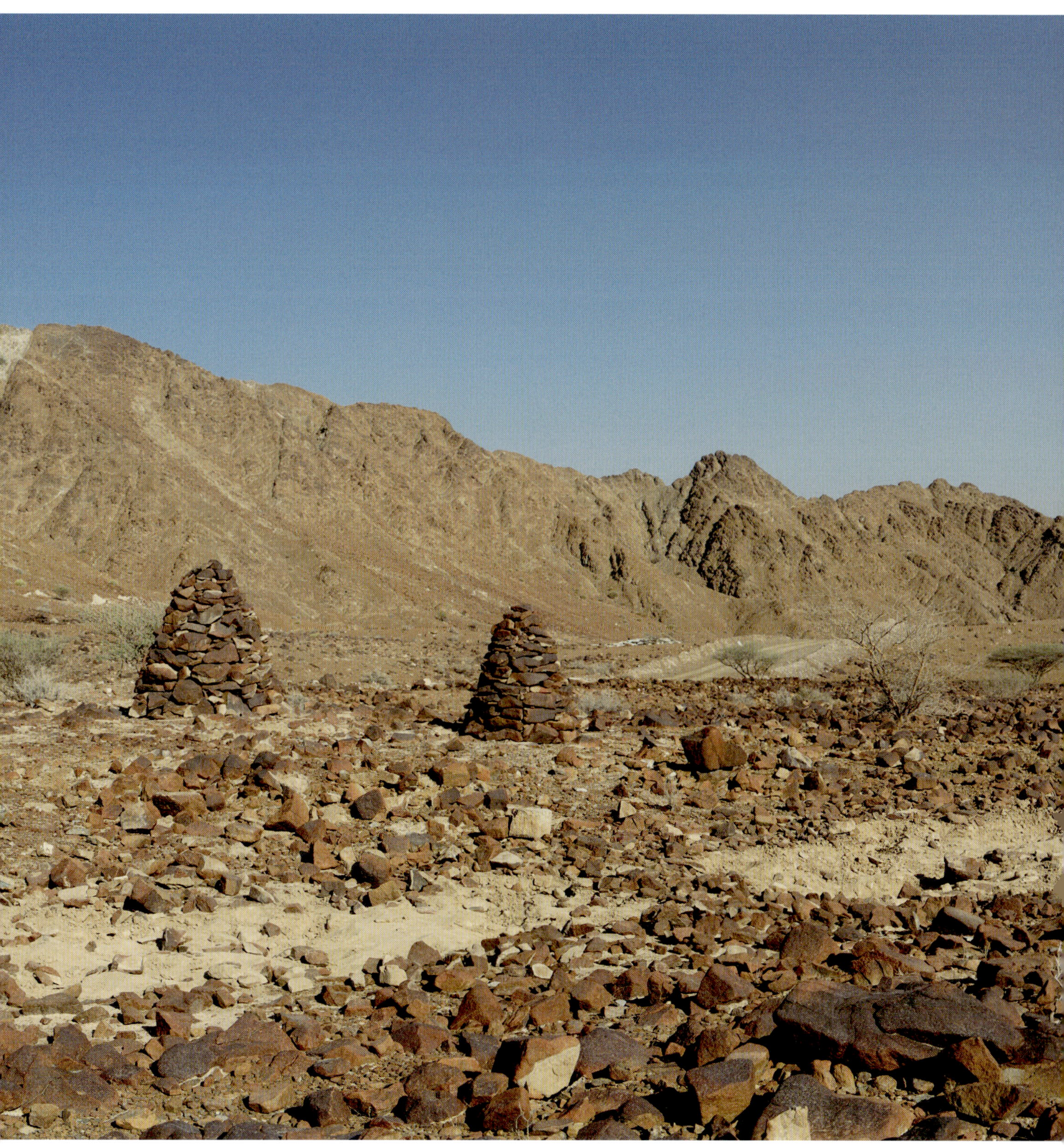

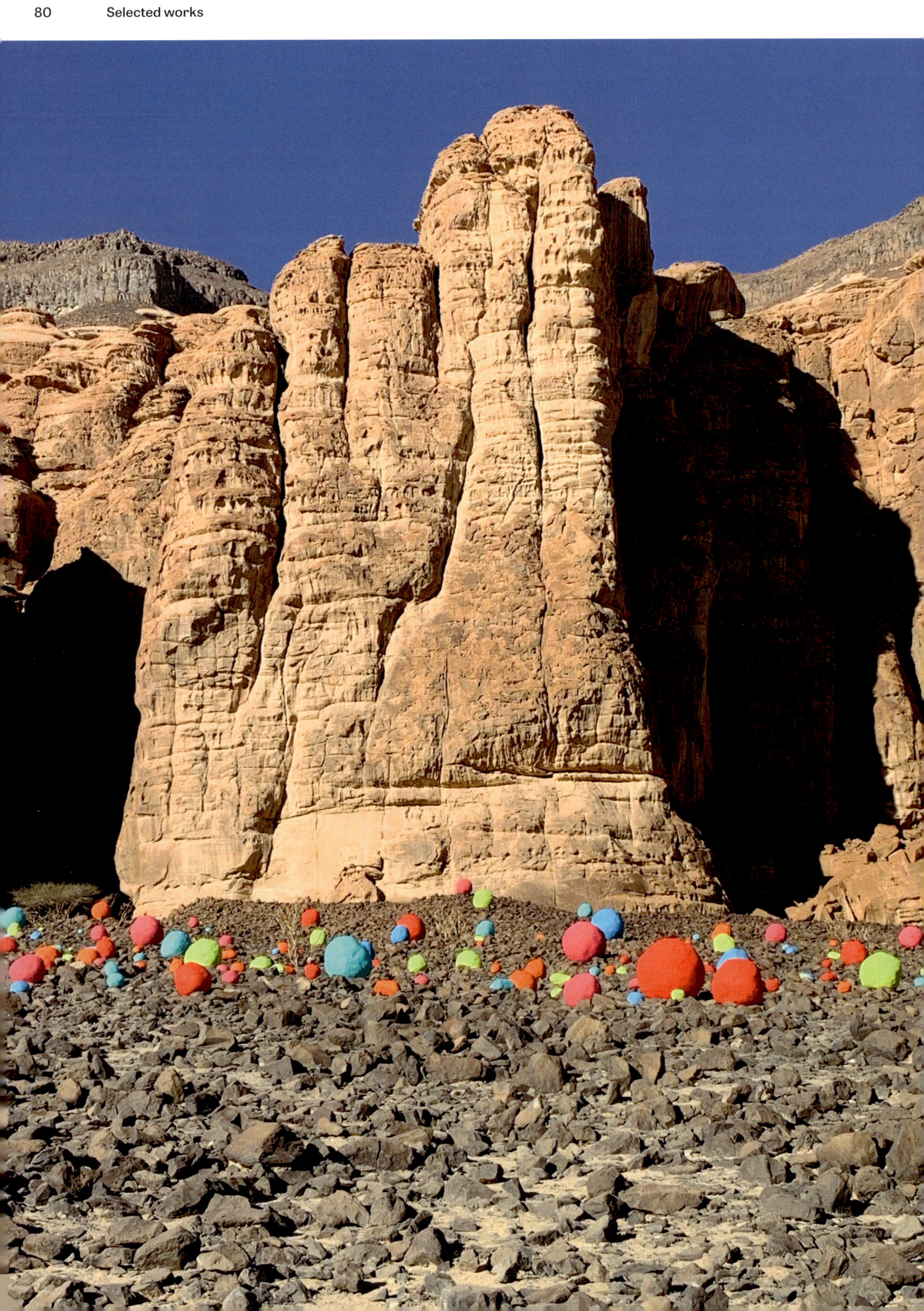

Falling Stones Garden, 2020
Painted fiberglass, 320 pieces,
dimensions variable
Site-specific installation at
Desert X AlUla, Saudi Arabia

Sunset

Fumio Nanjo

Early Days of UAE Contemporary Art

Next page
Installation view of Mohamed Ahmed Ibrahim's work at the 25th Annual Exhibition of the Emirates Fine Arts Society—Silver Jubilee, 2006 at the Sharjah Art Museum

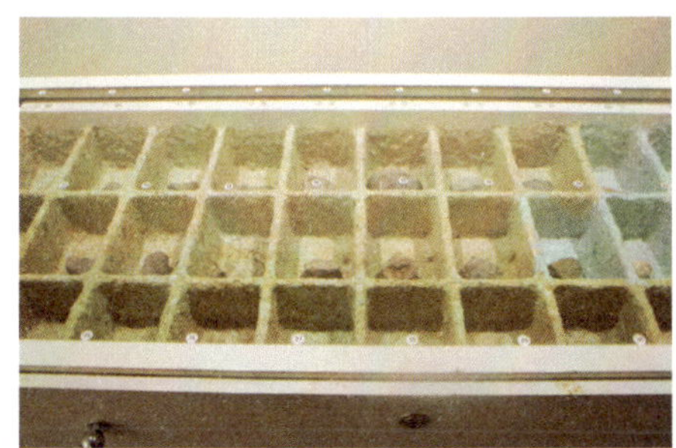

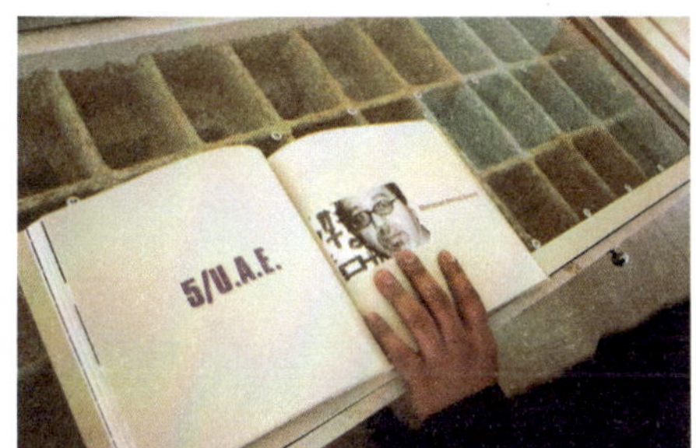

My first substantial visit to the Middle East and Gulf area was in the 1970s when the Japan Foundation gave me the job of organizing a seven-country tour for a traditional performing arts group. Traveling with the group, I spent over 30 days in the region. Then, in the 1980s, I became a contemporary art curator and was involved in organizing international exhibitions. I felt a growing desire to go back to the region that had such an impact on me when I was younger.

In 2004, I was appointed the artistic director for the first Singapore Biennale. My aim was to produce a Biennale that was truly international, so when researching potential artists, I divided the curatorial team to cover specific countries and regions. I particularly wanted to include Arab countries, as very few Arab artists had been presented at international art exhibitions at that time. Around January 2006, I planned a factfinding tour and the first country I visited was the UAE.

I can't remember the exact details of why the UAE was first on the itinerary, but it was probably because I had heard from Pat Binder and Gerhard Haupt of Universes in Universe that there was an exhibition of UAE artists in Sharjah (25th Annual Exhibition of the Emirates Fine Arts Society—Silver Jubilee). They had introduced me to Mohammed Kazem, so I met him as soon as I arrived in the Emirates. He took me to Hassan Sharif's place in Satwa—I think it was the same afternoon. I am not sure whether it was Hassan's home or his studio, but it was very small—a tiny space of perhaps five square meters. The room had a bare earth floor, connecting it directly to the ground outside. I wasn't sure what to talk about because I still did not know much about his work, and Hassan was a quiet person—shy. He spoke just a little at a time, lowering his head slightly as he talked. But he showed me an installation in his room that was a circular group of small sculptural objects that looked like scraps of paper, balled up silver paper. There were also sculptures made of rope and a work made from a pile of potato-like objects created by kneading paper. It was clear to me that he was using a contemporary art vocabulary, and I sensed that we had successfully established communication.[1]

In the early evening, I visited the Sharjah Art Museum. It was surrounded by stone walls as if it were a fortress. A long red carpet was laid out on the road to the entrance in preparation for the exhibition opening. After waiting for a while, Sheikh Sultan bin Muhammad Al-Qasimi, the ruler of Sharjah, walked up the carpet, along with his entourage. I watched from afar with the other people who were waiting. However, Mohammed Kazem, who was in the entourage, must have pointed me out as a guest from a distant country. I soon found myself ushered into the reception and seated beside His Highness for the next 15 minutes or so.

1. This marked the beginning of multiple encounters with this group of artists that continue until today. In particular, after the Great East Japan Earthquake in March 2011, Kazem and Sharif donated work for a fundraiser to provide aid for victims of the disaster. Those early research visits also led to *Arab Express: The Latest Art from the Arab World* at Mori Art Museum (June 12–October 28, 2012).

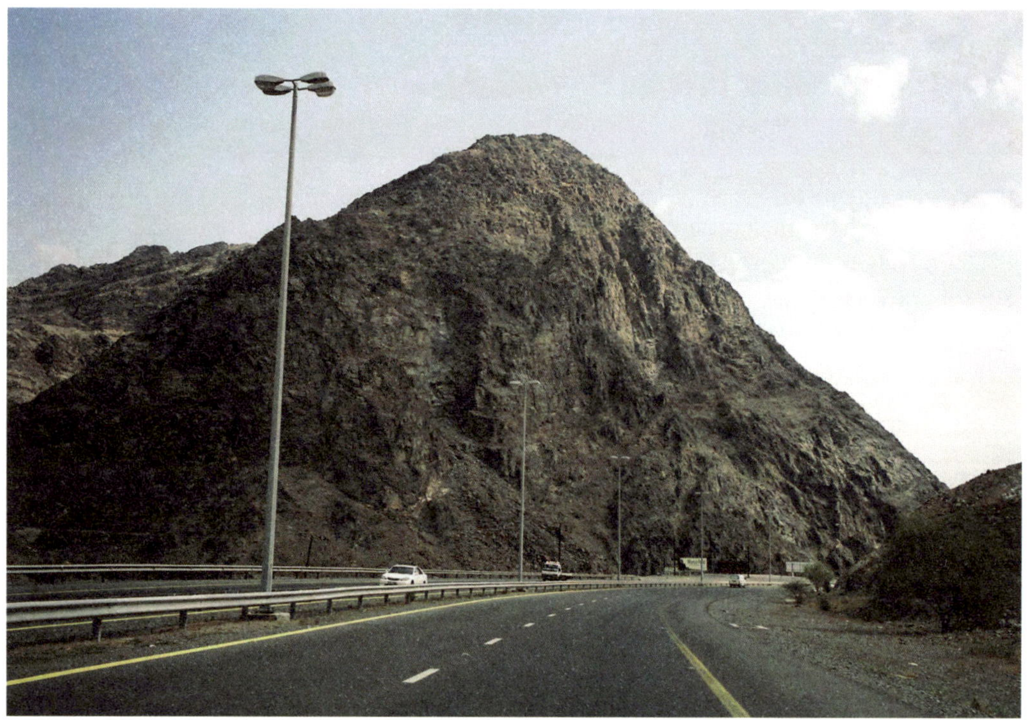

My photographs from the opening included the group of people guiding the Sheikh around the exhibition, and Hassan Sharif, Mohamed Ahmed Ibrahim, and Mohammed Kazem were all there.

I met Ebtisam Abdulaziz at the same exhibition. Her work incorporated a bank ATM and a display of chains of numbers in red light. It appeared to be a criticism of capitalism, and its very conceptual nature was striking.

Another artist who is clearly identifiable in the photographs is Mohamed Ahmed Ibrahim. Many of his works are also visible from the photos I took, including stones gathered in the desert and objects made of mud, placed on a grid. They looked like the sort of specimens you might find in a natural history museum, and they communicated the importance of the gaze with which you view your surroundings. They also embodied the message that art and life are together, that the environment is also art. I was surprised that this sort of conceptual work had already been produced in the Emirates for so long.

I think it was during the same visit that Kazem took me to the house of Abdul-Raheem Sharif, the brother of Hassan Sharif and fellow artist Hussain Sharif. He lived in a large house in its own walled compound, and inside the house, there were a large number of artworks. It was there that I heard how Hassan had become involved in contemporary art. After completing his fine art studies in the UK, Hassan returned to the Emirates in 1984. Along with a group of artist friends, he set about creating awareness of contemporary art in the UAE. Through effort and learning from each other, these artists successfully drove the growth of the conceptual art movement in the community. This story gave me an idea of how significant a role Hassan Sharif had played in

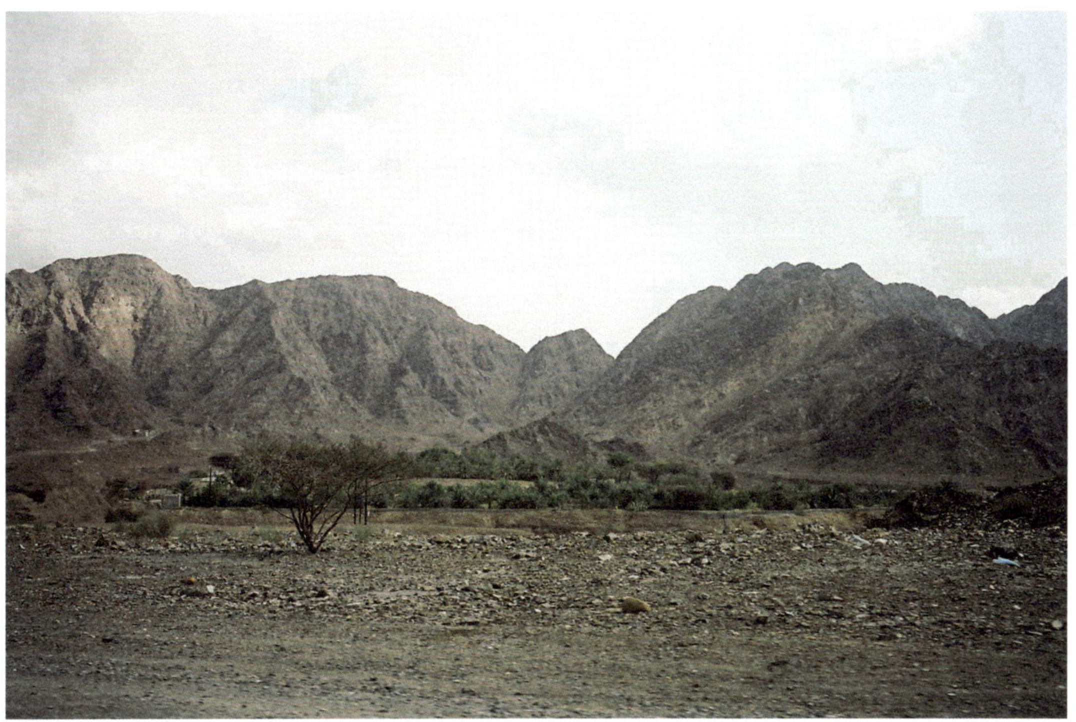

the early days of contemporary art in the Emirates.

Soon after this research trip, we decided on the artists for the Singapore Biennale, which was to be held in September 2006, eventually selecting Mohammed Kazem, Ebtisam Abdulaziz, and Nuha Asad. Kazem extended the work I had seen in Sharjah to produce a scaled-up version. Ebtisam presented a series of drawings with mathematical/geometrical arrangements, exhibited on the wall of a mosque in a manner that visualized the relationship with the venue. Nuha was still in the early stages of her career, but her photographic series of women covered in bright scarlet scarves left a vivid impression, incorporating a social metaphor that symbolized a characteristic of Arab culture.

In 2008, I was looking for artists for the second Singapore Biennale, and I returned to the Emirates. I was taken back to Abdul-Raheem's house and heard that it had become an official archive for Hassan Sharif's work as well as a small group of Emirati artists who had gravitated around him for decades. It was called The Flying House. Abdul-Raheem and Kazem showed me around in great detail. It felt much less like a house and had gained the atmosphere of an exhibition space. The central room on the ground level was an office with files full of documentation and other records. For this second trip, I had the objective of meeting more artists than I did on the first trip, so I made The Flying House my base for the research, which enabled me to meet many artists. This time I was interested in a younger generation, and I set up interviews with 10 male and 10 female artists. They each showed me their portfolios, and I took voluminous notes.

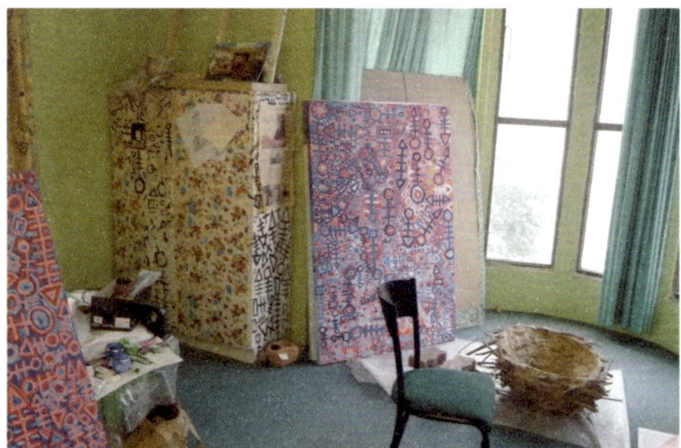
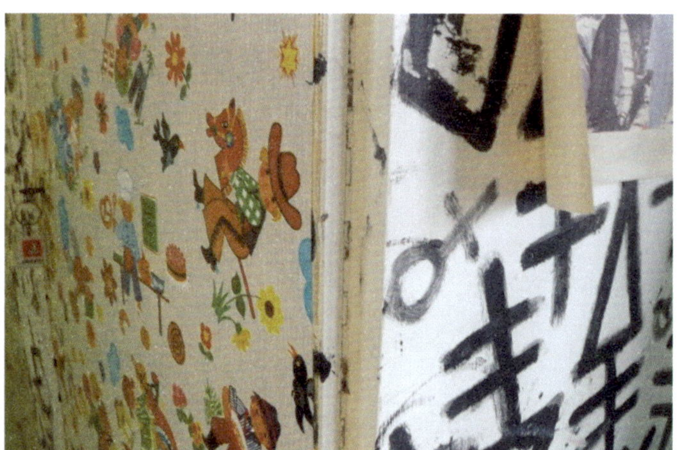

Eventually, I invited Layla Juma and Tarek Al-Ghoussein from the UAE to present at the 2008 Singapore Biennale.

During the January 2008 trip, I was also able to visit Mohamed Ahmed Ibrahim in Khor Fakkan, driven there in a 4x4 by Abdul-Raheem. Khor Fakkan is situated on the eastern side of the UAE peninsula, which juts out into the Strait of Hormuz, facing the sea. I recall the drive taking over an hour and a half, taking us for long periods on dry roads through the desert, kicking up clouds of dust behind us. Several times, we passed under massive power transmission lines, and occasionally hills came into sight. There were a few trees, here and there, making an effort to add some green to the scenery. Many of the buildings that we saw were still under construction. Eventually, we finished crossing the peninsula and arrived at the sea. I stood on the shore, thrilled to be there and impressed that I had come so far. The Strait of Hormuz was too wide to see the other side, so the sea spread out to the horizon.

We stopped the car at a restaurant close to Mohamed's house and waited for him. When he arrived, he joined us for coffee, and then we all headed to his house.

The house was on slightly higher land, set back from the coastline. There was a tower-like structure at the front with a circular wall curving away to the left. On the right side, a balcony was visible on the upper floor. The house number was written on the wall by the entrance. A garden swept around the house with lots of cacti on stones, and there was a child's bicycle.

I was invited into a reception room under the cylindrical tower, where we drank tea. The walls of the room were papered yellow, and there were yellow sofas, too. Afterward, we spent some time looking at Mohamed's artworks in the house. They were colorful, powerful works, and many were covered with arrow-like symbols. I noticed that there were similar symbols painted on drawers and other places in the room as well.

Views taken by Nanjo inside the home of the artist in 2008

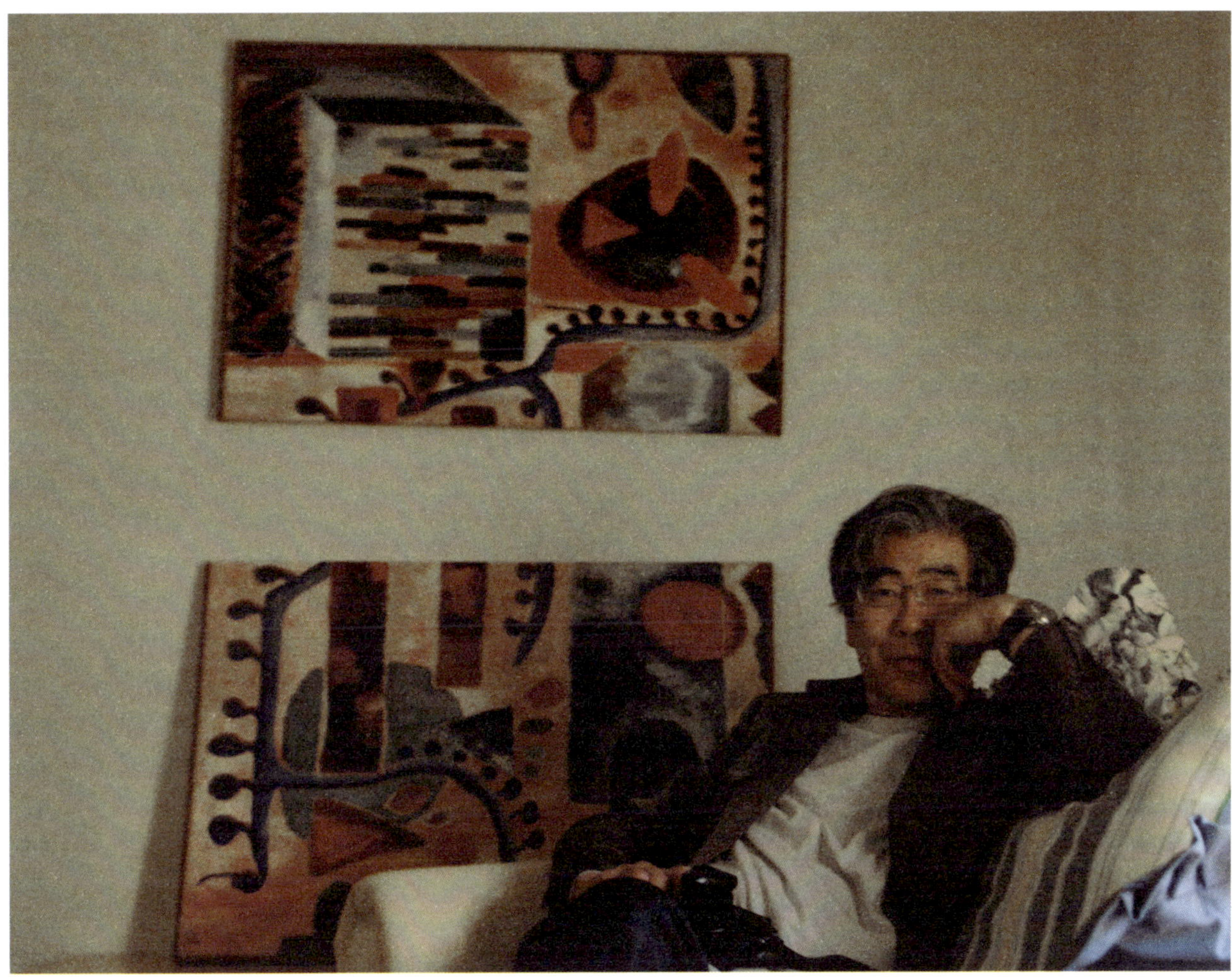

Fumio Nanjo at Mohamed Ahmed
Ibrahim's home in Khor Fakkan,
2008. Both paintings in the
background are by Ibrahim,
from 1986–1988

An extensive wall was covered with very representational oil paintings, and there were sketches and drawings here and there. There were also partially abstract works, paintings depicting symbols, and, on an easel, the beginnings of what looked like a painting of a sculpture. On a table was a colorful ball-shaped clay sculpture. There were stones wrapped in netting and a sculpture of what looked like a bird's nest made of earth. Interestingly, there wasn't anything resembling the specimen-like works that I had seen at the 25-year jubilee exhibition. I began to think about how nature, the distinctive colors and shapes, the air, and the vegetation of this town near the strait, an hour and a half away from Dubai, were appearing in his works. Mohamed's way of living was formed from the land, the light, the air, and the plants of this district. He used them in his works. And the themes that he chose were probably connected, too.

When we left, the evening was already approaching. The western sky gradually took on a purple tint as we headed back to Dubai.

What you present is
is read within the c
The art allows you t

**message that
text of art.
find your kind.**

Adel Khozam

Mohamed Ahmed Ibrahim:
Sculptor of New Concepts

<u>His Works Are a Monument to Nature Itself</u>

Is the artist subject to the power of time? Does the work of an artist necessarily reflect his or her present moment, reality, environment, and place? Or is the function of art essentially to go beyond these questions and follow exploration to its extreme? Can an artist break free from the limitations of space and time as well as open up to infiniteness in physicality and consciousness?

These are the first fundamental questions that come to mind as we stand before the works of the Emirati artist Mohamed Ahmed Ibrahim, whose practice is known to be visibly and intimately connected to land, environment, and place. From his city in the mountains, he borrowed his artistic instruments: stones, broken branches, ash, and clay, to create new works of contemporary art.

The journey of this artist began in the late seventies in a mountainous city called Khor Fakkan, overlooking the sea in the United Arab Emirates, which was established as a federal state in the year 1971. A high school student looking to enhance the spirit of art burning within him, he began spontaneously painting views of the sea, mountains, trees, and the sun. However, the lack of possibilities, materials, and artistic references in the city initially hindered the development of his understanding of the world of art.

His real journey began in 1980, after graduating from high school, when he tried to pursue the study of ancient art and archaeology. He spent a year in Pakistan, where he searched for the secrets of the vast world. He returned only a year later, having found that the archaeological monuments, despite their historical importance, were not the world he was looking for.

In 1982, he enrolled in the United Arab Emirates University (UAEU) to study psychology, likely due to visual arts not being available as a degree at the time. There, in the library of his university, books, references, theories, and new philosophies fell into his hands, and he drowned in research. He also met and joined a circle of young poets and artists, a generation who were hungry for transformation and innovation. He tried to write with them, and illustrated the covers of their magazines and books in a unique style, consisting of sketches and miniatures in the form of symbols, circular and square markers, and overlapping inscriptions in black-and-white visual compositions. This seemingly hieroglyphic aesthetic would go on to become the defining feature and artistic imprint of Mohamed Ahmed Ibrahim in many of his paintings and drawings.

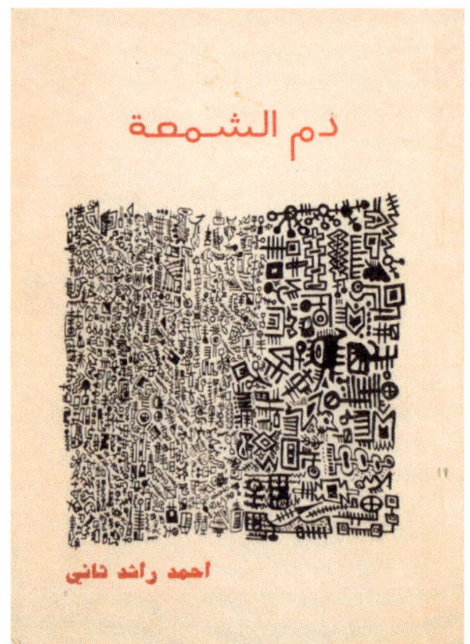

Front cover of *Candle Blood* (1991), a book of poetry by Ahmed Rashid Thani. Illustrations by Mohamed Ahmed Ibrahim. Published by the Department of Culture and Information, Sharjah

Mohamed Ahmed Ibrahim's Writing Experience

Ibrahim was a close companion of Emirati modernist poet and playwright Ahmed Rashid Thani (1962–2012), the son of the city of Khor Fakkan. Inspired by this friendship with him and other poets, Ibrahim tried his hand at literary writing with experimental poetic texts. He also wrote a single play that, unfortunately, did not see the light of day. His literary style showed potential and raw talent if he had continued as a writer, as seen in a piece from 1982:

Will you be like my heart?
Will you declare disobedience to me?
You're strong, and my heart is weak.
You're a master, and I'm a slave.
There's a difference between the two of you. . No
There's no difference between the two of you.
My heart loved you and loved your soul.
Is there a difference?
Between slavery and worship?

He continued to write for a while but later abandoned writing and became obsessed with going to art exhibitions in Abu Dhabi, Dubai, and Sharjah. The early 1980s were a golden age of culture in the UAE that came to life after oil sale revenues brought economic prosperity to the region. A surge in urbanization, education, and information had taken place, accompanied by the emergence of cultural and artistic institutions. In 1980, the Emirates Fine Arts Society (EFAS) was established and started organizing an annual exhibition for its member artists and residents of the UAE. Emerging cultural institutions were interested in organizing new and distinct exhibitions. Similarly, the first generation of artists who had traveled to study art in the universities of Egypt, Iraq, and Britain began to return to the country, and newspapers became devoted to following artistic activity within the country. It was during this period that the UAE started to hold book fairs that provided specialized art references.

Ibrahim experienced all these rapid transformations in lifestyle, and with it, his awareness, maturity, and questions increased. His experiences have evolved into paintings brimming with color while retaining the same themes, shapes, and symbols. He presented murals bearing his mark, used different colors, and participated in the collective exhibitions held annually by EFAS, but the obsession with renewal, breaking patterns, and searching for his own style continued to occupy him. He had nourished this passion when he was studying psychology, reading philosophy, and engaging in heated debates about literature in the UAE society. That society had moved very quickly from being centered around a simple life to living in the intensity of the modern city. Artists had to confront this rapid development and ideas of modernity, as it related to their understanding of what art is.

In the Heart of the Battle

At that time, progressive advocates were engaged in intense conflicts with the traditional and conservative mainstream. Poets were accused of trying to subvert the language because they broke the conditions of rhyme, and artists were attacked similarly because they presented abstract painting and experimental, conceptual art. The questions surrounding art flowed endlessly, schools, ideas, and artistic currents overlapped, while concepts of change extended to everything. Newspapers saw arguments between the two sides, and the battles reached out to seminars, poetry evenings, and art exhibitions. It was natural for Ibrahim to take the progressive side in this battle: that was part of his rebellious nature against traditional art and reflected his philosophical understanding of the essence of art. He began to think of producing works of art that went beyond the rigid and narrow concept of a painting, and from there, went up onto the mountains. Finding only stones and scattered trees, he said: "It's OK, I will make art from them."

In 1986, Ibrahim was introduced to Hassan Sharif (1951–2016), the UAE's leading conceptual artist, who had just returned from the United Kingdom with a diploma in visual arts from the Byam Shaw School of Art in London. Upon his return to the UAE in 1984, Sharif created conceptual art through his art installations made out of mundane and mass-produced materials. He also publicly challenged the traditional concept of a painting as decorative. Sharif embraced Marcel Duchamp's vision and understanding of the nature of art, particularly his rejection of the idea that artwork should be produced only to satisfy the eye. Instead, Duchamp wanted to use art to serve the mind. As he adopted this perspective, Sharif faced rejection and disapproval from many community groups and institutions.

The moment they met, Ibrahim entered Hassan Sharif's world and soon became one of his close friends. He felt this artist had a vision that was similar to his own soul and ideas, and that is exactly what he was looking for. With great strides, Ibrahim began to shorten the distances in this beautiful space of poetry, art, philosophy, theorizing, and experimentation. He mingled with many Arab and foreign artists residing in Dubai, Abu Dhabi, and Sharjah. On one hand, Ibrahim found himself in the middle of a great cultural battle in the Arab world, beginning from his immediate surroundings in the UAE and expanding into bigger battles in broader Arab culture. On the other hand, he felt a sense of belonging to global culture, in

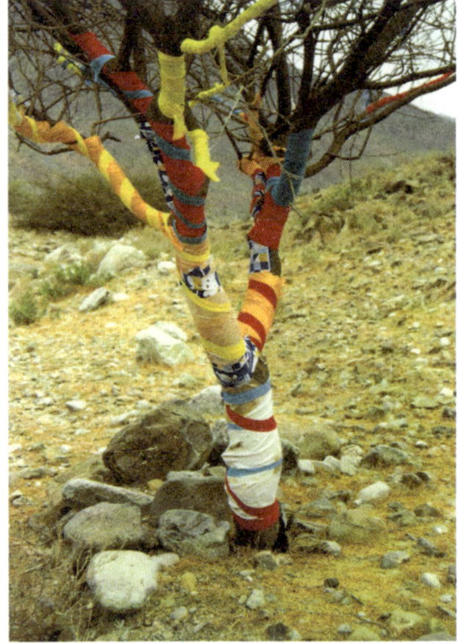

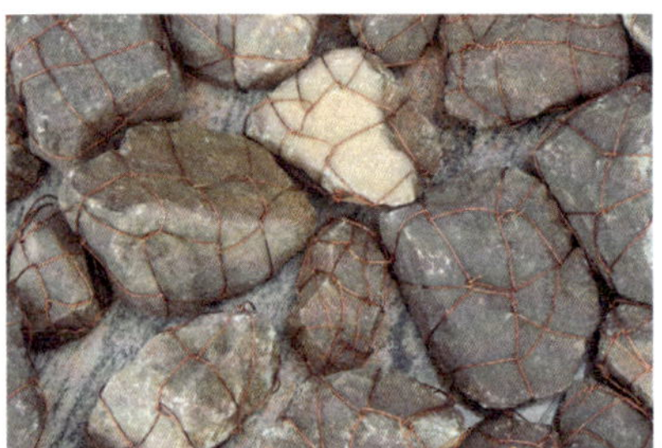

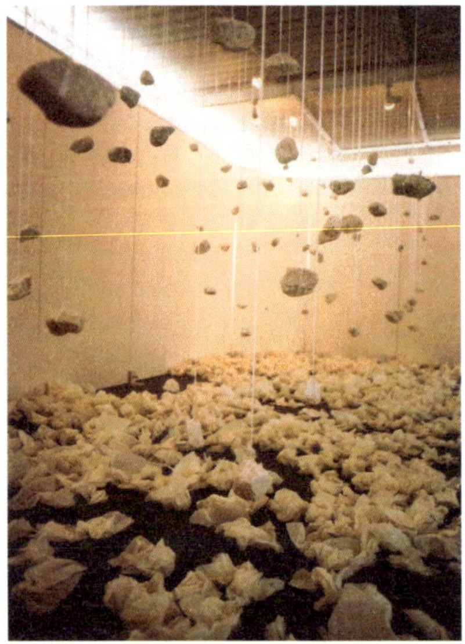

Draped Trees (Ashjar Muqammasha), 1996
Textiles, dimensions variable

Stones Wrapped in Copper (detail), 2007
Stones, copper, wire, dimensions variable

Hanging Stones, 1994
Installation at the EFAS Annual Exhibition

thought and through his research into art, and, with time, he was able to feel his own voice.

Returning to the mountains of his distant city, he wrapped the mountain trees and palm trees that were scattered in public streets with pieces of colorful fabrics related to the colors of his early childhood. That was a deliberate provocation to those who saw art as just a painting framed on a wall. It was a visual concept that rebelled against its reality. The idea also translated into painting on mountain rocks, engraving them with amulets and symbols resembling drawings from ancient caves. He then brought ropes and materials and wrapped large and small mountain rocks with plastic and metal wires in an artistic practice that shocked traditional taste. The entire city of Khor Fakkan became his art studio, and the foot of the mountain became the place where his works were displayed. He had dreams of coloring an entire mountain and would have done it if the opportunity had been available. I met him during this period and began to learn about his ideas in art and his perspective on life.

Sculptor of Concepts

These projects were somehow close to the concept of Land Art, which typically refuses to imprison works of art in museums and instead presents them in nature. Ibrahim would not have accepted a very limited concept of Land Art: he believed in the philosophy that art could be produced and exhibited anywhere. So, he flipped the equation and insisted on presenting his works (with elements taken from the earth) in many exhibition spaces, including a set of stones he took from the foot of the mountain and wrapped in pieces of fabric, placing some on the floor and hanging others in the exhibition hall. I vividly recall being present with him, seeing that exhibition.

Ibrahim continued drawing shapes and symbols in paintings and participating in group exhibitions. He created a middle ground between traditional sculpting and painting by collecting cardboard papers, tree bark, leaves, and broken branches and then crushing them to form a paste for molding out his works. In the second half of the 1990s, Ibrahim was in the throes of experimentation, moving among styles and shapes, developing his own concepts at the intersection of art philosophies.

Ibrahim was not satisfied with materials found in the landscape or only taken from nature. He also included materials such as corn flour, papers, boxes, sawdust, dyes, spices, and tea leaves to form a mixture and paste for his artwork. At its core, this approach anticipated contemporary notions of environmentally friendly art. These practices added a spiritual dimension to these works, which he started producing in the 1990s, continuing to this day.

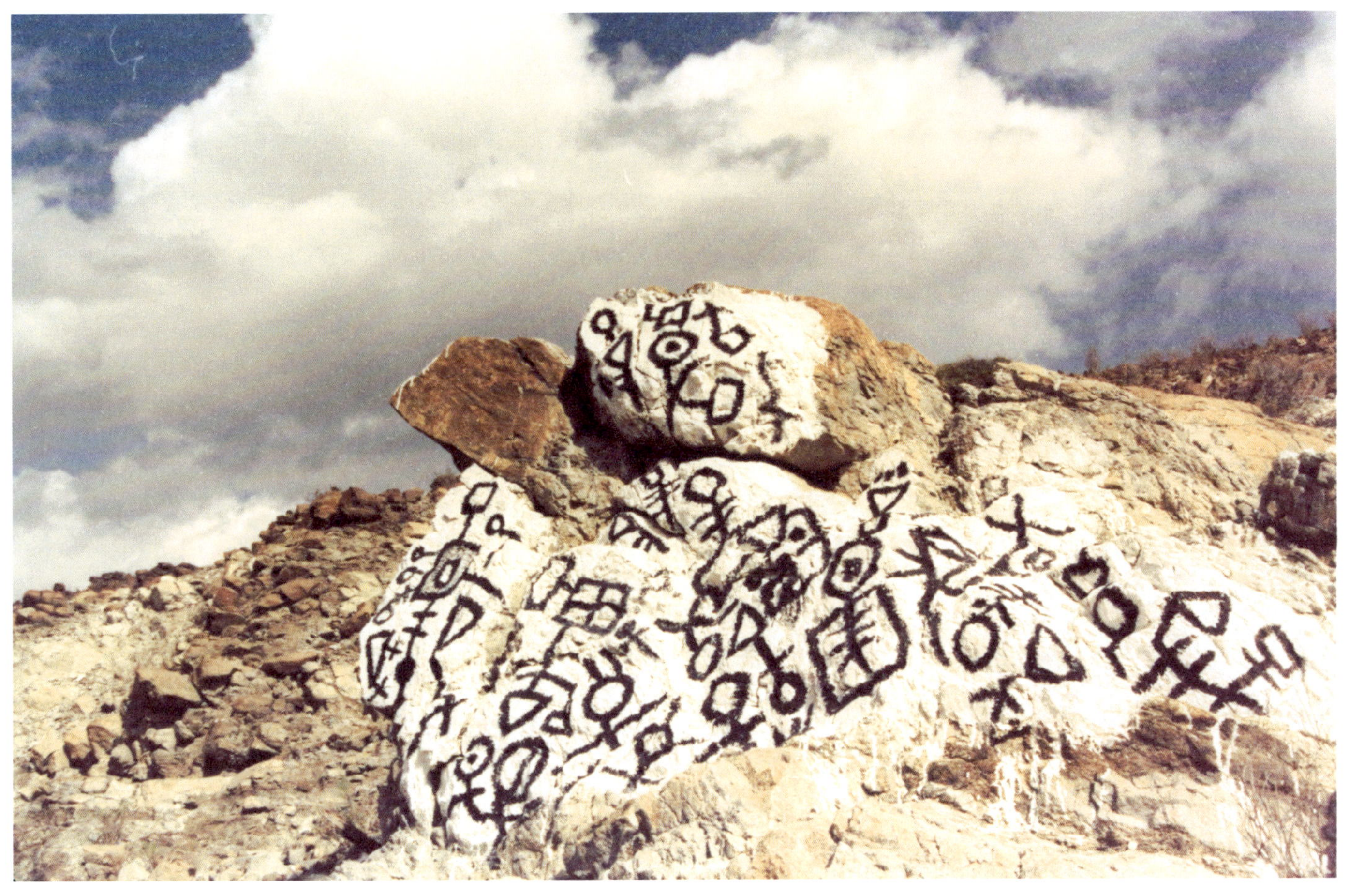

Painted Stone, 1991.
Paint on rocks in Khor Fakkan

The Question of Shape

The other question that persisted in the imagination of this artist was about the shape of the sculptural material. In other words, what does he want to embody in his works? Does he imitate by creating configurations of human or animal forms? Does he adhere to the classical dimensions and conditions of the sculptural work in terms of the relationship of mass to emptiness? We see that he gave himself complete freedom: the sculptural masses were created as if they did not embody particular features but were free compositions that take their own shape from the present moment of the artist at work, as he ventures in the creative process. A viewer can imagine a link between these formations and the embodiment or form that is imagined in their mind, but when they look closely and move around the object, they will discover nothing more than that the piece represents itself and rarely resembles the forms of humans, animals, or plants. They are mostly memorials to nature itself. Some of these sculptures are rough to the touch due to their material composition, such as remnants of twigs and sawdust, and some are smooth and coated with materials that hide the apparent roughness.

After struggling, Ibrahim began to reap the fruits of his labor, and his reputation and artistic career grew. He participated in exhibitions within the UAE and presented his practice for the first time in a solo exhibition in 1991. He

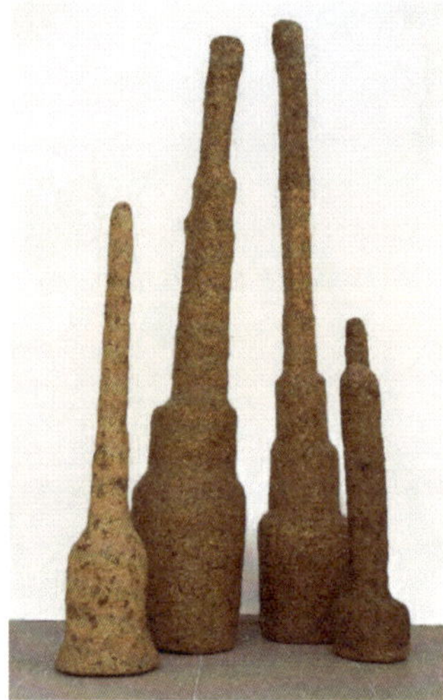

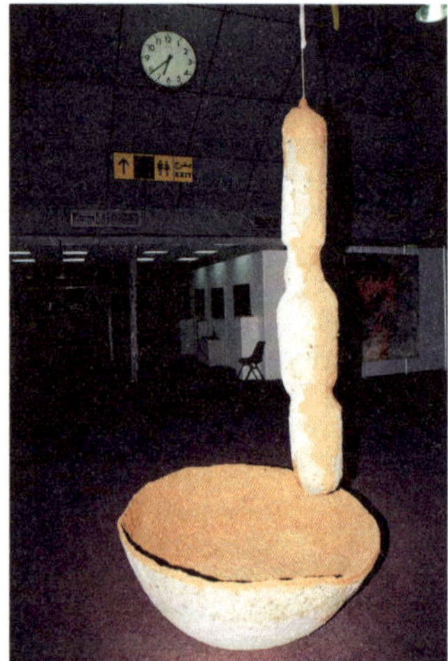

Leaf, Paper, & Glue, 1998
Leaf, paper, glue, dimensions
variable

Leaf, Clay, & Glue, 2001
Leaf, clay, glue, dimensions
variable

showed his work in an exhibition in Moscow, and he took part in the Sharjah Biennial from 1993 onward. There he was awarded the first prize in sculpture in both the 1999 and 2001 editions for his works derived from nature, bound by paper, wood, and glue. In the work that won the 1999 Sharjah Biennial Prize, the concept of time manifests in these sculptures on two levels. First, physical temporality: the artist adjusts the rhythm of his production and the movement of his hands, which affects the way the materials are mixed and what type of shape is possible. It is an improvisational process that harmonizes with the second level: psychological temporality. The moment of production exists in the art itself, creating a portal via the artist's imagination that renders time eternal through the flow of the moment—the moment of production. Long after the work is complete, that moment continues and moves with the work from one exhibition to another. There is a fundamental point in this concept that appears in the details of each work: no piece is similar to the other, in shape, in color, or in its construction and composition. Therefore, they are separate cases in their own right, although they appear to the viewer to be harmonious and integrated.

The second time Ibrahim won the Sharjah Biennial Prize was in 2001. I remember being with him during this moment of victory. He had tried to create a new form that highlighted the relationship between the object's mass and its surrounding emptiness by hanging a part of the work in the air with a rope while its counterpart was left on the ground. The intelligence of this compositional development continued, and over time, he grew more focused on ideas and concepts, always avoiding a ready-made model for sculpture. His works do not beg for prestige or luxury. On the contrary, they destroy these imposed categories if one was to look at the concept of sculpture as a display of the aesthetics of traditional composition and geometry.

Toward Universalism

In the 1990s, his participation expanded to several important international exhibitions, including the Dhaka, Havana, and Cairo Biennials, and other exhibitions in Germany and the Netherlands. Within the UAE, his battle for progress in art continued, and he became a key member of a small group that included four other artists, namely Hassan Sharif, Hussain Sharif, Mohammed Kazem, and Abdullah Al Saadi. They all participated in exhibitions dedicated to the conceptual dimension of art. They adopted this approach, and they wrote about it and experimented with shocking and controversial works. Ibrahim also developed a deep and strong friendship with Dutch artist Jos Clevers, which started in the early 1990s. Clevers organized an exhibition for the five artists in his quiet city of Sittard. I attended the exhibition and felt the admiration of the Dutch public for the work presented there.

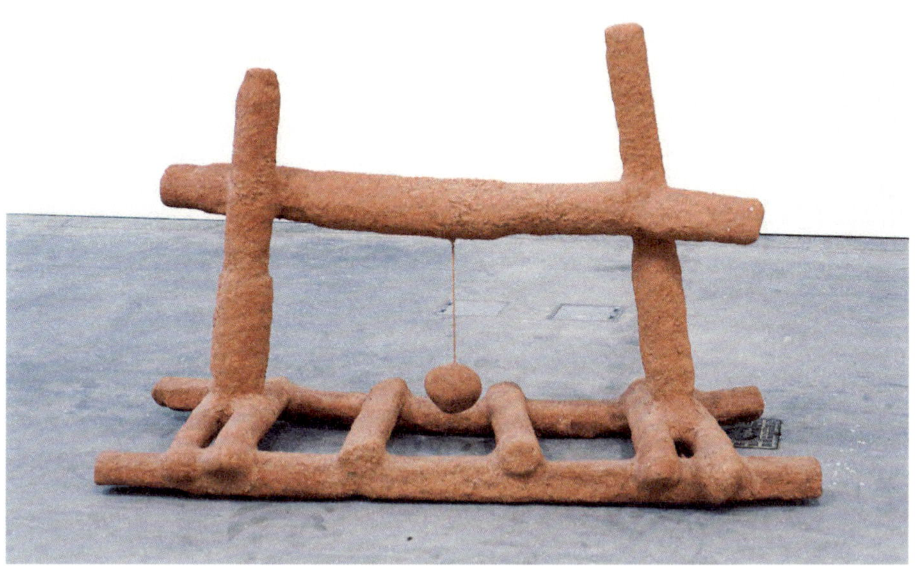

Khor Fakkan (detail), 2002
Leaf, glue, clay, dimensions
variable

At the Sittard exhibition, as well as in other shows, Ibrahim entered the exhibition space and began to cover the walls with paper to start immediately drawing straight lines on the entire wall. Ibrahim presented artworks based on the concept of linear dimension that began in the 1990s and continues to the present day. The idea of his work is based on the improvisational drawing of straight lines, from the top of the wall to the ground, which are sometimes connected and sometimes separated. The lines are cut off but appear to be connected. Most importantly, these works are not transported or shipped, but the artist comes to the space to create them there. He started this lines artwork in the Emirate of Sharjah and developed it further for the exhibition in the Dutch city of Sittard, and he returned and repeated it in more than one city and location. This repetition of the concept recalls a quote by Archimedes of Syracuse, who said that "the shortest distance between two points is the straight line." It also relates to the idea of infinity and, therefore, the idea of the infiniteness of time and space and of thought and consciousness.

Artistic and sculptural ideas continued to develop with Ibrahim's experiences and expanded to an endless horizon. In the beginning, the materials he collected had their own natural color, close to dirt and sandy clay, but later he began to include other colors in many of his sculptures. Ibrahim developed specific types and a certain quality of color. His first sculptures had a singular color dimension, but he introduced bright colors and made them part of the texture and material of the sculpture. The bright colors in the work break the monochromatic stereotype that one associates with traditional sculpture. In contrast, the works of Ibrahim allow color to enter as a disruptive element, introducing new perspectives. This is the same concept that is repeated in his paintings, where the bright colors are remarkable. Instead of rigidity, these pieces are displayed in a childlike and simple way to the point where they approach the forms of toys. This is a deliberate break of the rhythm of the

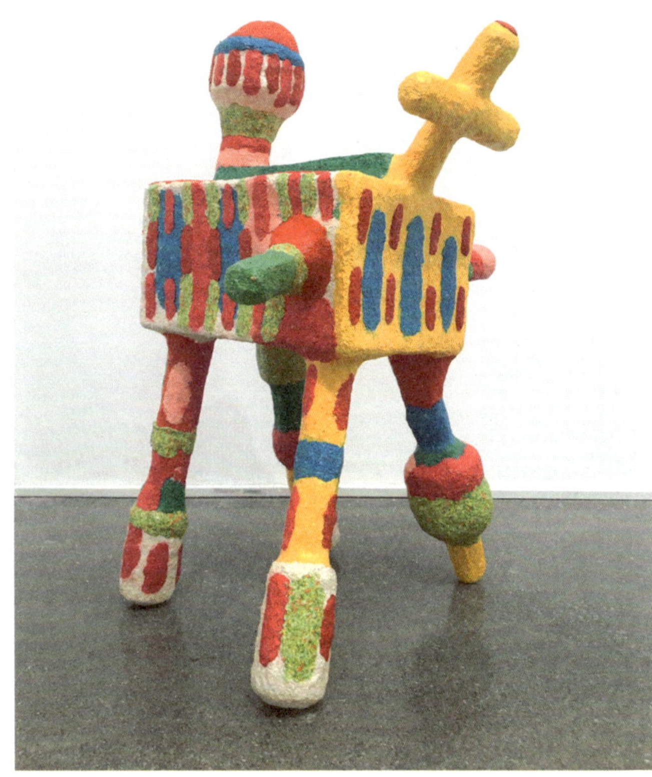

sculptural mass and an introduction of a new rhythm based on spontaneity and unequal relationships between the dimensions in the material itself.

For more than 40 years, Mohamed Ahmed Ibrahim has had dozens of experiences, traveling widely, including artist residency programs in many European and Asian countries. He participated in some of the largest art exhibitions in the world, and his works have been acquired by leading museums, but his spontaneous voice has remained the same. He stores in his heart the deep simplicity of childhood, and his works continue to be his greatest treasure that goes beyond the rigid view of life and existence. From this awareness, he integrates the spiritual dimension into his artistic practice that gives everything a new life.

Today, with his artwork at the Venice Biennale, this artist stands to say something new about the nature of art while his concepts continue to expand and develop the more deeply you look at them and delve into their meanings.

Robot, 2020
Sliced cardboard, wood, fabric,
papier-mâché, 72 x 42 x 51 cm

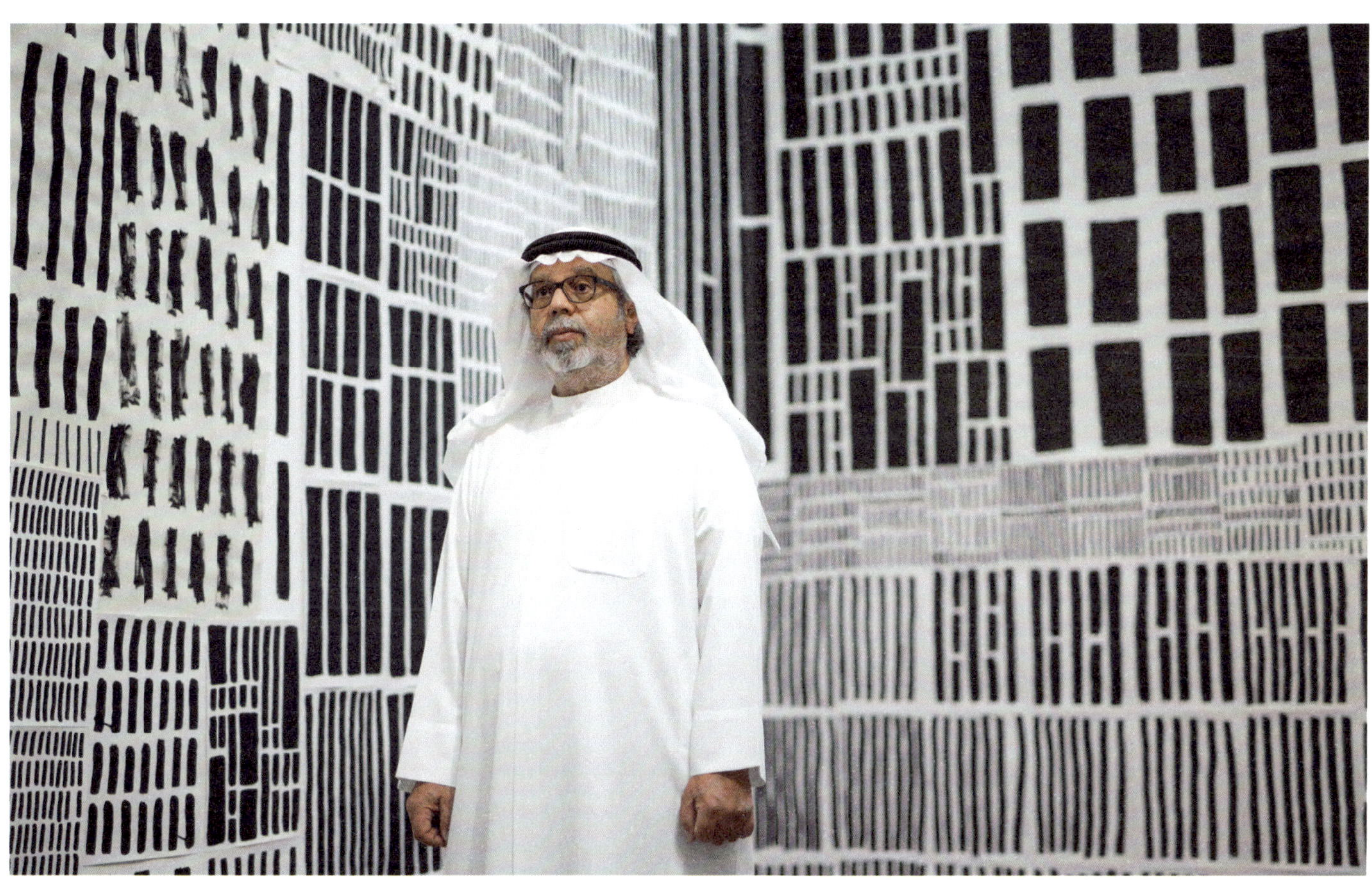

Mohamed Ahmed Ibrahim in his
exhibition *The Space Between
The Eyelid and the Eyeball*, 2019
at Lawrie Shabibi, Dubai

I found a place that
with, as an artist, af
"against" for quite s

could identify
er struggling
me time.

Vivek Vilasini

Leaning on the Edge

Next page
Piled Rocks No. 2, 1995
Clay, stones, carpet,
100 x 300 x 200 cm

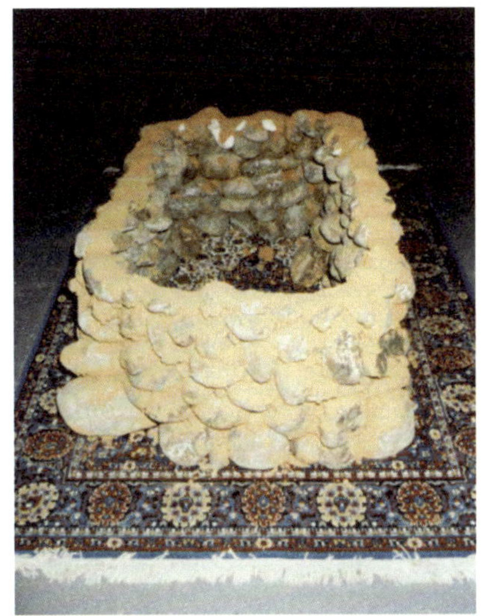

During the Sharjah Biennial in 1995, I noticed a work that stood out like an island, questioning the sensibilities and aesthetics of the art around it. I felt like most of the other works were very ornate, embellished, and decorated, but this artwork was much more organic and contrasted with the surrounding aesthetics. I was standing near it for a long time, taking in the sensory experience and reflecting on how the work resonated with my thoughts. As I was leaving, I noticed a gentleman wearing a dishdasha approaching the work. I casually greeted him and did a "thumbs up" while pointing at the work. When he came closer, I nodded and whispered, "great work." Sensing my enthusiasm, he smiled and said, "it's mine." This was my first meeting with Mohamed Ahmed Ibrahim. We talked at length about art, life as an artist, and even life in general. There were so many similarities in our approach, understanding, ideas, and in the artists we admired.

A year later, I was thinking of going back home to India because the plans I had of showing my work at a gallery in Dubai were canceled. After years of preparation, I was left with so many works and no place to exhibit. I knew I had to leave them behind as most of them were pretty monumental. But before I left, I wanted to show my work, at least, to this gentleman that I had met at the Sharjah Biennial from the year before. I just wanted to show it to someone who might appreciate my efforts. After a bit of a search, I traced him through a journalist friend and found out that he often visited a library in Sharjah, and I managed to meet him there. The meeting rekindled our old conversation, and we began again, where we had left off.

Soon after, Mohamed Ahmed Ibrahim introduced me to Hassan Sharif, Hussain Sharif, Mohammed Kazem, and Abdullah Al Saadi. After seeing my works, they invited me to exhibit alongside them in a now-historic exhibition at the Sharjah Art Museum.[1]

After becoming friends, I had the opportunity to visit Mohamed's studio in Khor Fakkan several times, observe his practice, and better understand his approach to making art. I also saw many of his Land Art pieces in the hills of Khor Fakkan and documentation of his work.

Mohamed is continuously working. His fascination for found and recyclable material, and new ways of engaging with it, is intriguing. He has made fantastic use of everyday materials from plastic, newspaper, pebbles, cardboard, and corrugated sheets. I found that in Mohamed's work there is a constant search for inspiration from the material itself. He often incorporates the ever-increasing amounts of packaging materials that are thrown away from shopping malls and supermarkets. Everything comes in so much packaging, whether it is water, food, or any other goods. His sustainable practice of reusing and upcycling is sometimes understood as a commentary and critique of the consumer world.

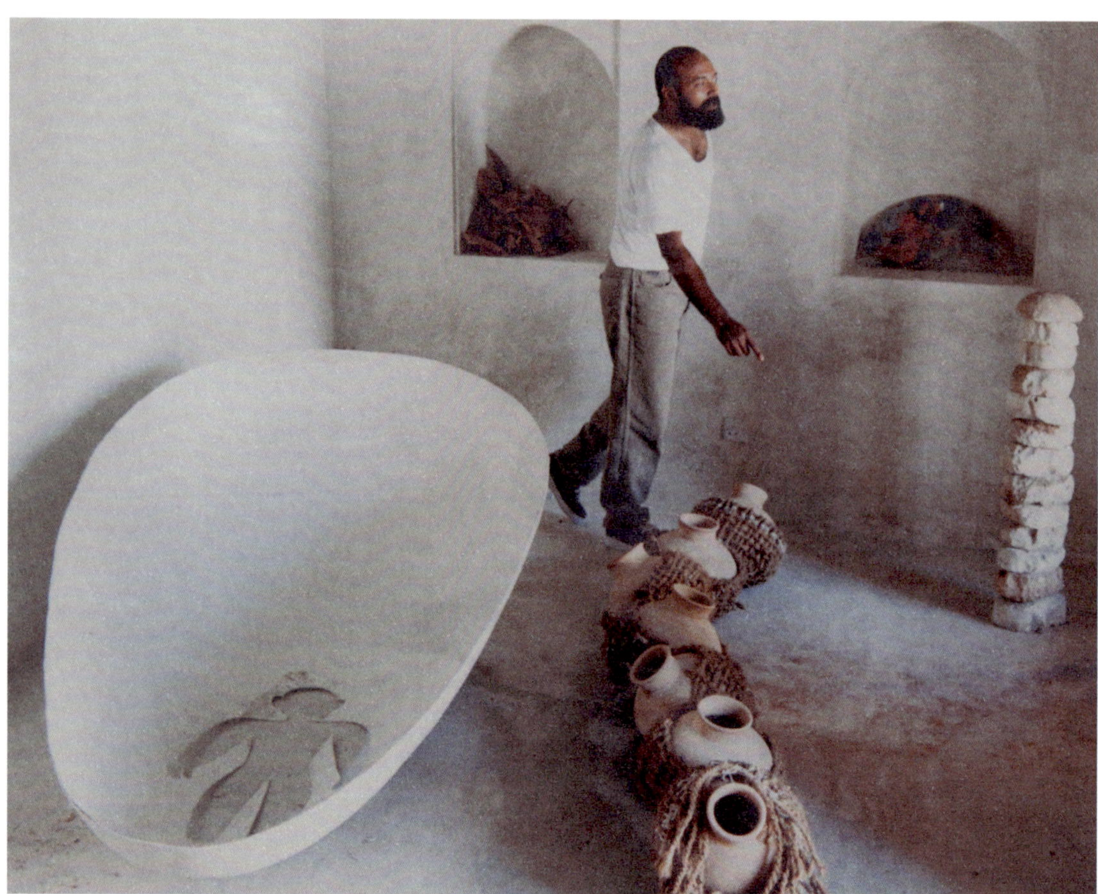

For example, paper starts out its life as a tree, then becomes packaging material that travels from across the world and finally lives in Mohamed's artistic narrative. He creates the interaction of these materials through his practice, asserting the aesthetic character and value of the unnoticed objects around us. In this process, he restores the material's wonderment. To paraphrase a successful commercial, he is "giving ordinary material its moment of glory."

We have been friends and collaborators for a long time, connecting even across our distant locations in the UAE and India. He visited me in Kerala and participated in the planting of fruit trees as part of my art project to create a food forest in Munnar. Discussing that project in length, it resonates with the Land Art that he has developed in Khor Fakkan. Today, bridging those two projects, we are dreaming of creating a food forest in Khor Fakkan to adapt to climate change in the future.

Vivek Vilasini installing his work for the exhibition *6 Artists*, 1996 at the Sharjah Art Museum

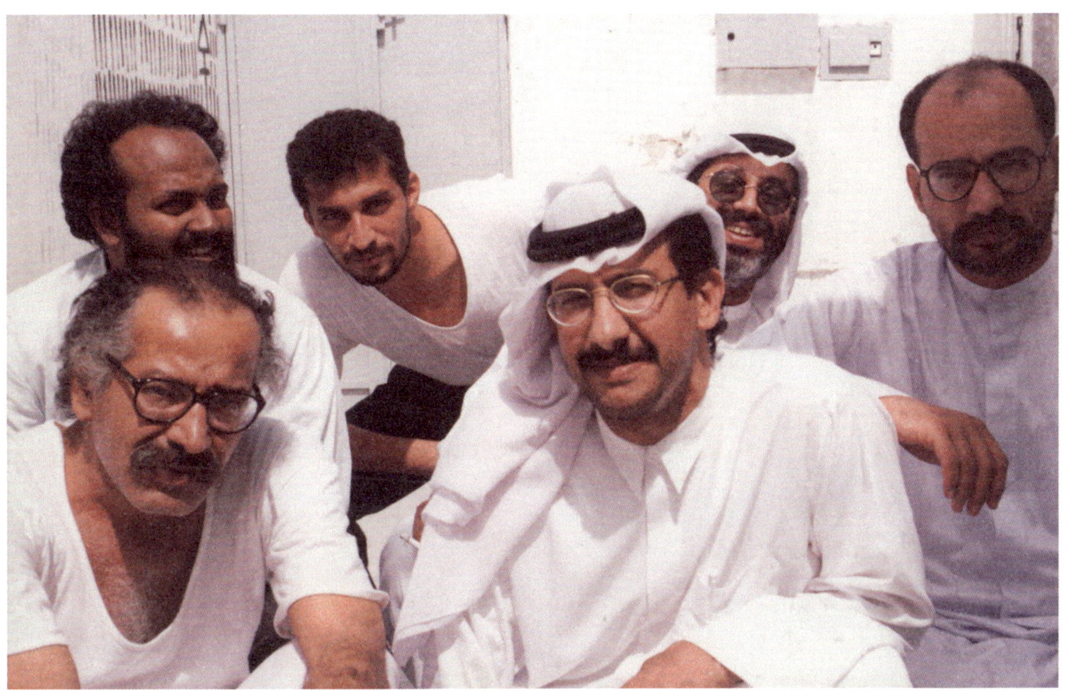

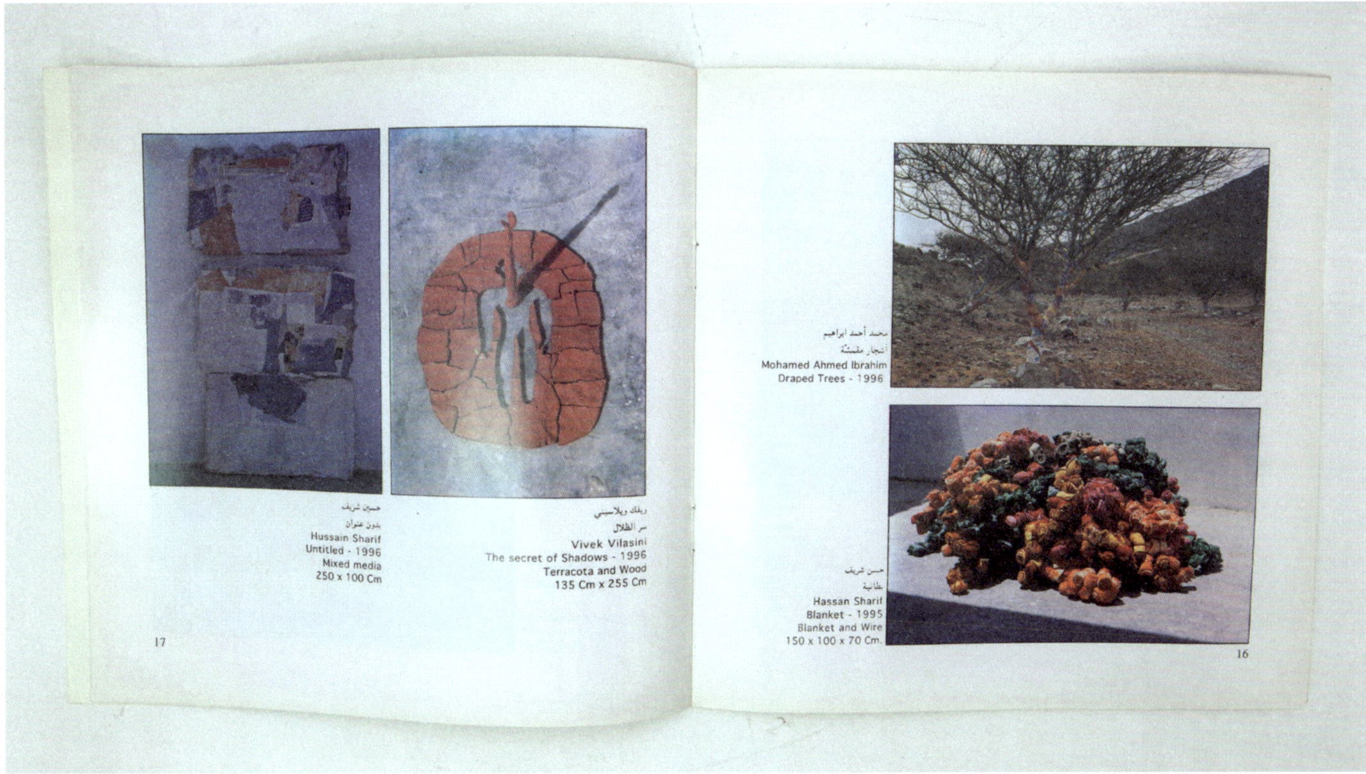

Left to right: Hassan Sharif
(front), Vivek Vilasini (back),
Mohammed Kazem (back),
Abdullah Abdelwahab (front),
Mohamed Ahmed Ibrahim (back),
Hussain Sharif (back). In the
courtyard of Hassan Sharif's
home in Satwa, Dubai, c. 1996

Pages from the exhibition
catalog for *6 Artists*, 1996
at the Sharjah Art Museum

When the viewer st
form he does not re
connection is lost b
doesn't know what
however, made me
myself. Going back
feeling different tha
and so on. Going ba
I'm doing now. I'm d
to you to like it or no
real question.

nds before a
ognize, this
cause he
is. […]. This,
ow closer to
the idea of
your peers
, this is what
ferent, it's up
, this is the

Munira Al Sayegh

Rising Mountains and Setting Suns

Next page
Fresh and Salt (detail), 2015
Copper wire, stones from Caspian
Sea, coral from Khor Fakkan,
dimensions variable

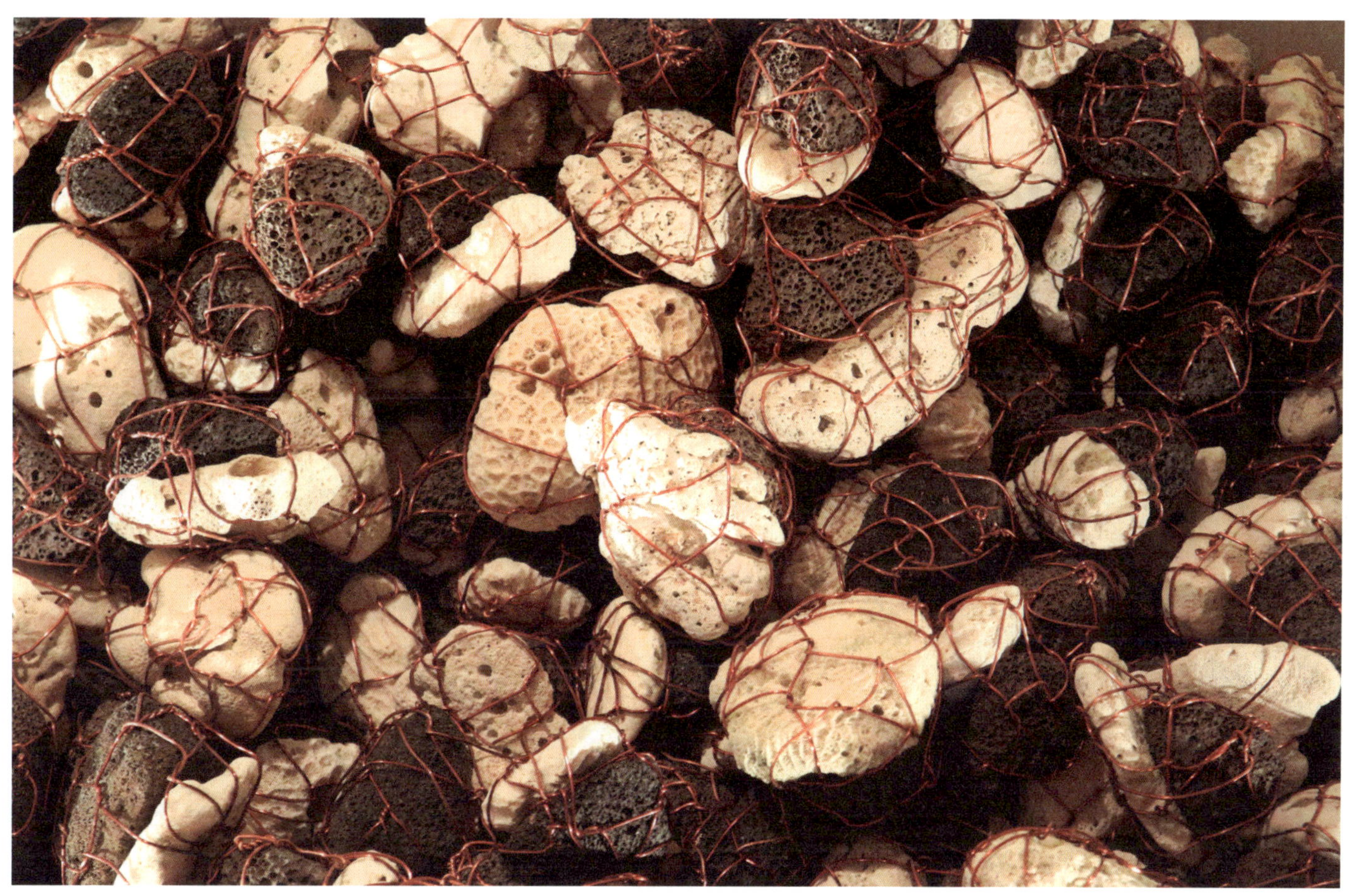

1. The 2015 residency program was run by the Dubai Culture and Arts Authority, Tashkeel, Delfina Foundation, and Art Dubai. That year Art Dubai Projects commissioned new, site-specific works, that were exhibited at the Art Dubai fair, March 18–21, 2015, as part of an expansive not-for-profit program.

In 2015, I learned about the United Arab Emirates' history of art through an encounter that pivoted my understanding of the contemporary world. This contextualized both the history and landscape that surrounds me in ways that I was otherwise unaware of (in spite of having grown up in the UAE). It became the basis of my thinking and started the foundation of my curatorial practice, highlighting the importance behind the locality of voice and the understanding of place. That year, I was introduced to a group of artists from the A.i.R Dubai residency; one of them was Mohamed Ahmed Ibrahim.[1]

The expectation for all the artists was to create works in time for Art Dubai. The production was organized to be in conversation with the curators, including Lara Khaldi as the head curator for that edition. It was my first curatorial undertaking and I was drawn to the narrative that Mohamed was unfolding for me. Looking at his work, it was as if each of his stories was tied to a rock being turned and a landscape understood and then expanded. The studios were in the Al Fahidi district, a UNESCO World Heritage Site in the heart of old Dubai, located in a traditional liwan house in which the rooms are clustered around a central courtyard. On the top floor, there was one room and a rooftop. Mohamed quickly went up to this peak and inhabited the space quietly, with the only sounds coming from the flick of his lighter. An accumulation of rocks sat silently in his studio, the space where an unloading of history would take place, from one generation to the next.

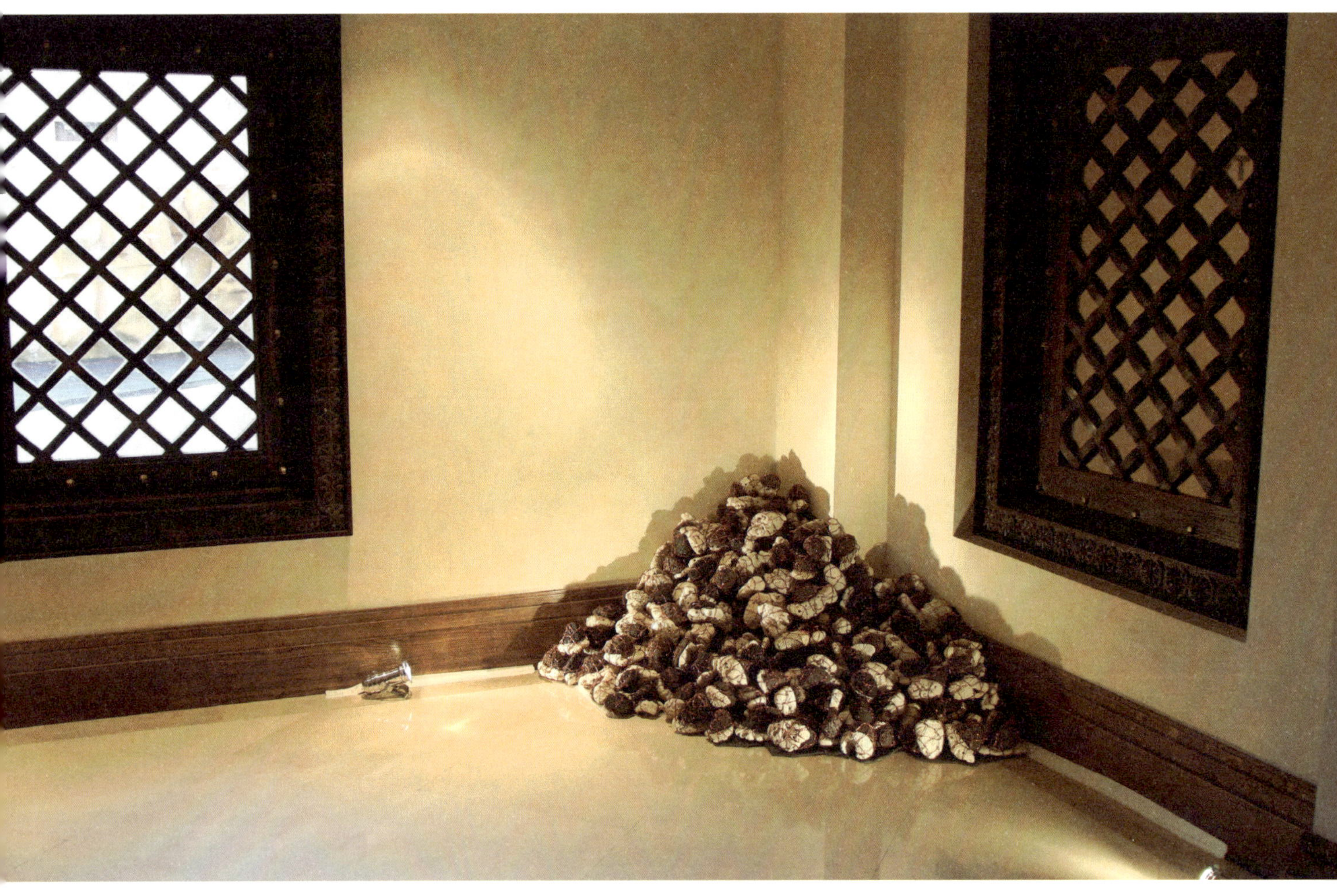

Fresh and Salt, 2015
Copper wire, stones from Caspian
Sea, coral from Khor Fakkan,
dimensions variable. As shown
in the Art Dubai Projects

When the conversations began, they came in brief spurts. Mohamed would tell me about his practice of Land Art while pointing to the rocks in his studio. He told me which of the rocks came from freshwater versus those that came from saltwater, explaining the differences in their physicality, and also asked about their nature, personality, and their contexts. He asked what happens when they are removed from their context and placed next to one another. It wasn't until the first road trip with Mohamed that I understood this question of context and the role of the self as a mirror of the surrounding environment. This was my introduction to the landscape of the rest of the Emirates.

Mohamed constantly negotiated with his surroundings. He questioned how he could add to the mountain landscapes or dissect them. The conversation around his art was always about the give and take of the land, which quickly became a natural dialogue between us. Although the exchange and thinking process was in my mother tongue of Arabic, I struggled to find the words to communicate at the time. I was always listening and curious, sitting on one of the two chairs in his studio. Leading up to the fair, Mohamed was contemplating a question, how does one value land? Furthermore, how does land become valuable?

Mohamed wanted to intervene in the land. He wanted to know what would happen if the land from the rocky mountainscapes were introduced into the city and vice versa. Who has the right to this land? If land is valued only as a monetary means, what is stripped from it? How can land become static when, of its own accord, land has the right to move and shapeshift? Mohamed continued to explain that the land is something that is in constant motion or readjustment; something that is in a state of reinvention and accession; something that exists on its own, but also in response to its context and time. This conversation quickly moved from concept to a working list of items needed for his intervention for the fair. The list read:

- Approval to take 1x1 meter of earth, a few inches deep, from the management of the Madinat Jumeirah team, in Madinat Jumeirah, Dubai
- 5–7 empty rice sacks
- Shovels
- A measuring unit
- A pickup truck
- Approval to take 1x1 meter of earth, a few inches deep, from Abdullah Al Saadi's house, Sharjah
- Gas
- Coffee

After much explanation to the Madinat Jumeirah team, who were reluctant to accept the proposal of their land being taken and exchanged, a small plot was finally assigned to the intervention with the timeline of its physical life to be the duration of the art fair. Mohamed was to take a 1x1 meter plot from behind the shrubbery of the hotel in Dubai and swap it with a 1x1 meter plot from Abdullah Al Saadi's house in a mountainous area of Sharjah.

Leading up to the art fair, all the necessary approvals were taken. Then came the arrival of the pickup truck carrying big empty rice sacks, so with his list of items fulfilled, Mohamed was ready to start. Instead of a measuring tape, he used a rope that measured 1 meter in its length to draw his square. He estimated the depth in accordance with what he assumed would be enough. We started with the grass and could hear the sound of its attempted rooting being pulled out of the ground. Soil that otherwise would have been foreign to Dubai's landscape where the grass grew pristinely was actively being removed one rice sack after the other until the square was emptied. As the land was being dug, we watched the ants that had been hiding under the earth run around frantically. After filling the rice sacks full of Jumeirah earth, I loaded them into the back of the pickup. Before the peak of the hot sun, we started to drive north, first in silence, then in anticipation.

On our drive, the landscape changed in three phases. We moved from the cityscape of Dubai into the desert, then we followed the road that tore through the rocky mountains of Sharjah, leading us toward the sky. The bumpy drive

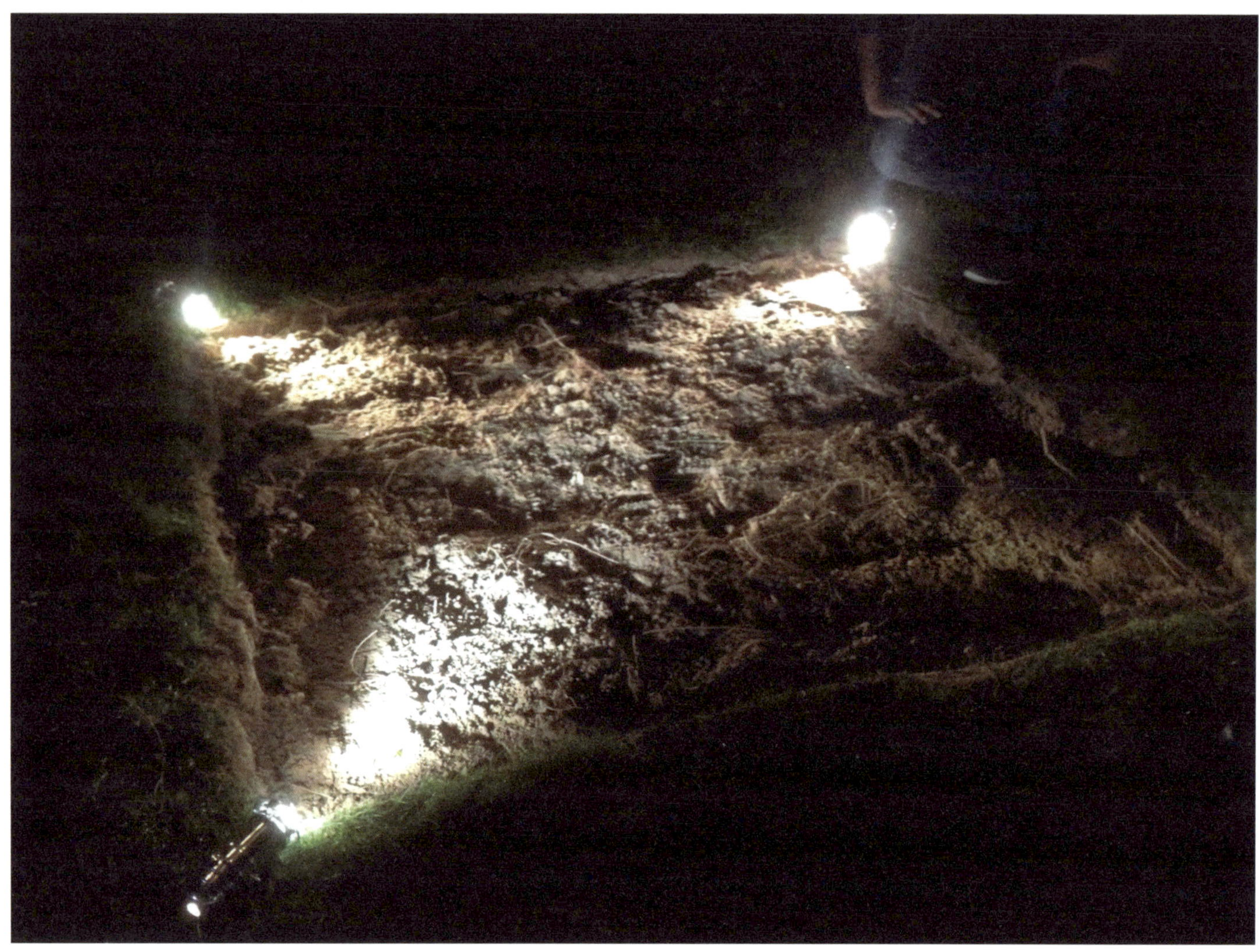

Land Shift, 2015
Documentation of the intervention
underway in Madinat Jumeirah,
Dubai

Land Shift (detail), 2015
Earth from the landscape of
Khor Fakkan. Intervention,
Madinat Jumeirah, Dubai

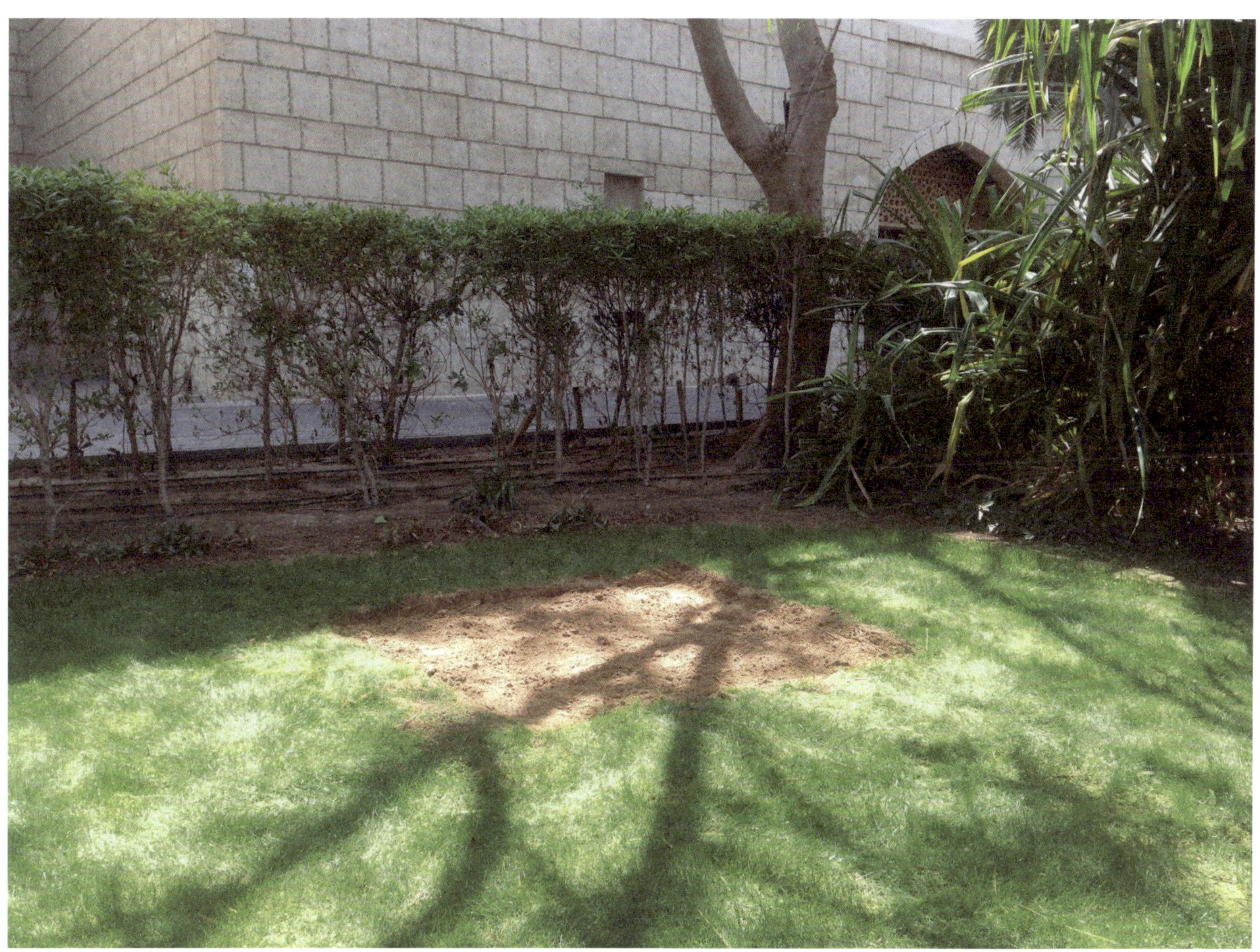

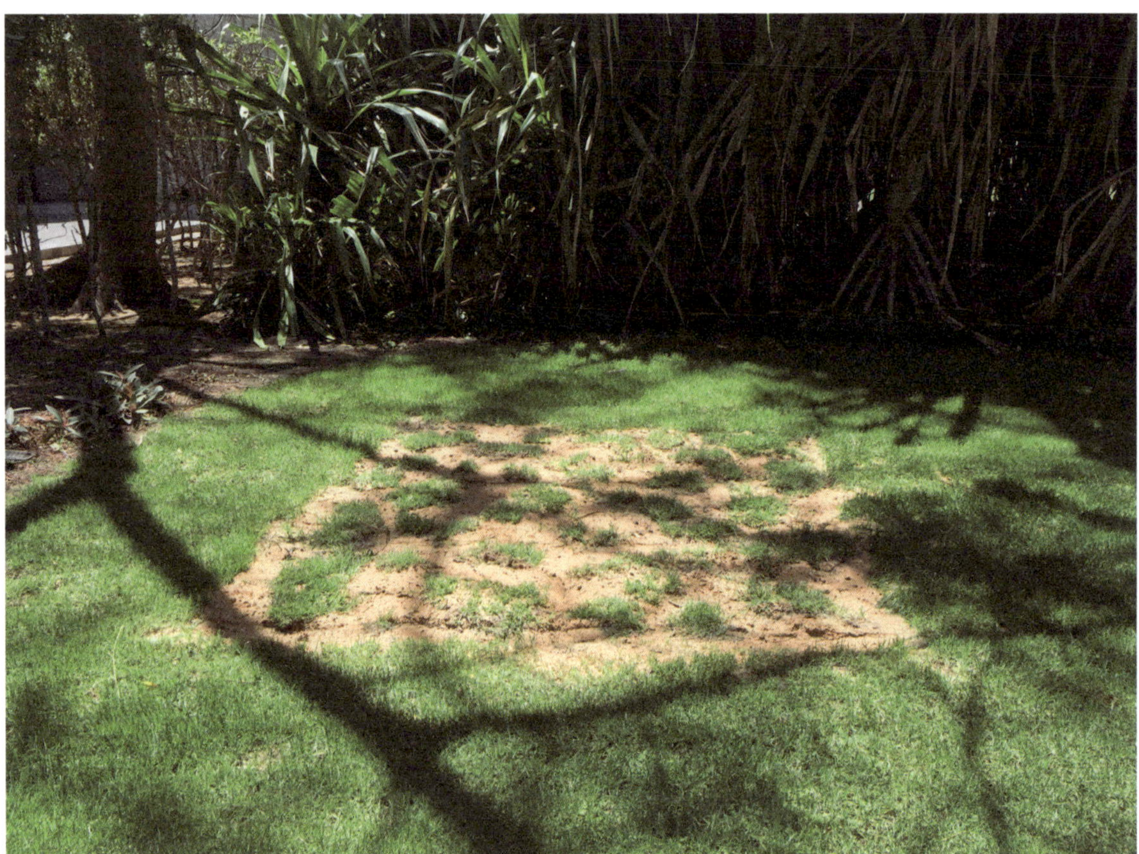

Land Shift (detail), 2015
Earth from the landscape of
Khor Fakkan. Intervention,
Madinat Jumeirah, Dubai

was full of stories. I listened intently as I watched the sun change the color of the mountain's skin. The pores of the mountains began to breathe through the stories painted by Mohamed. The present tense mixed with the histories he told of the people and the land, their change and stability, set the stage for our arrival at Abdullah Al Saadi's house.

Our destination was a humble home set in a larger outdoor space filled with trees. The house was further dwarfed by the mountains governing the valley town. Abdullah stood auspiciously but with minimal words of exchange: he pointed us to a corner under a Ghaf[2] tree and told us we could start. We offloaded the rice bags filled with the land extracted from Madinat Jumeirah and allowed them to sit and witness the exchange that was about to take place. The same rope measuring 1 meter in its length was used to draw up his square, and again he estimated the depth in accordance to what he assumed would be enough.

The land, dry and rocky, reacted differently to the land extraction from earlier that day. It responded with varying degrees of easy movement, almost like flour moving through a sifter. Small rocks, grainy soil, and no grass, one shovel full after the next, the land was being actively taken and placed into the rice bags. The 1x1 meter square stood empty, and the remaining earth showed a color that was richer in tones than at the surface. The land presented itself with no externalities, no interjections, just varying depths of the color brown mixed with the rocks broken off from the mountains, which were a dusty grey. We began to empty the land that we transported into this square. The final juxta-position of the land in its new habitat versus its surroundings was that of two strangers, separate in their weight and their presence. The Madinat Jumeirah land was compactly held together in a way that spoke foreignly in its new context, and the land from Abdullah Al Saadi's house existed estranged in the context of the fair at Madinat Jumeirah. The rocky and somewhat sandy earth contrasted with the manicured gardens in which it was now homed.

In Mohamed Ahmed Ibrahim's gestures of exchange and extraction, I received the answers to the questions initially proposed. The stage he set, of the rising mountains and the setting suns, explored localities in their hyper presentations and their truths. It explored the discomfort of change and the necessity for movement where movement is negotiated. It highlighted the importance of conversation in the attempt to understand the unfolding of the self, reflecting the drastic arrangement of the landscapes that composes our ground. In this process, I learned that in the same way the water moves on the coast of Abu Dhabi, the mountains of Khor Fakkan come to life. In between, I began to understand that for all the differences that are created by the environment, there are also similarities that encapsulate and tie this conundrum of the stability of land to the inconsistencies of the sea.

2. Prosopis Cineraria, also known as "ghaf," is a species of flowering tree in the pea family, Fabaceae. It is native to arid portions of Western Asia and the Indian Subcontinent.

In the beginning, th looked like they wei be like people. As I s work, I found that, i become a forest, as were becoming tre

figures
going to
arted the
, it has
he figures
s.

Selected Works

Just Lines

Lines, 1995
India ink on paper, 48 x 36 cm

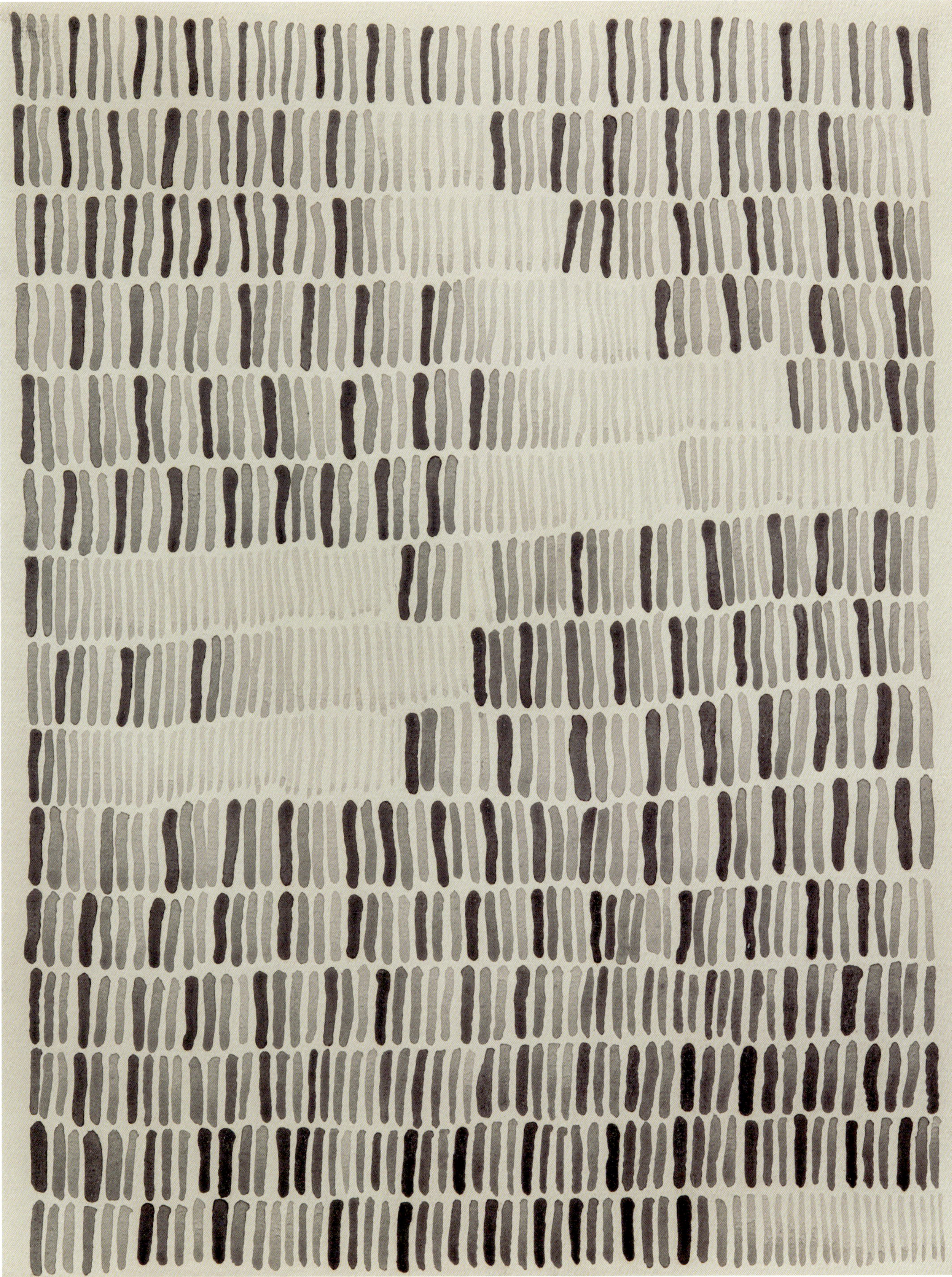

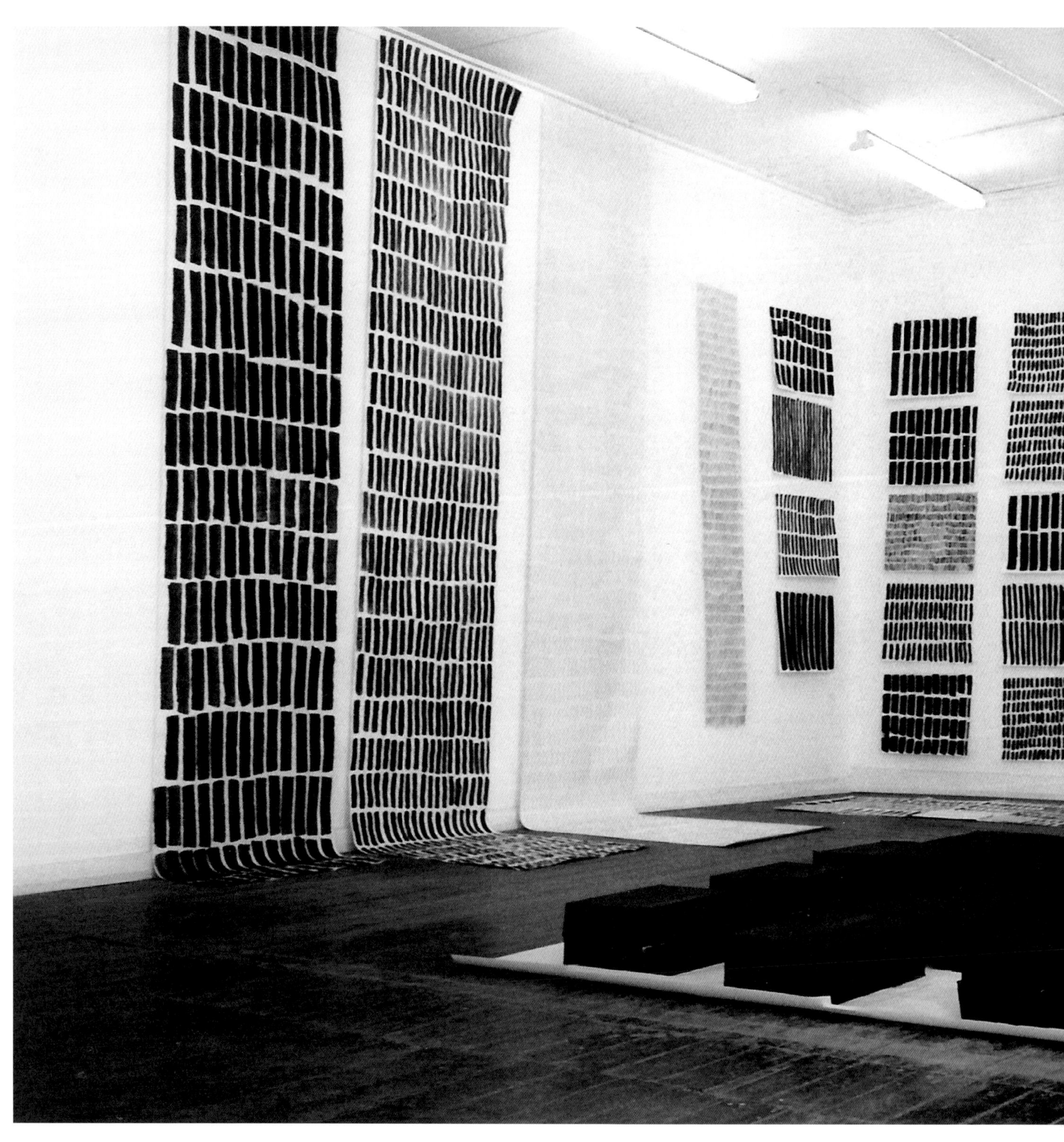

Lines, 1995
Acrylic on paper and cardboard
boxes. Site-specific installation
at the Sittard Art Center, the
Netherlands

Next page
Lines, 2017
Acrylic on paper, papier-mâché,
cardboard. Site-specific installation
at Manarat Al Saadiyat, Abu Dhabi,
UAE. Commissioned for the Gateway
exhibition at Abu Dhabi Art

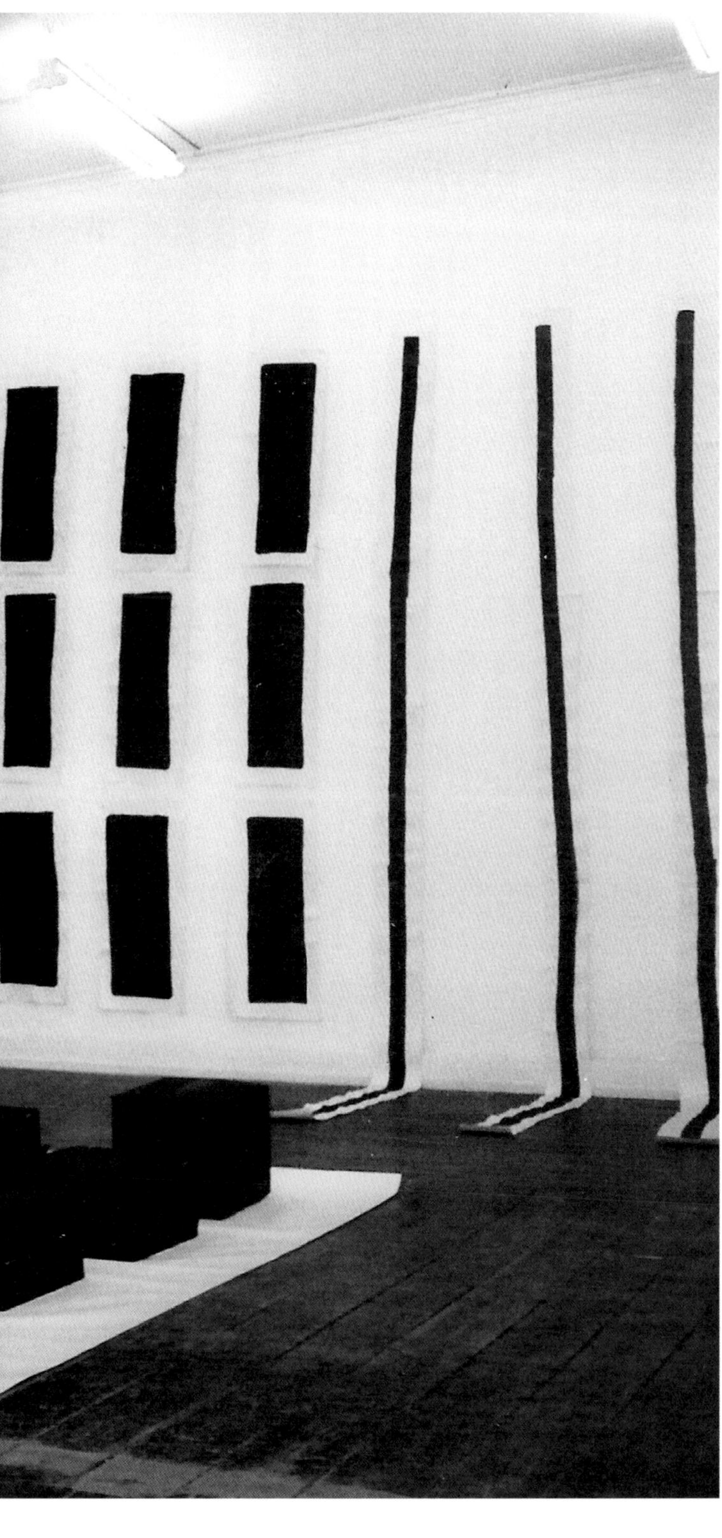

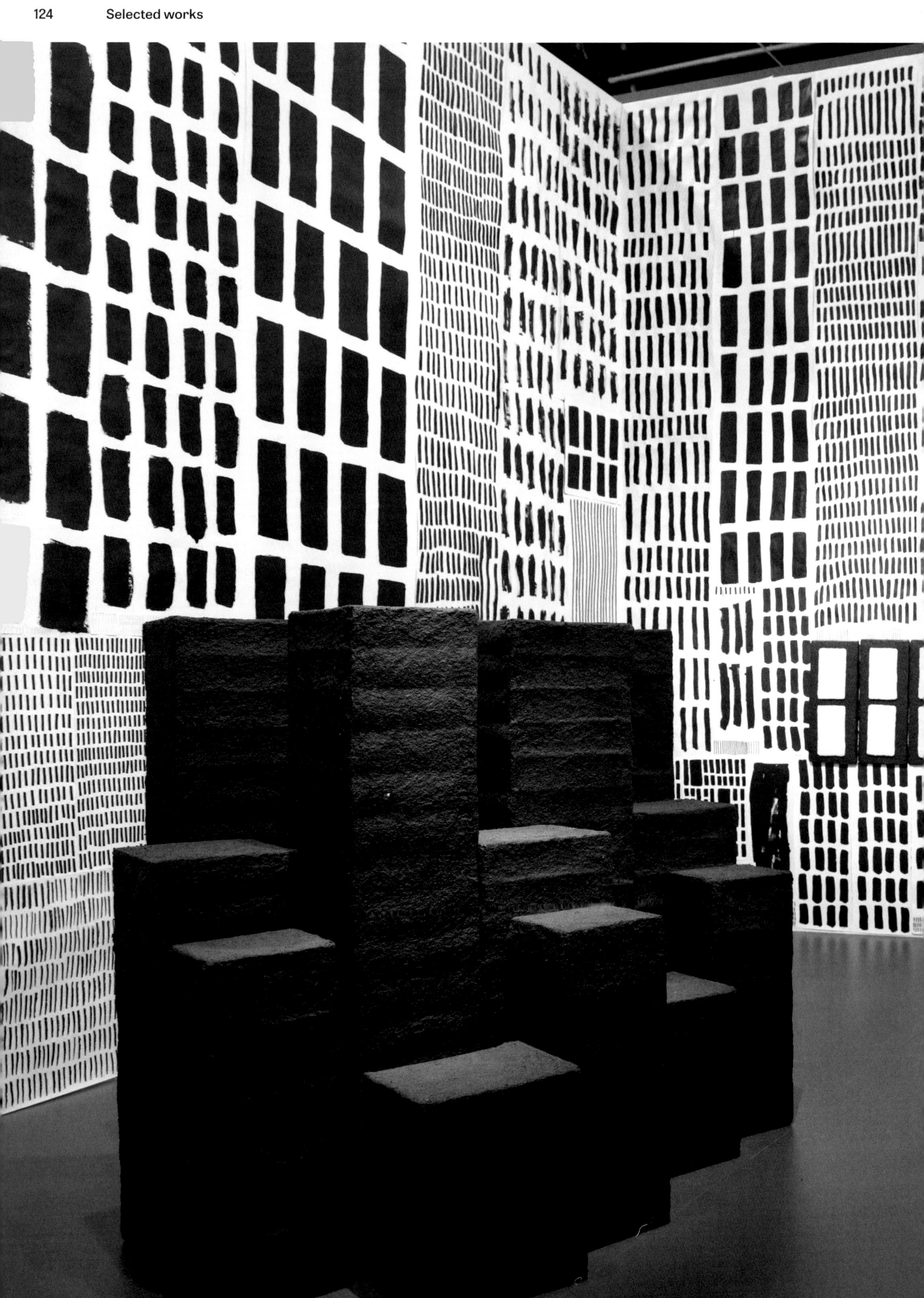

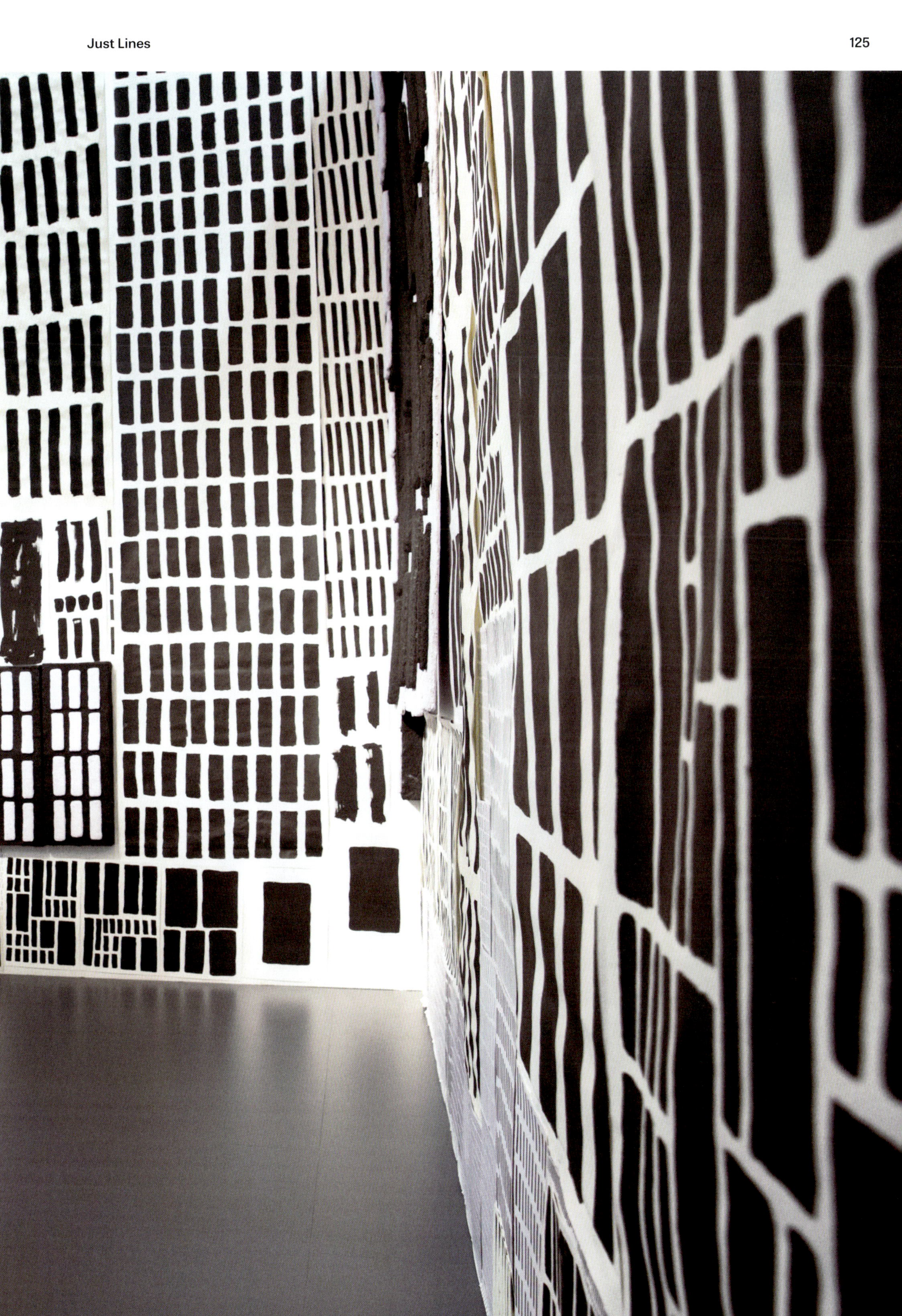

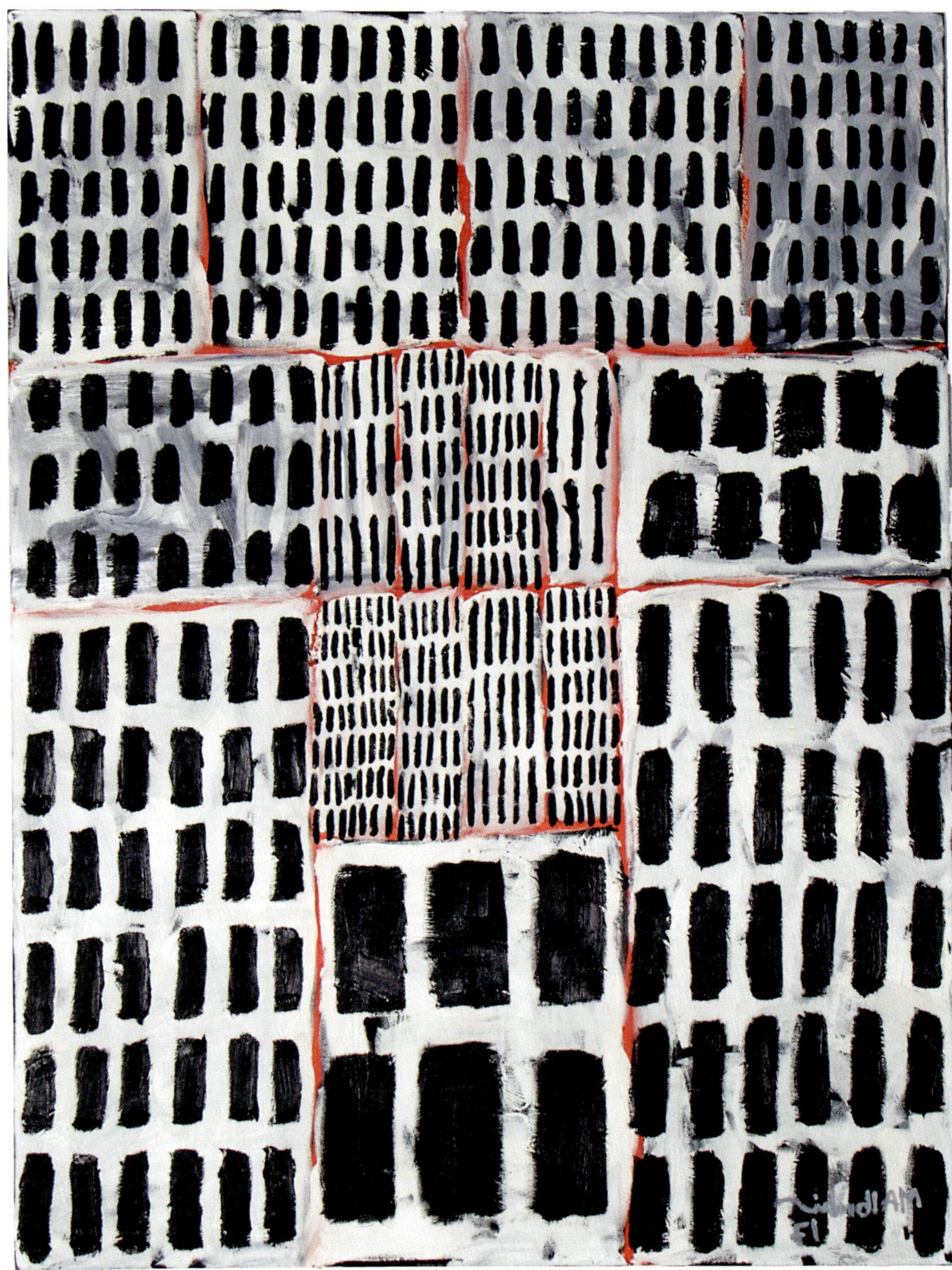

Different Lines, 2017
Oil on canvas, 122 x 91 cm

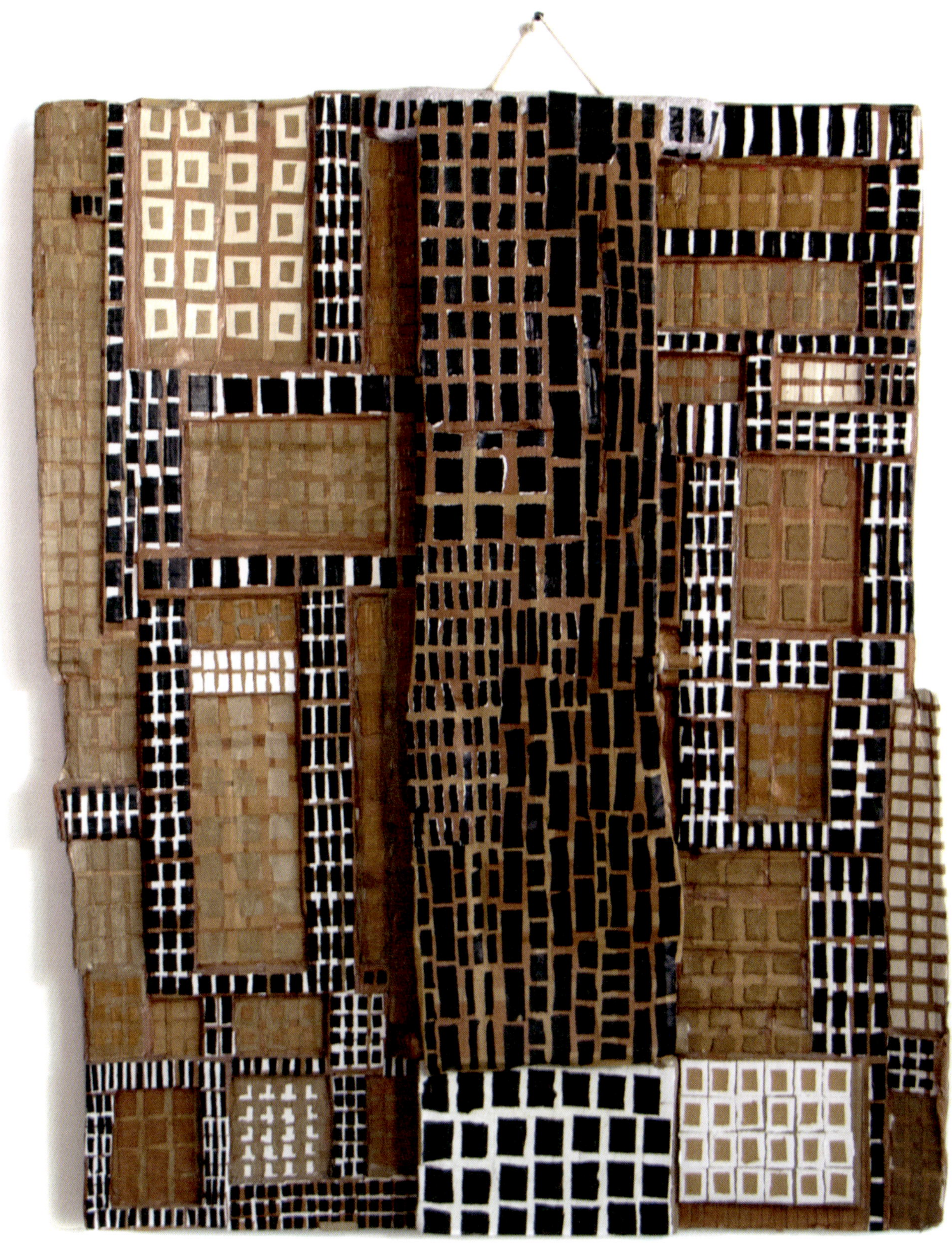

Untitled, 2015
Cardboard assemblage,
148 x 116 x 10 cm

Untitled, 2015
Sliced cardboard, papier-mâché,
58 x 48 x 4 cm

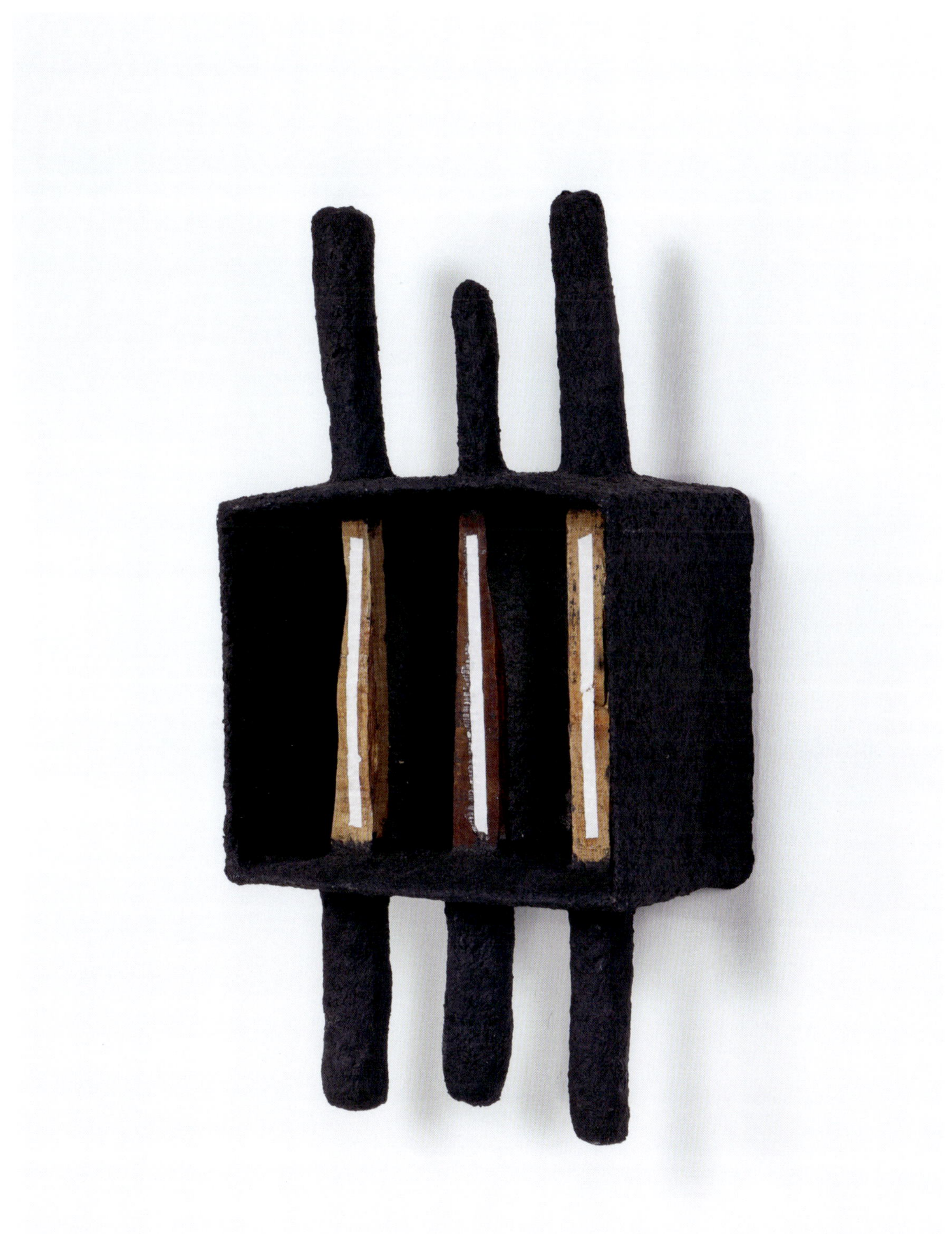

Window, 2015
Cardboard box, wood, papier-mâché, 60 x 33 x 18 cm

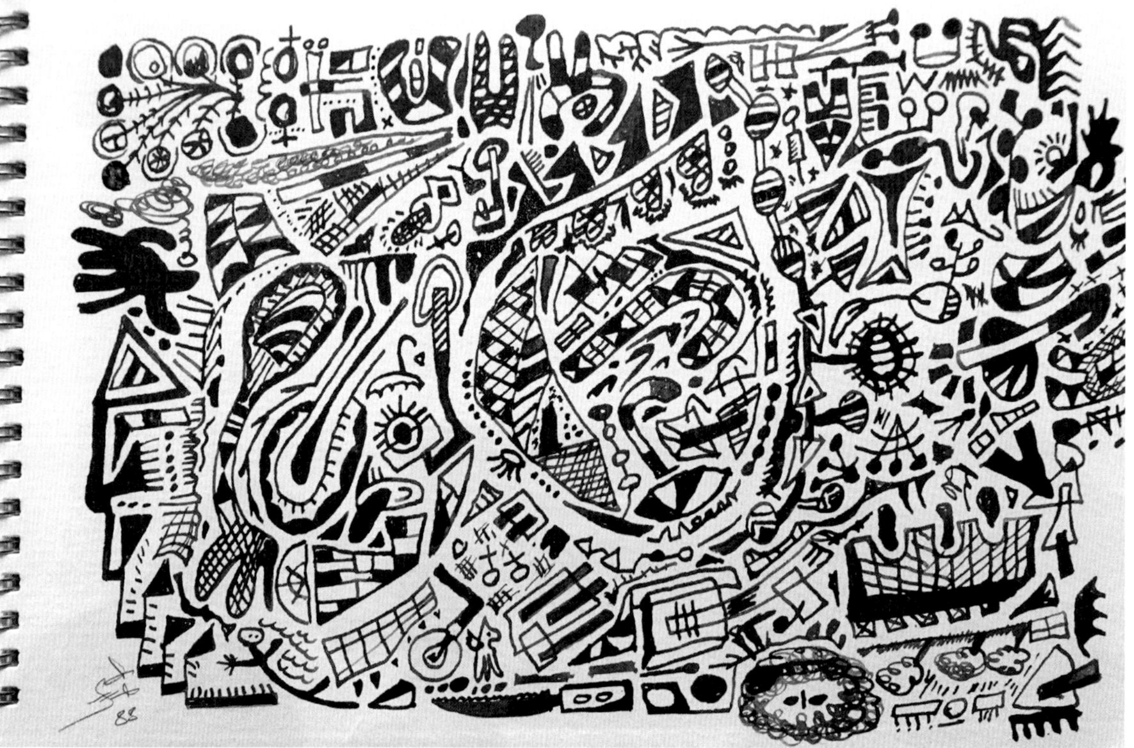

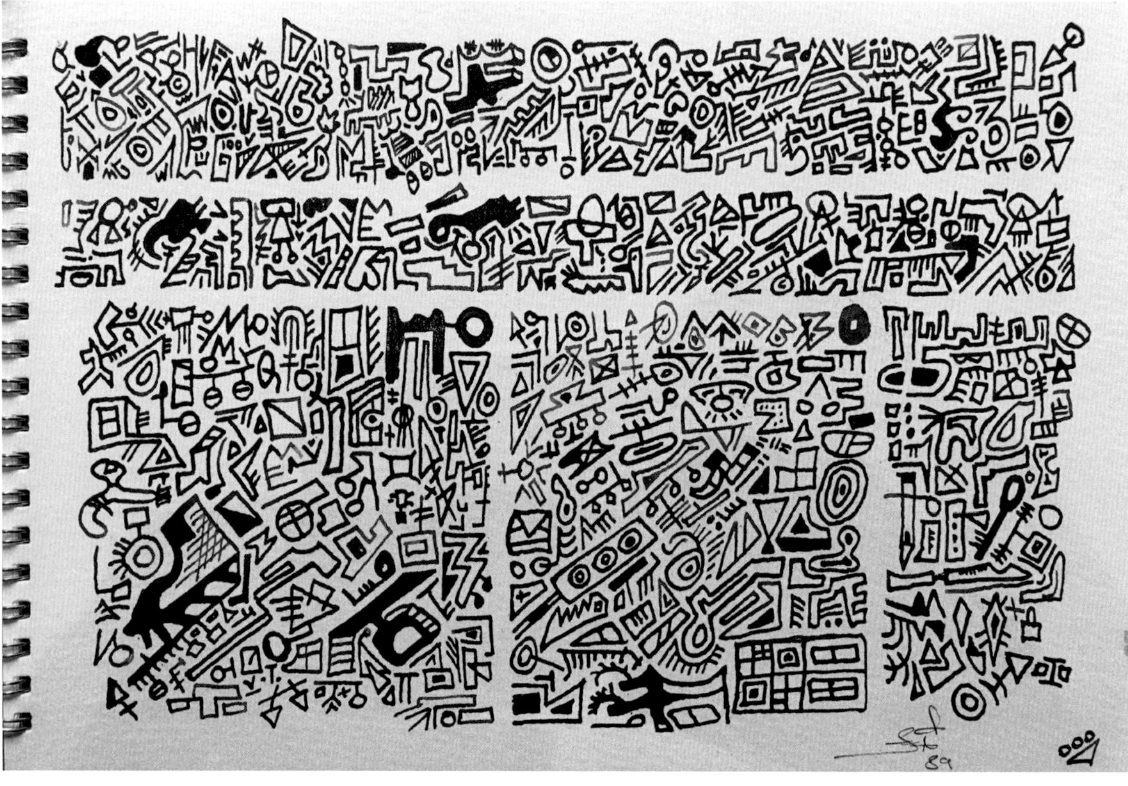

This page and next, all images are from:
Note Book No 01, 1988–89
India ink on paper, 18 x 25 cm

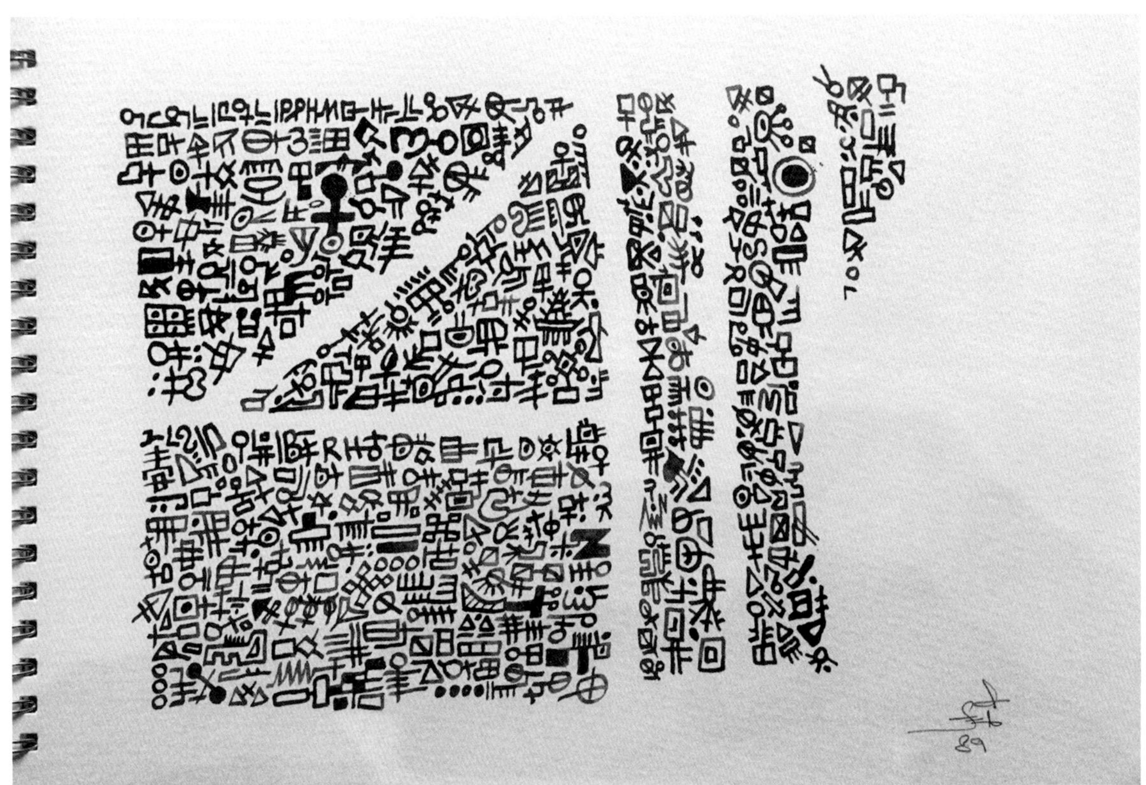

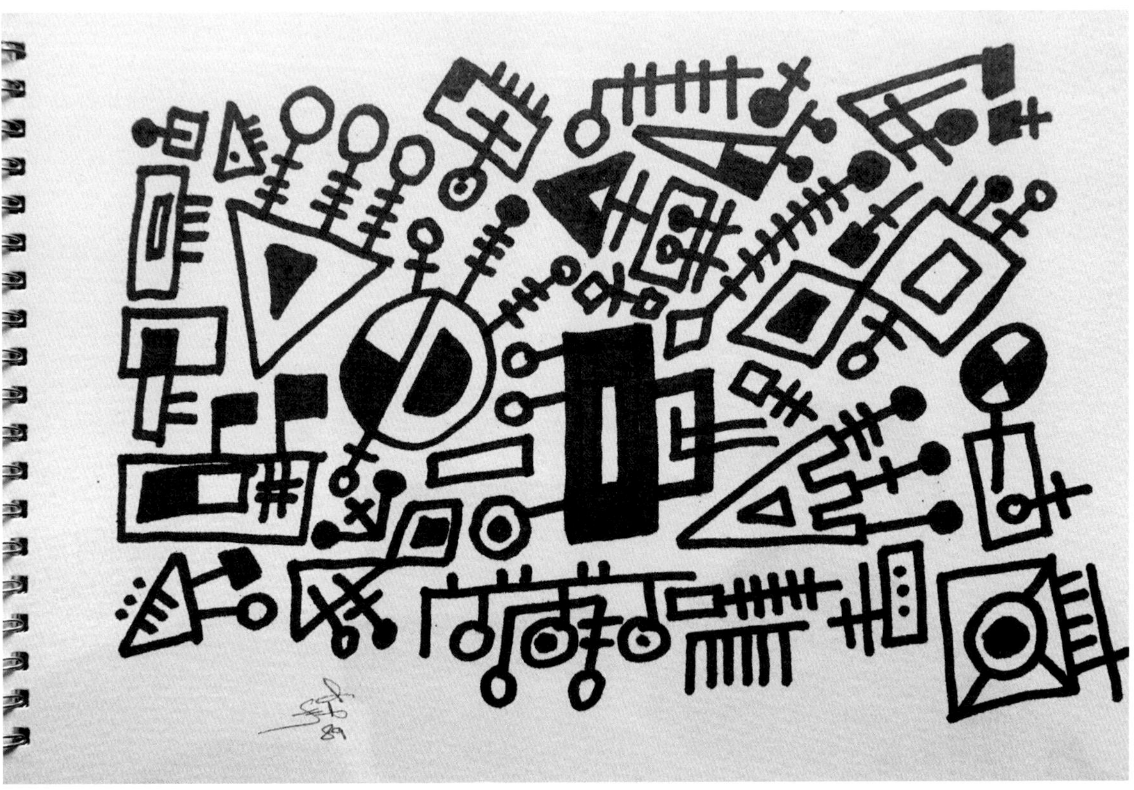

Pages 132–135
Installation view of *Mohamed Ahmed Ibrahim: Elements*, 2018 at the Sharjah Art Foundation

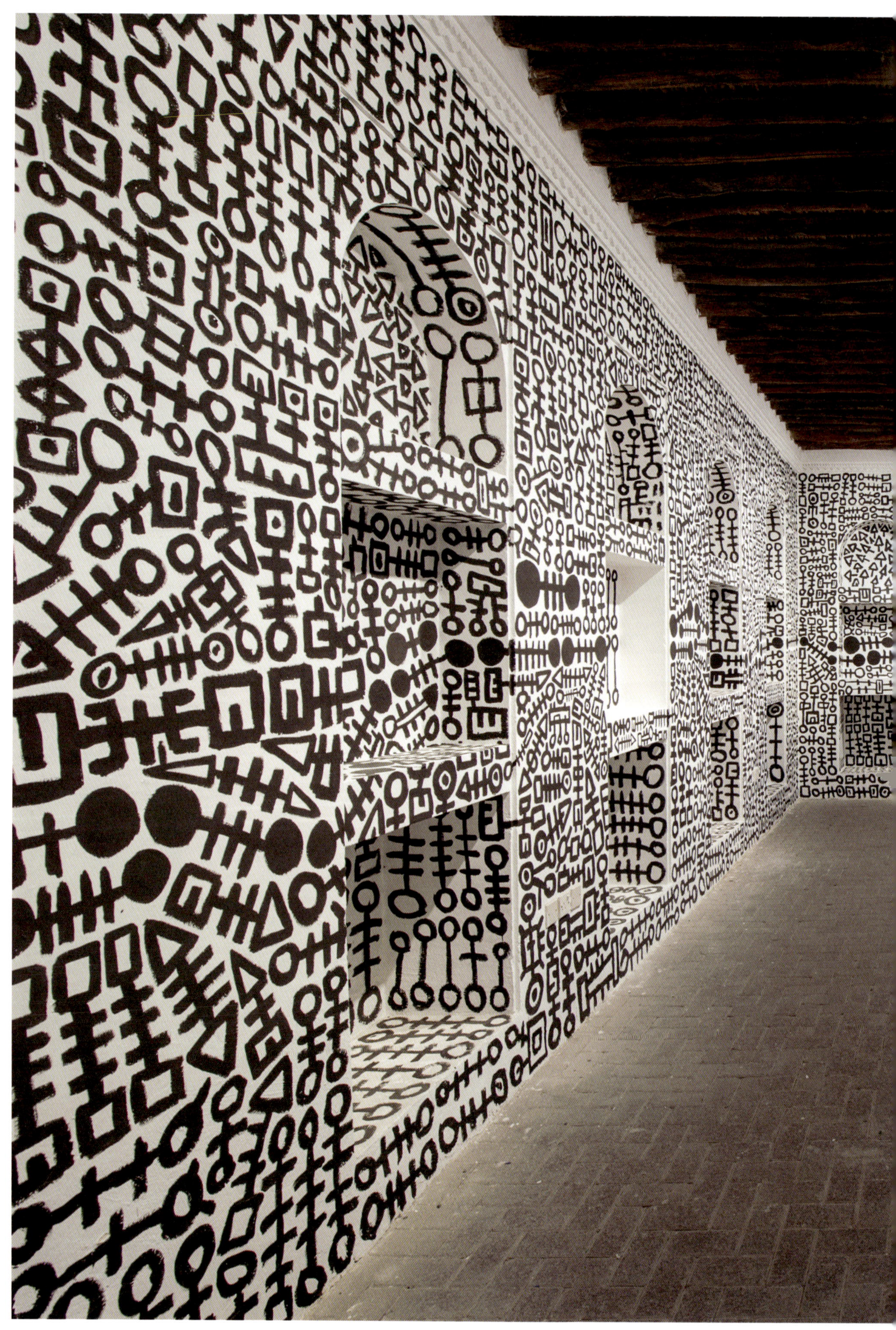

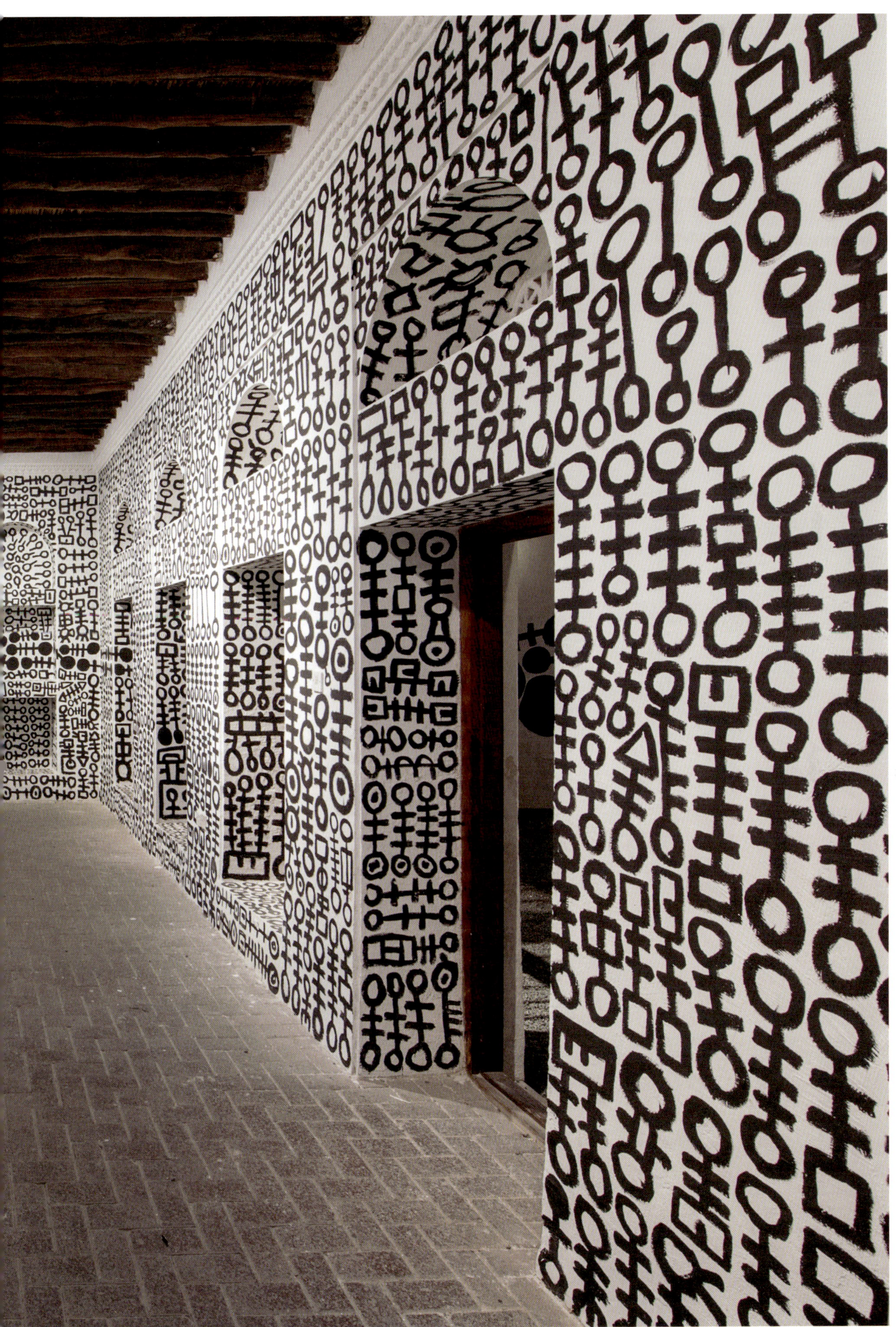

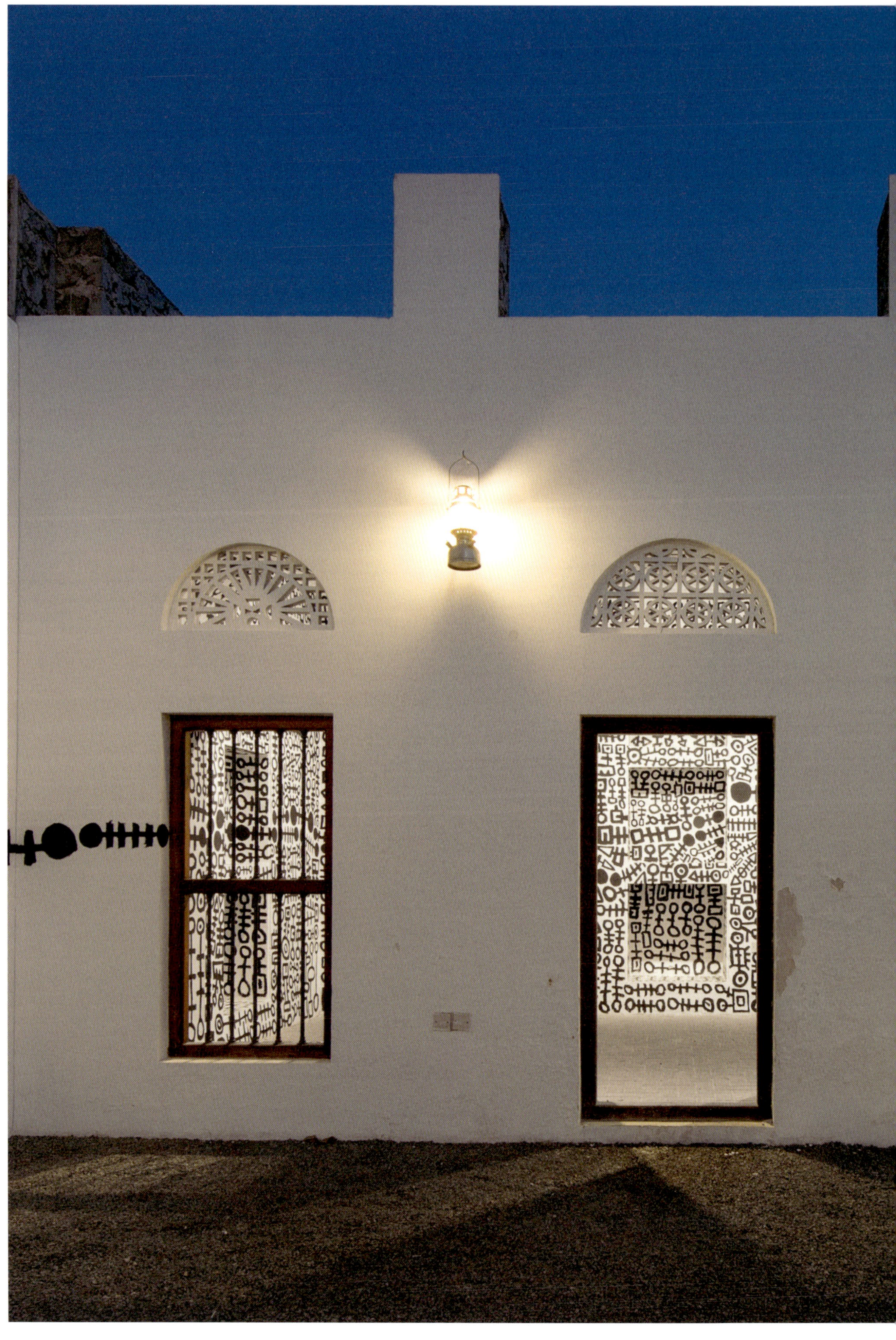

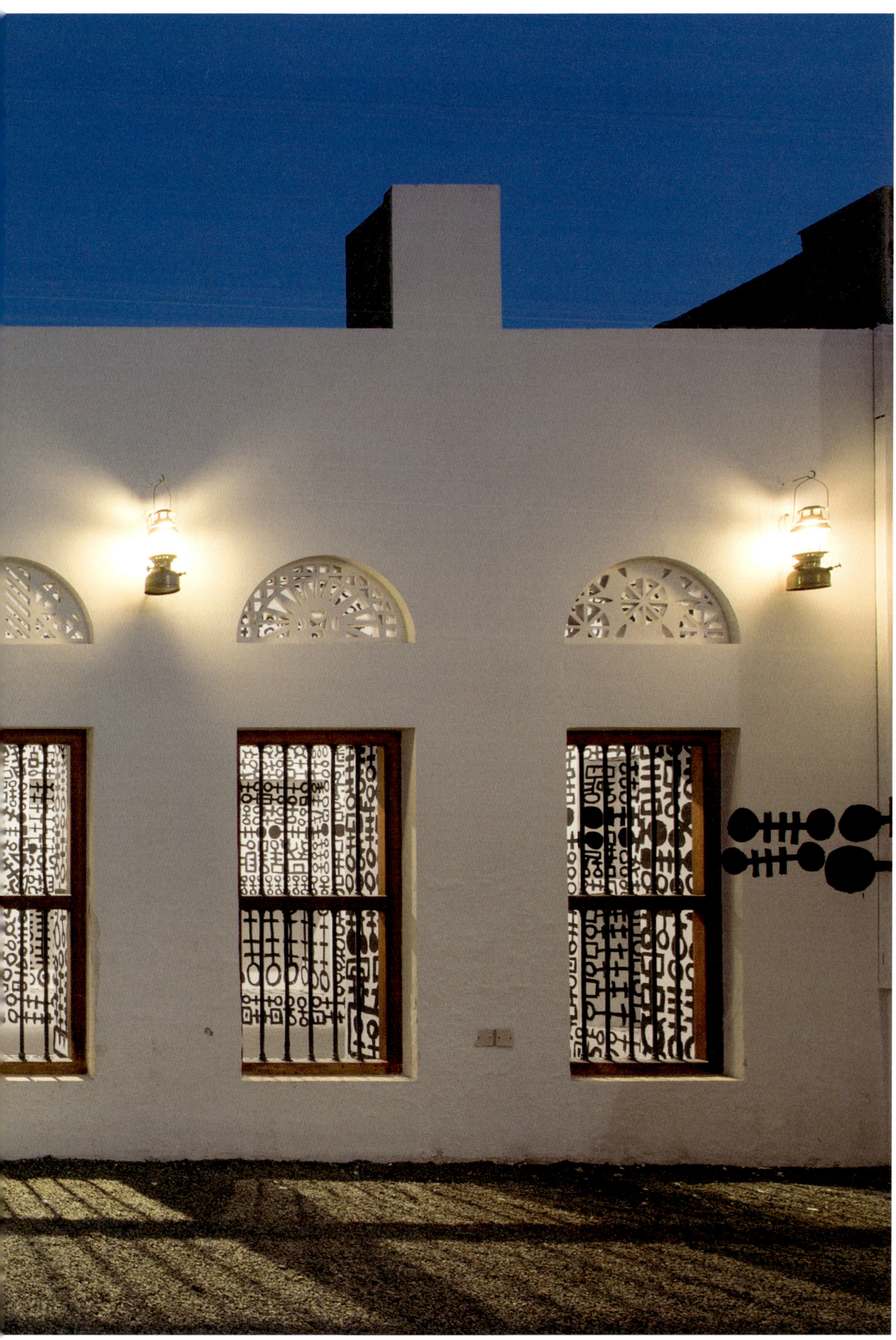

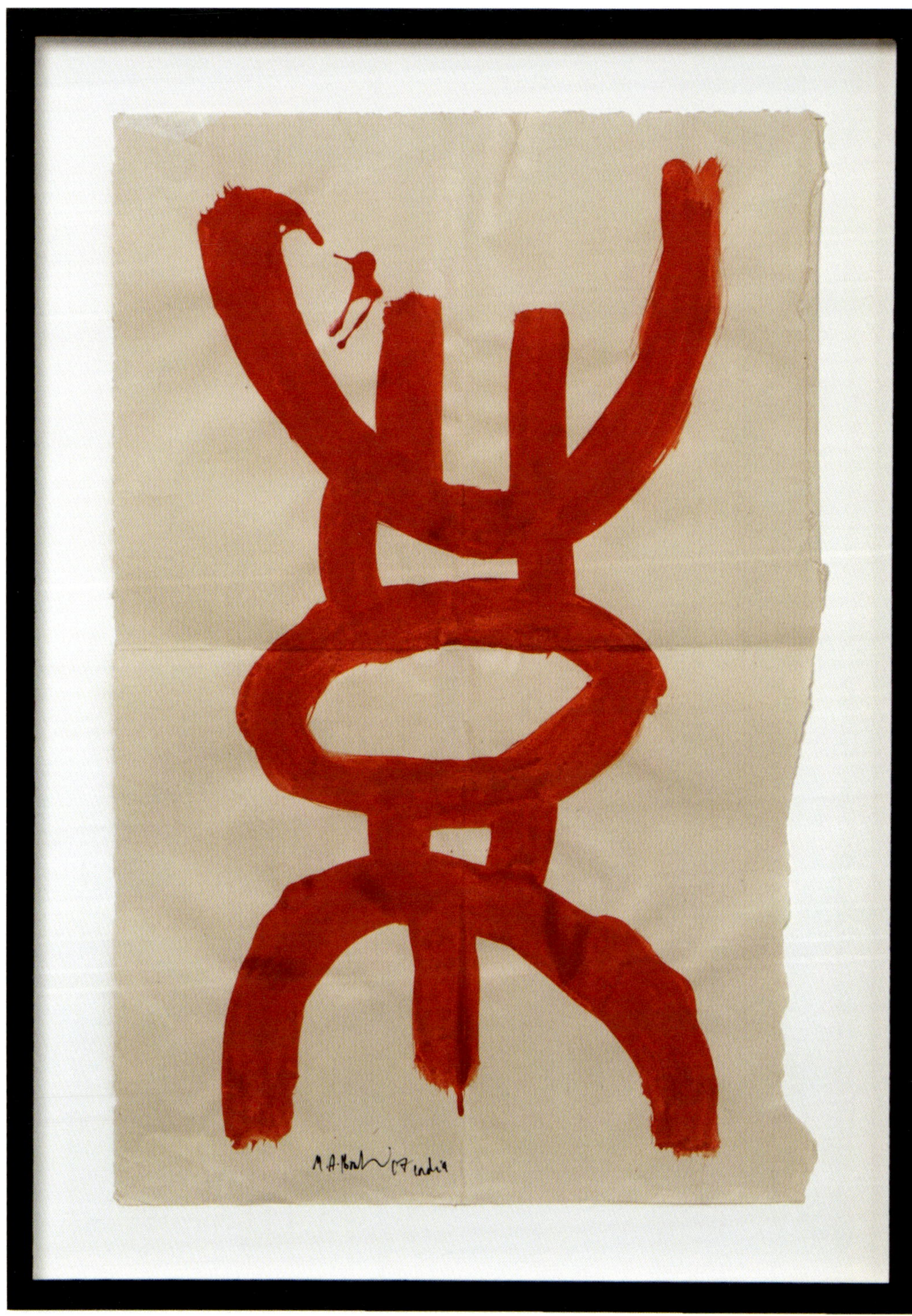

Form in India, 2017
Acrylic on paper, 45.5 x 30 cm

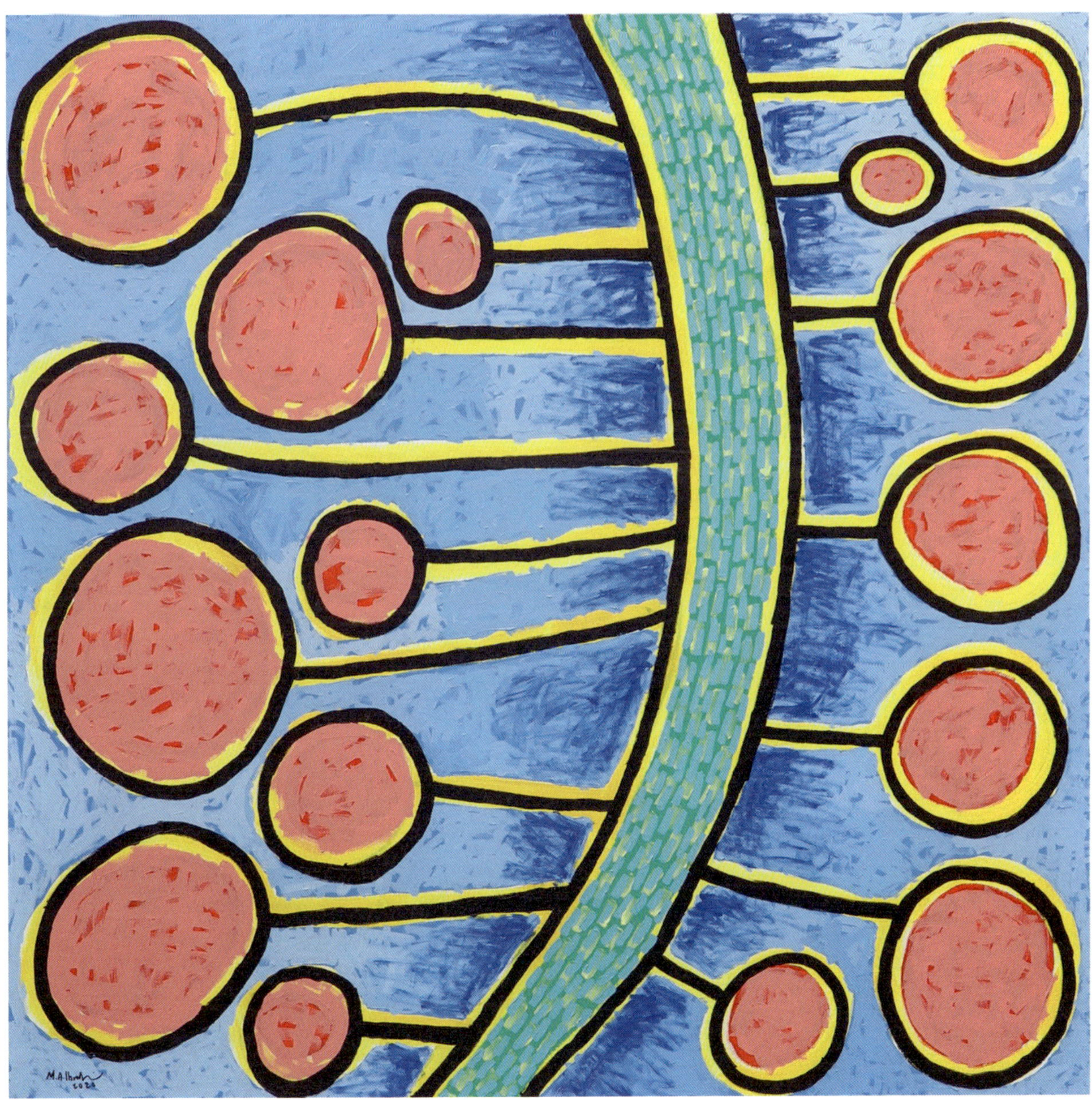

Green Boulevard, 2020
Acrylic on canvas, 155 x 155 cm

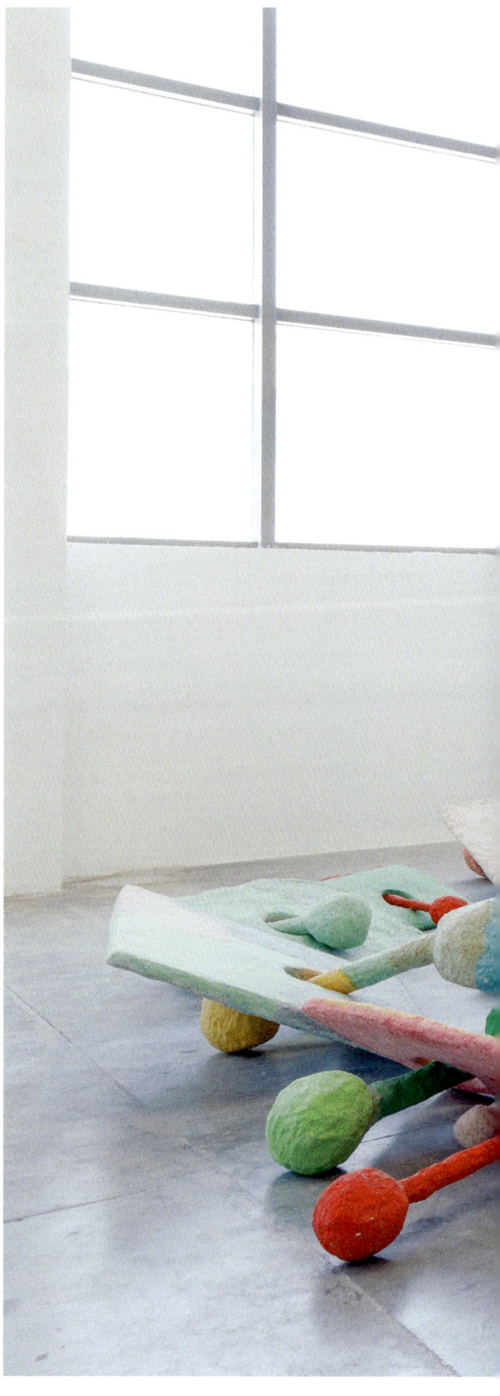

Khorfakkan number-2, 2007
Cardboard, papier-mâché,
wood, variable dimensions

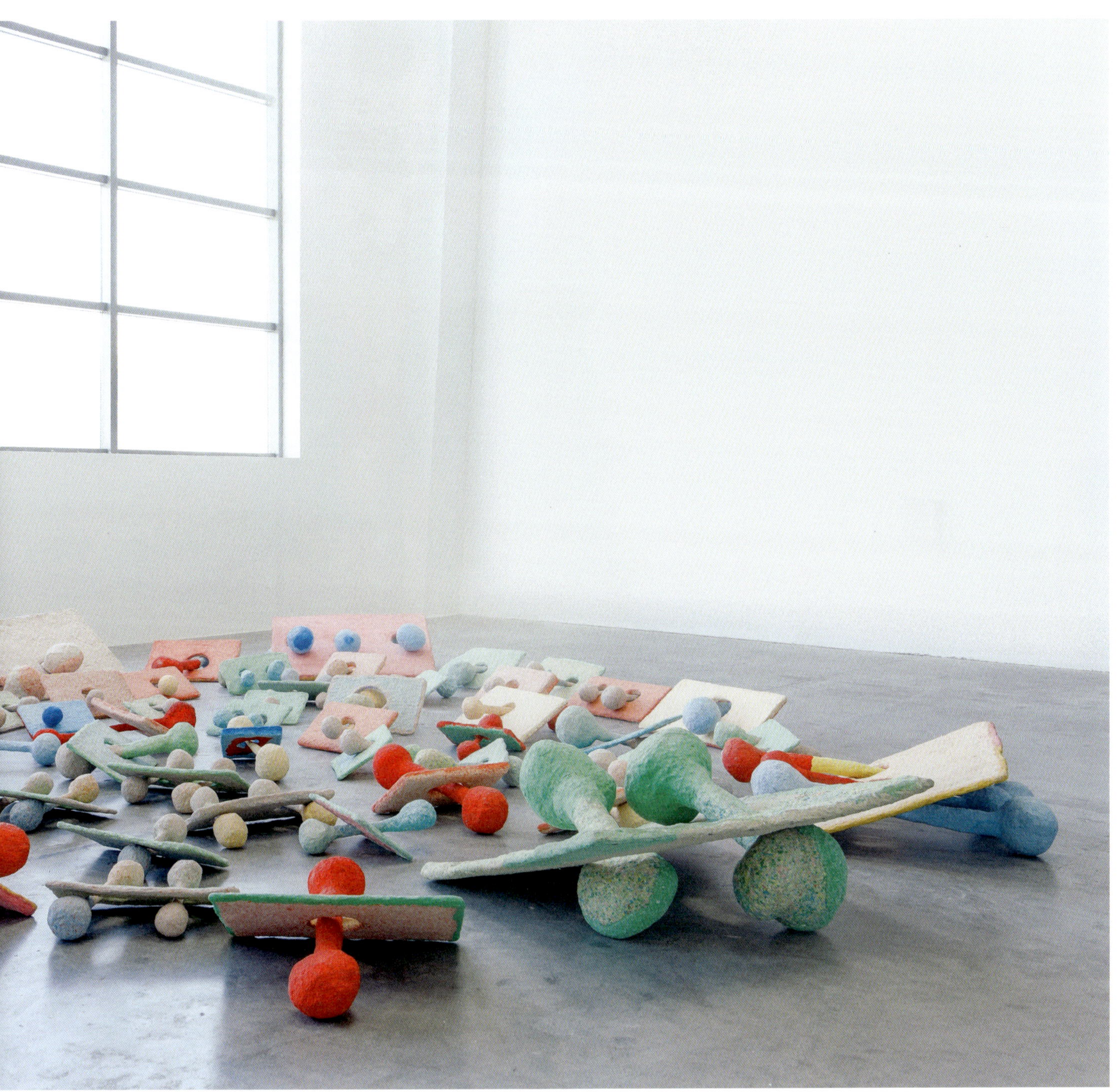

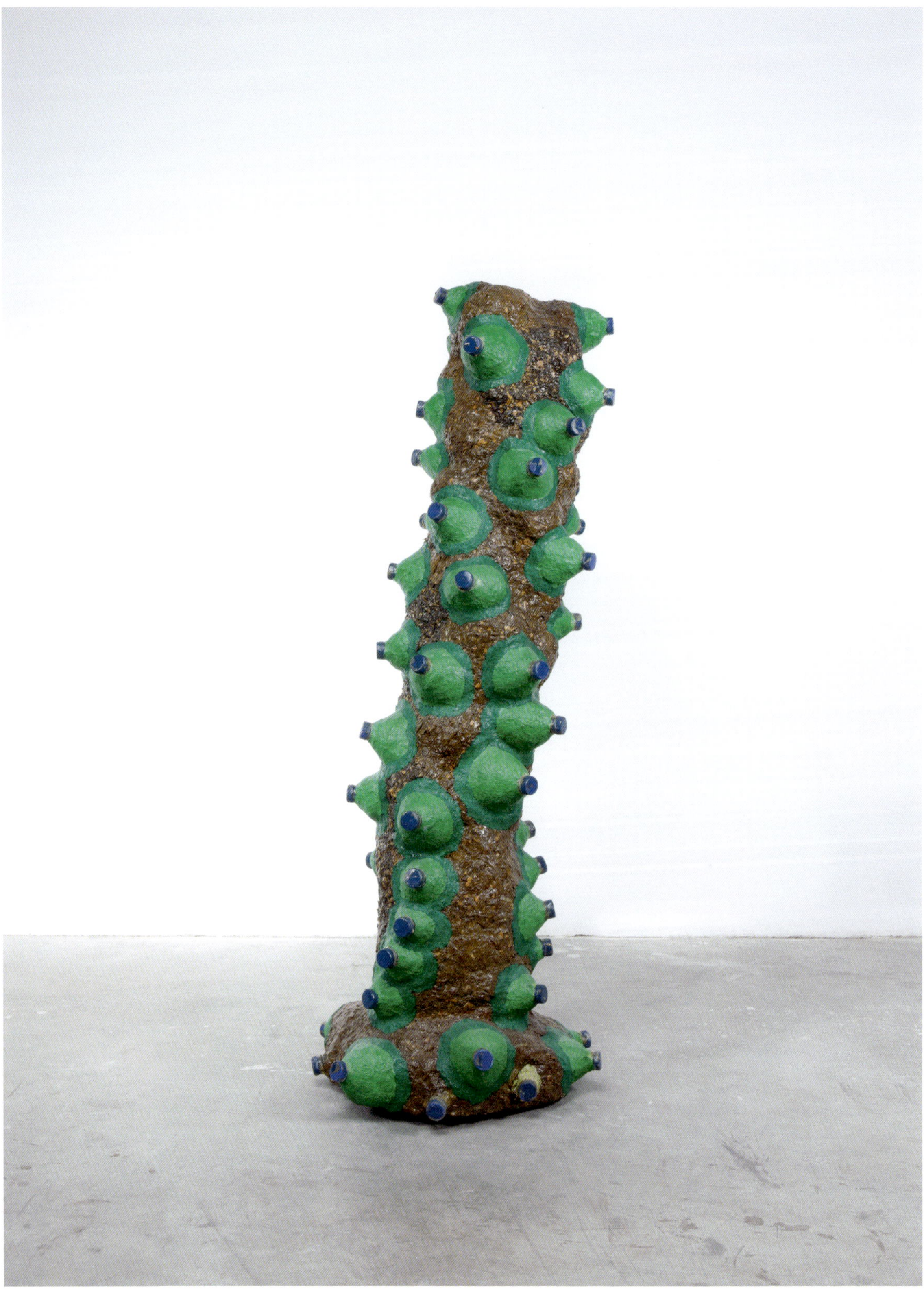

Green Apple Tree, 2013
Plastic bottles, papier-mâché,
140 x 50 x 50 cm

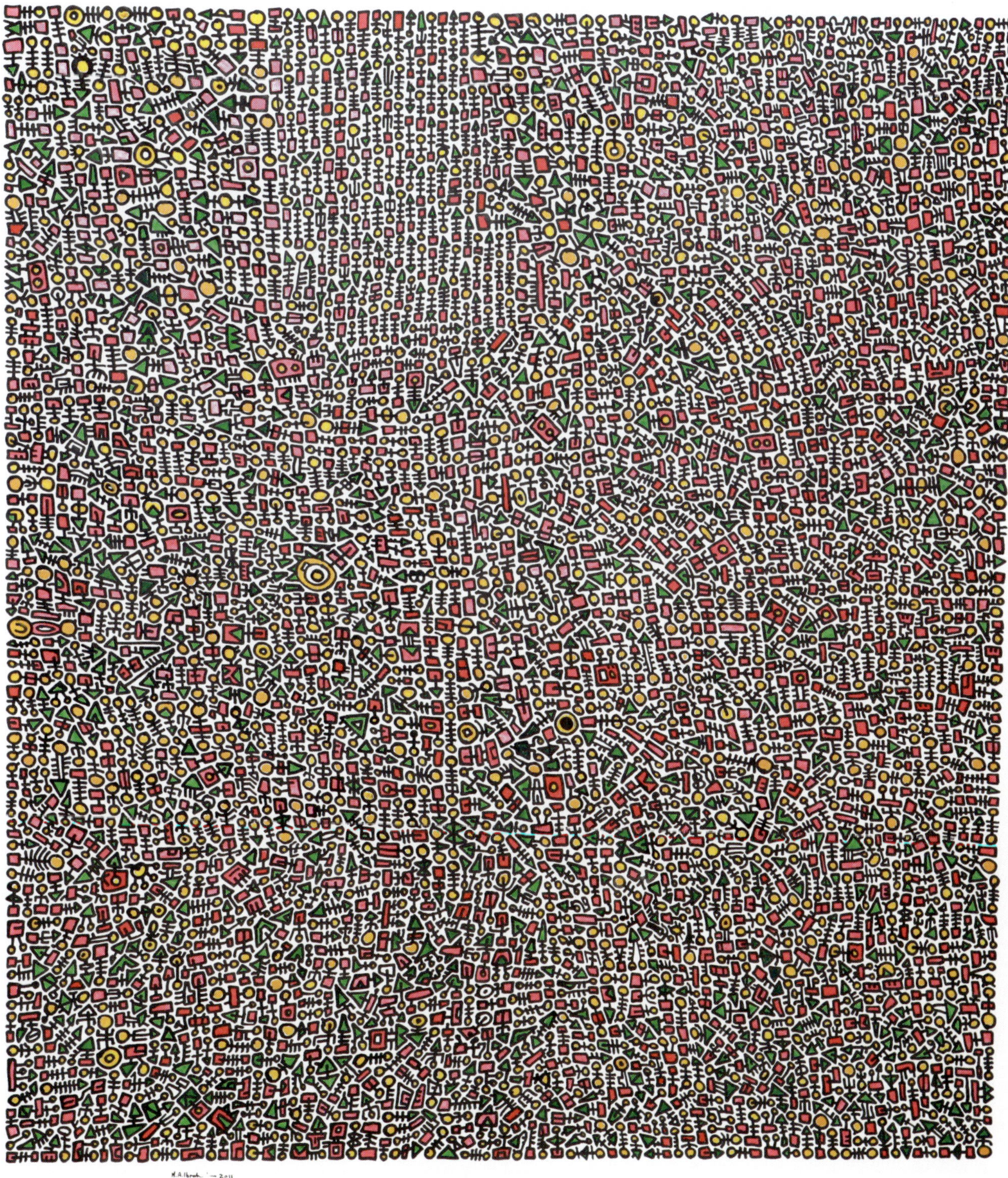

Untitled 1, 2011
India ink on paper, 115 x 100 cm

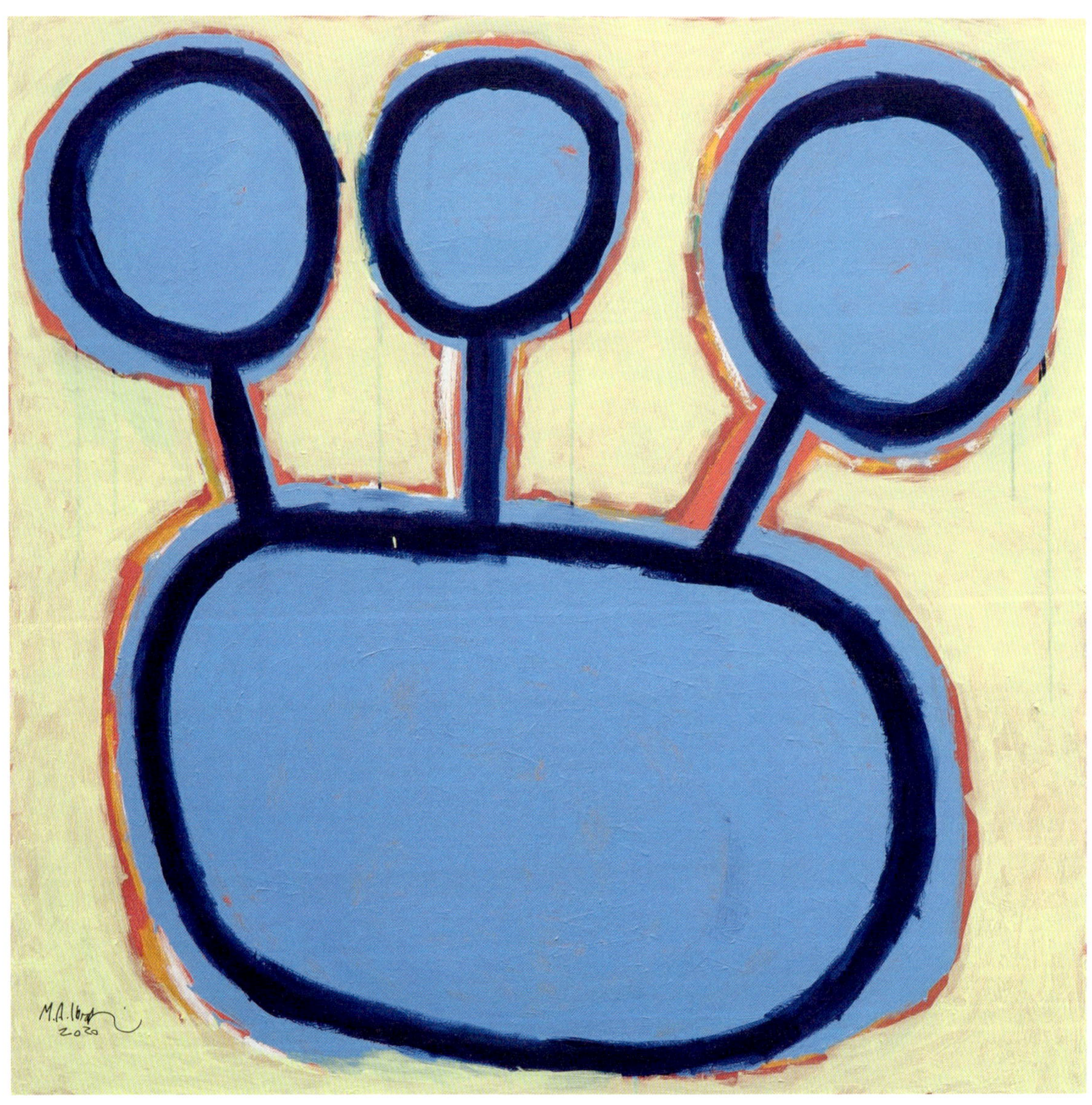

3 Blue Flowers, 2020
Acrylic on canvas, 155 x 155 cm

Next page
Dancing Woman, 2019
Cardboard, papier-mâché,
127 x 46 x 46 cm

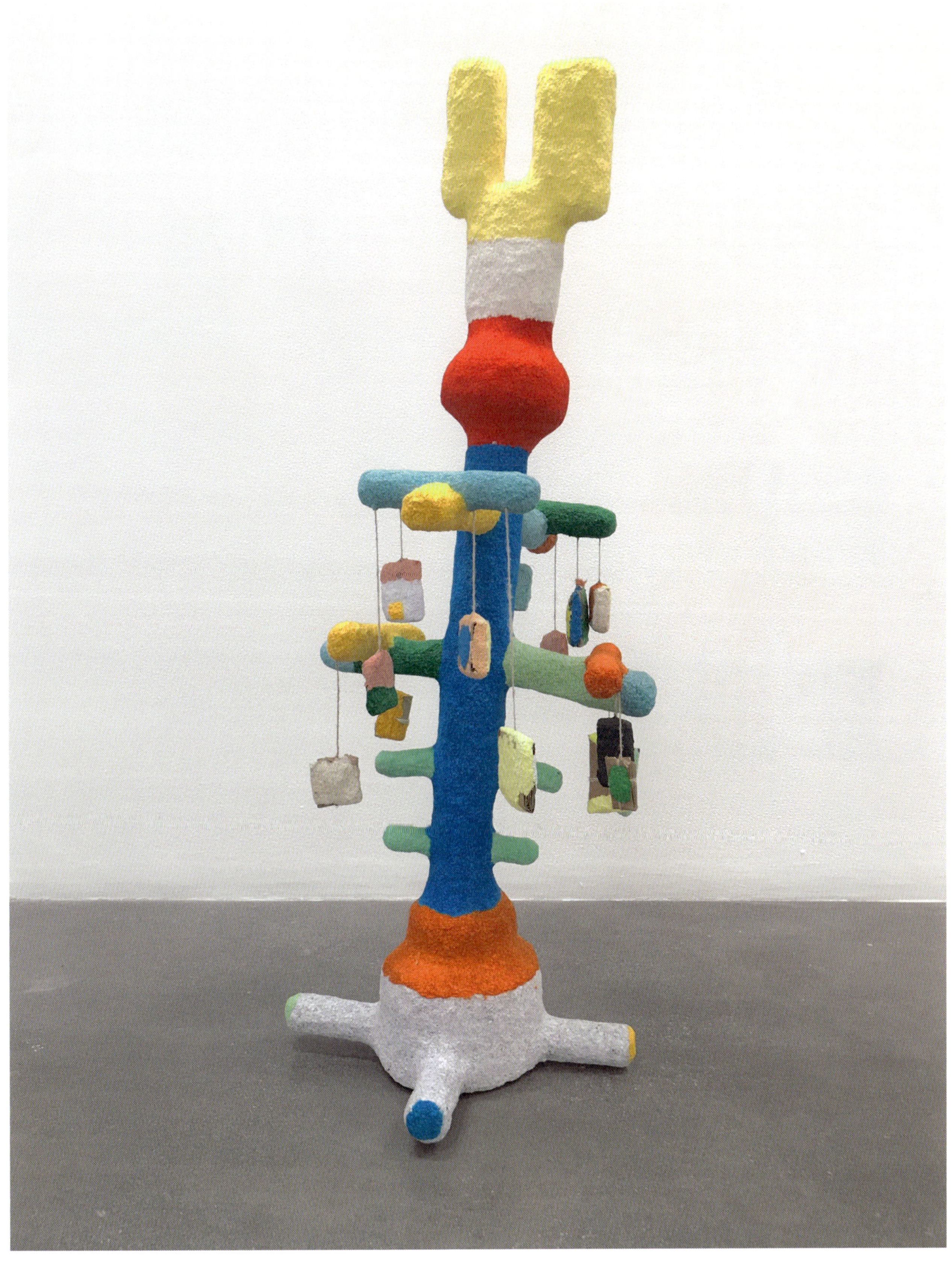

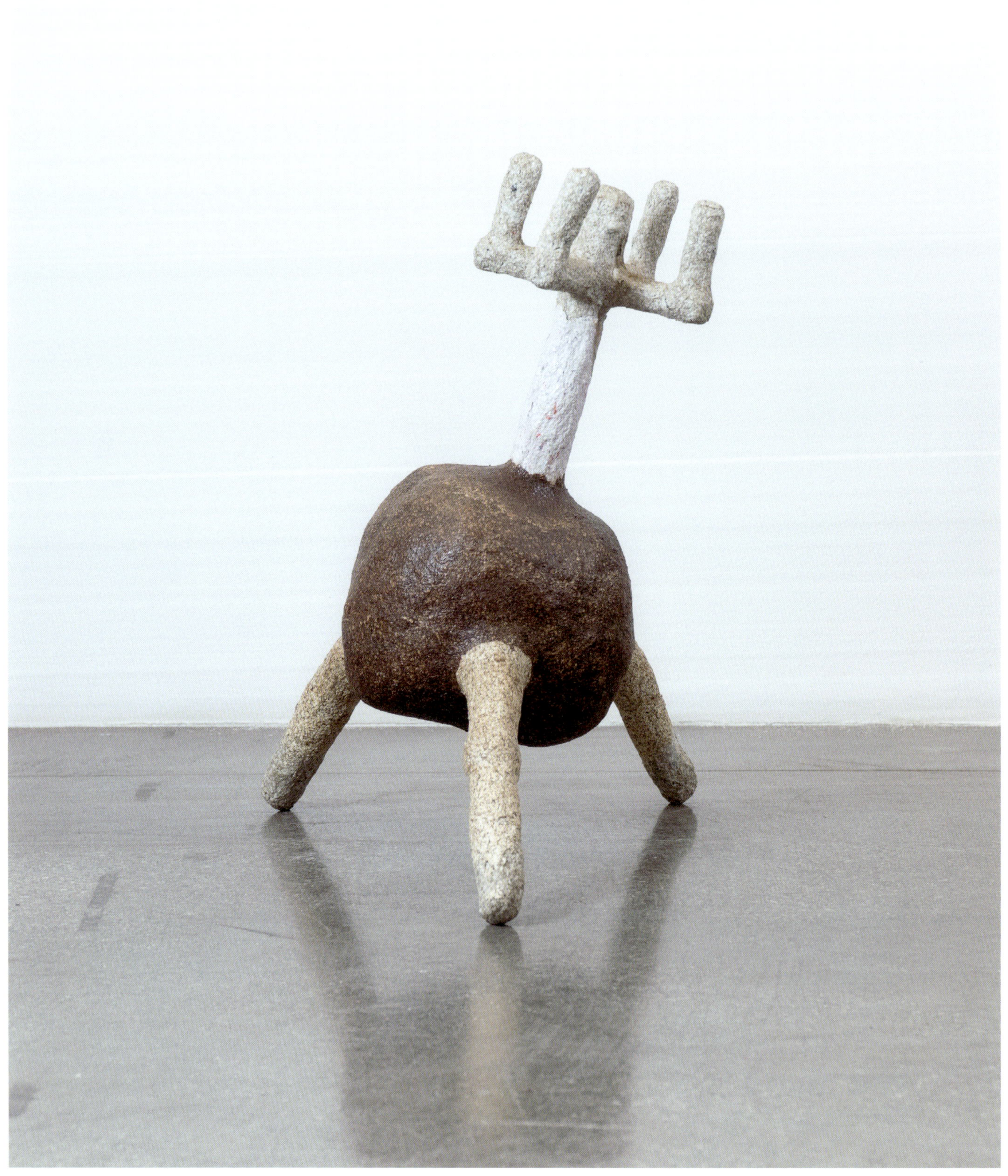

Bud, 2020
Cardboard, papier-máché,
coffee, tea, grass

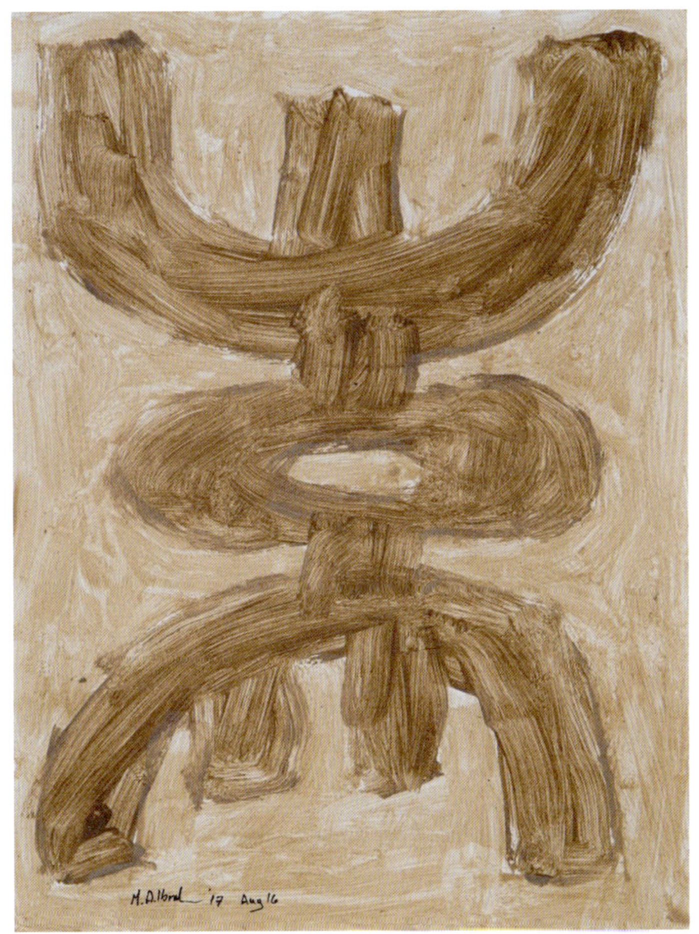 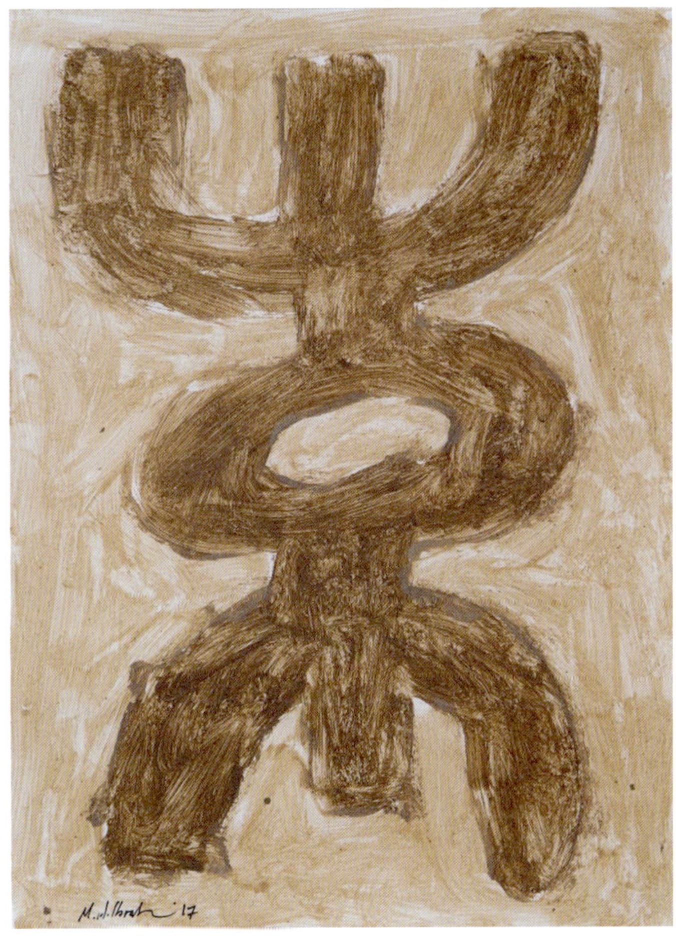

Left
Untitled, 2016
Clay on paper, 40 x 27.5 cm

Right
Untitled, 2017
Clay on paper, 40 x 27.5 cm

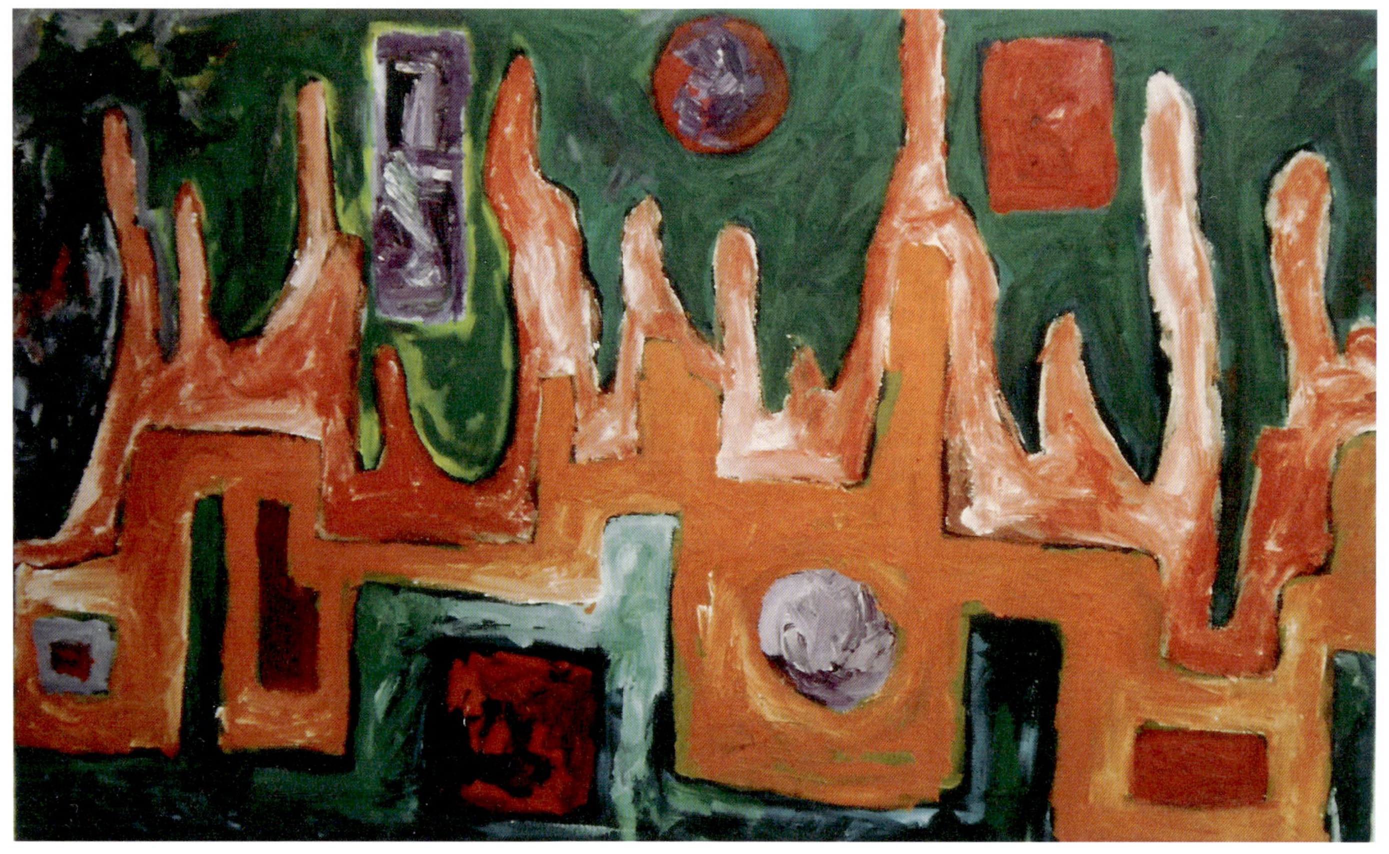

Form 2, 1989
Oil on canvas, 90 x 120 cm

Next page
Leaf, Paper & Glue, 1998
Leaf, paper, glue, dimensions
variable

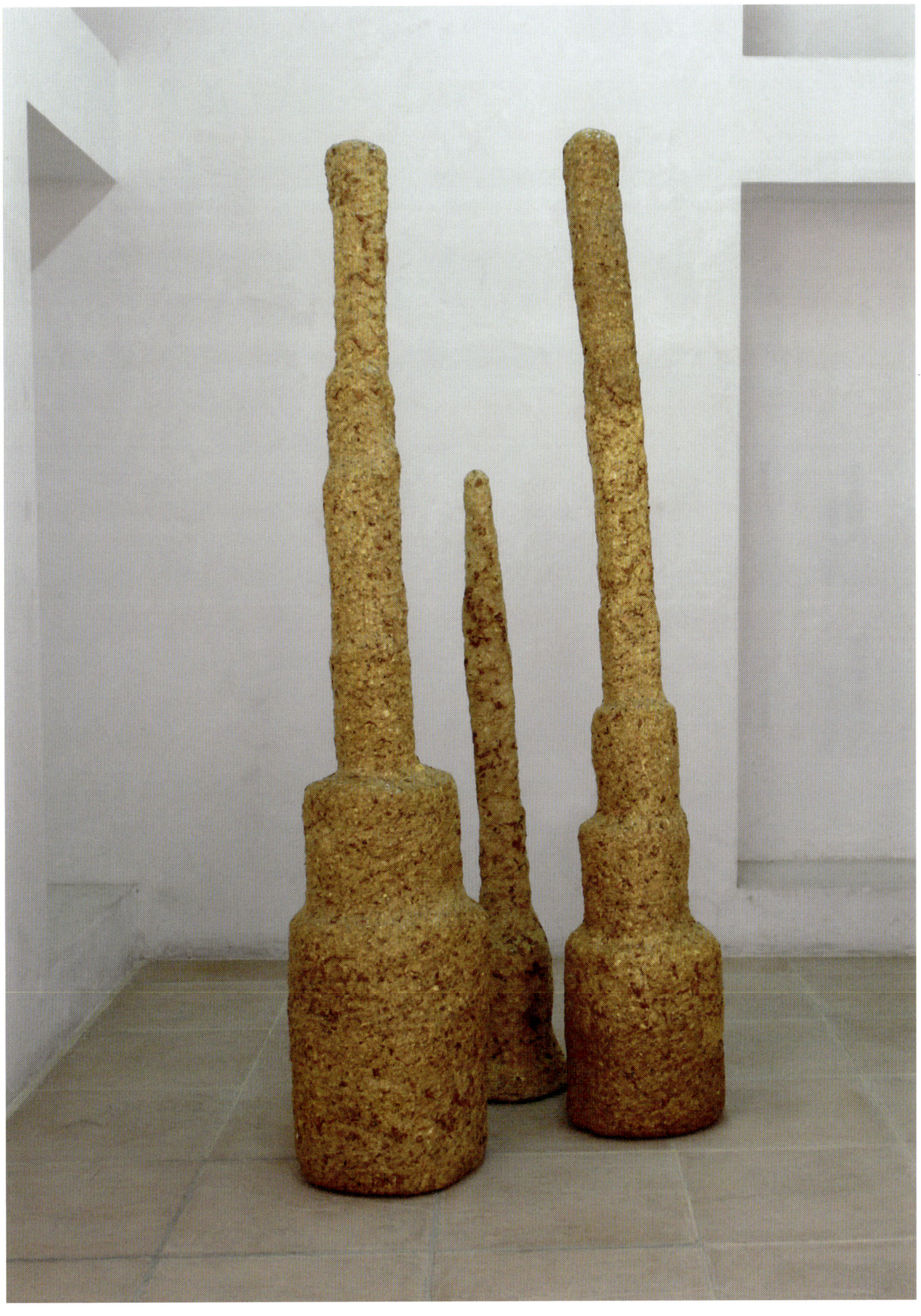

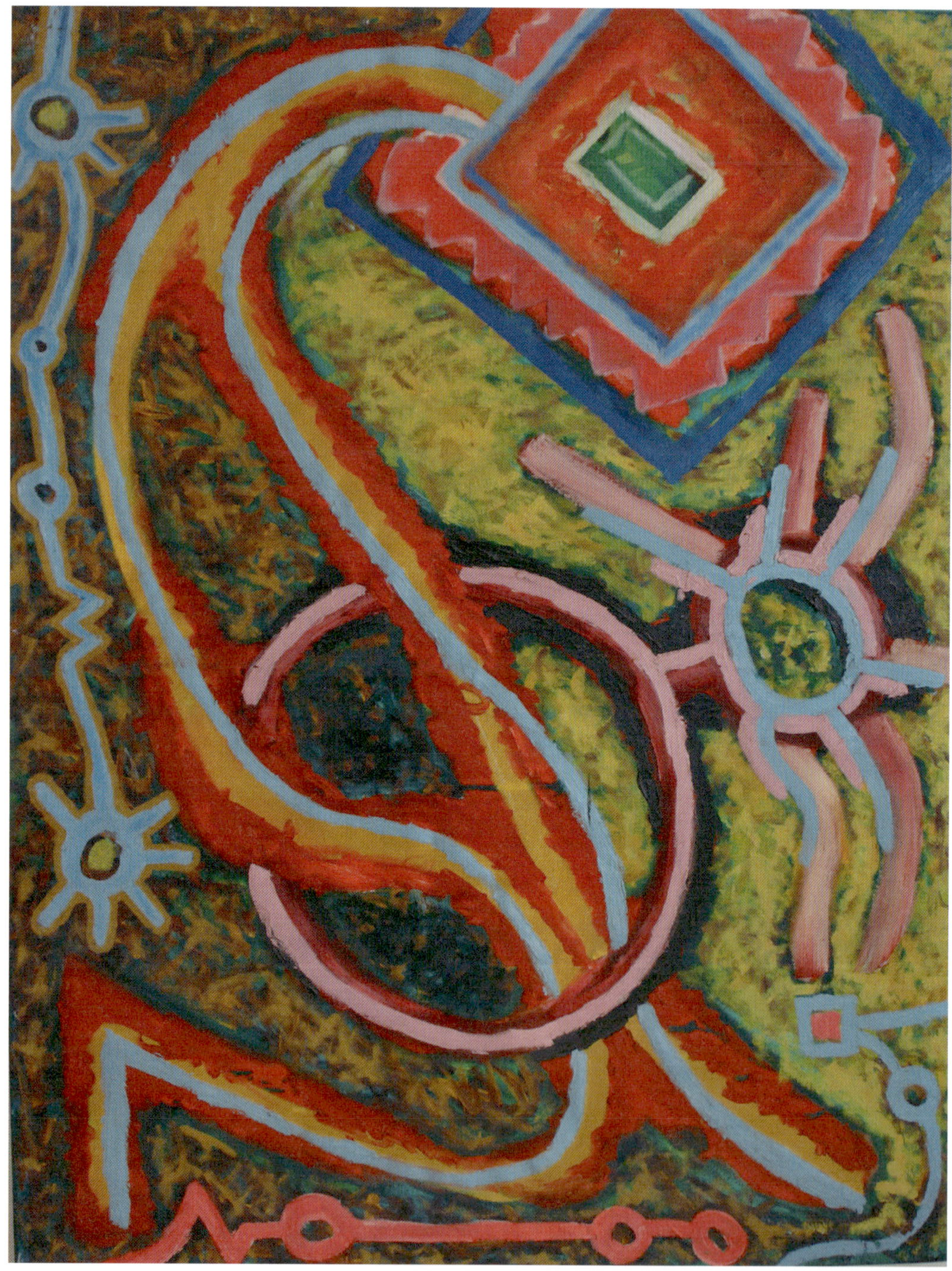

Abstract 1, 1986
Oil on canvas, 120 x 90 cm

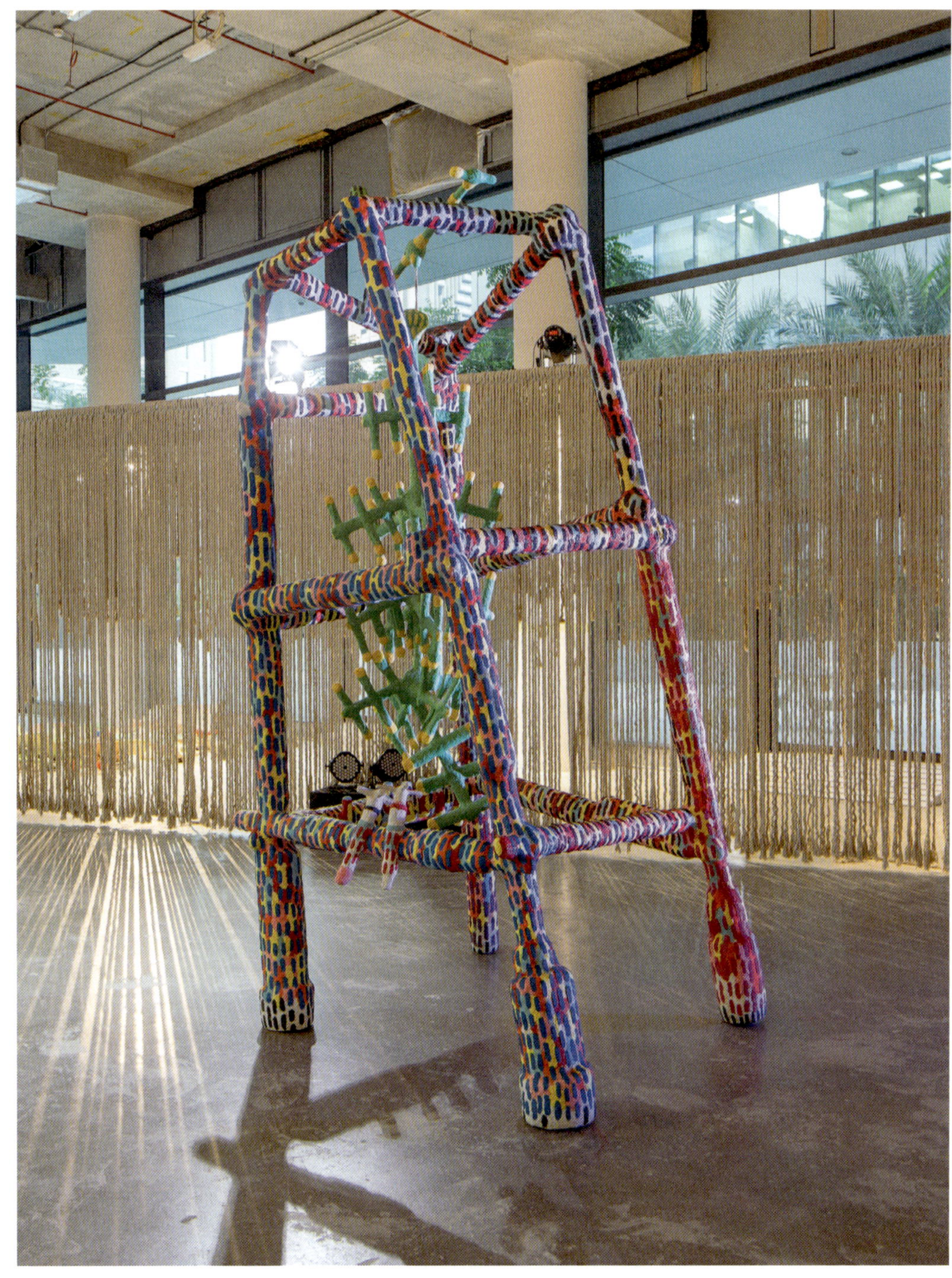

Palm Tree, 2018
Papier-mâché and wood, 400 x
150 x 150 cm. Commissioned by
the Department of Culture and
Tourism – Abu Dhabi

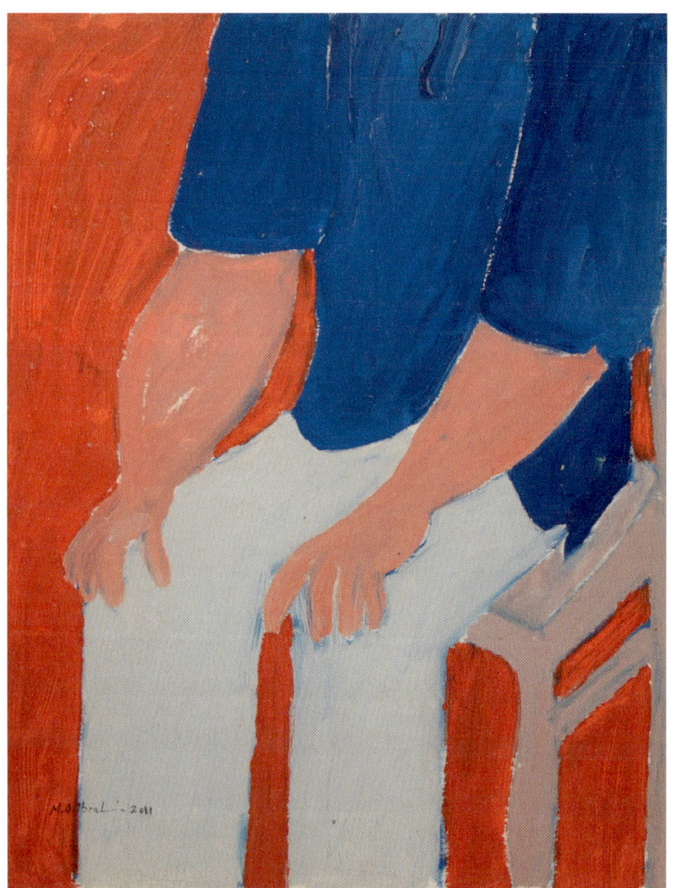

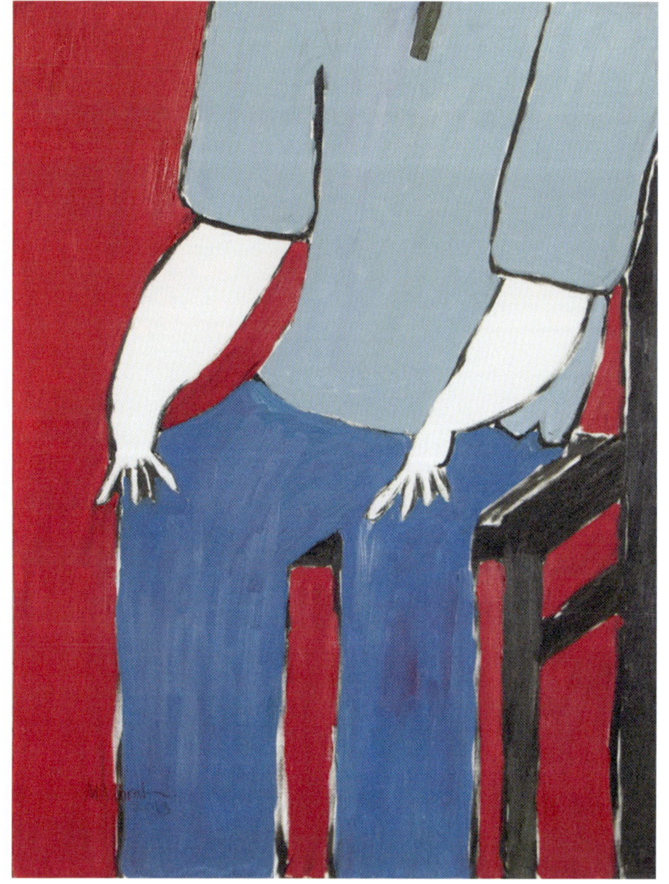

Sitting Man, 2011
Oil on paper, 47.8 x 35.8 cm

Sitting Man, 2013
Oil on canvas, 80 x 60 cm

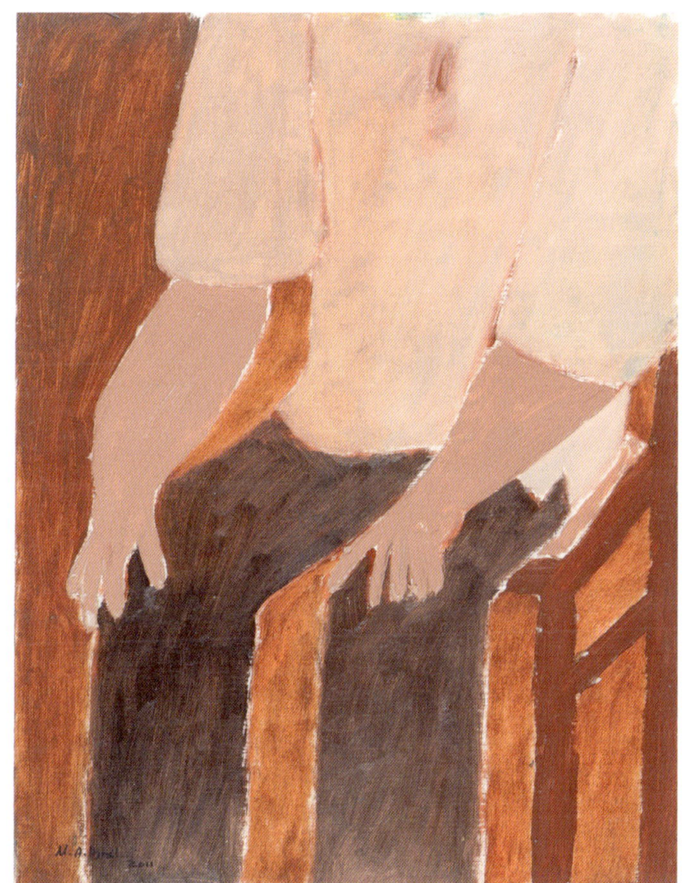

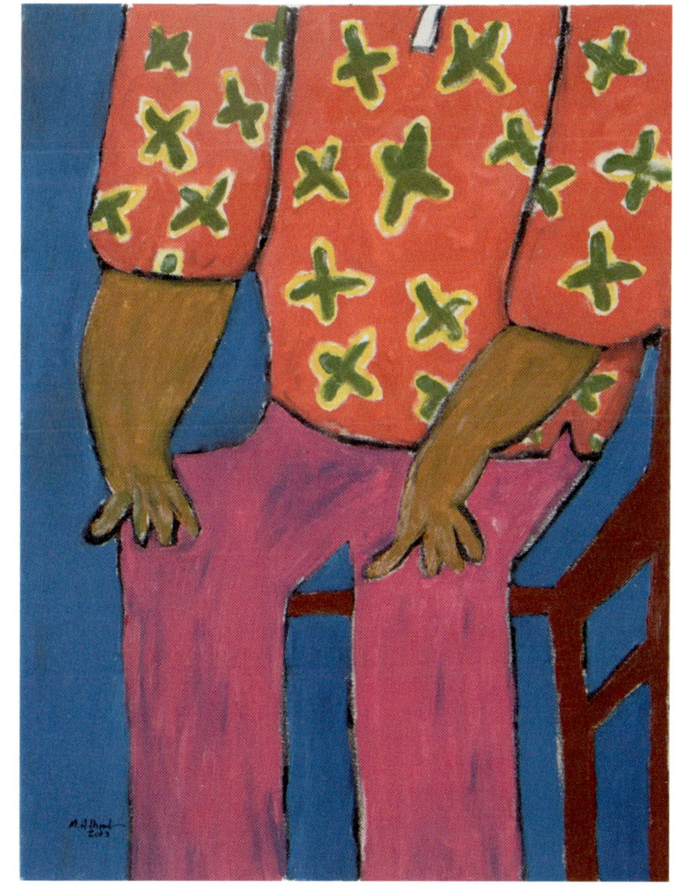

Sitting Man, 2011
Oil on paper, 48 x 36 cm

Sitting Man, 2013
Oil on canvas, 80 x 60 cm

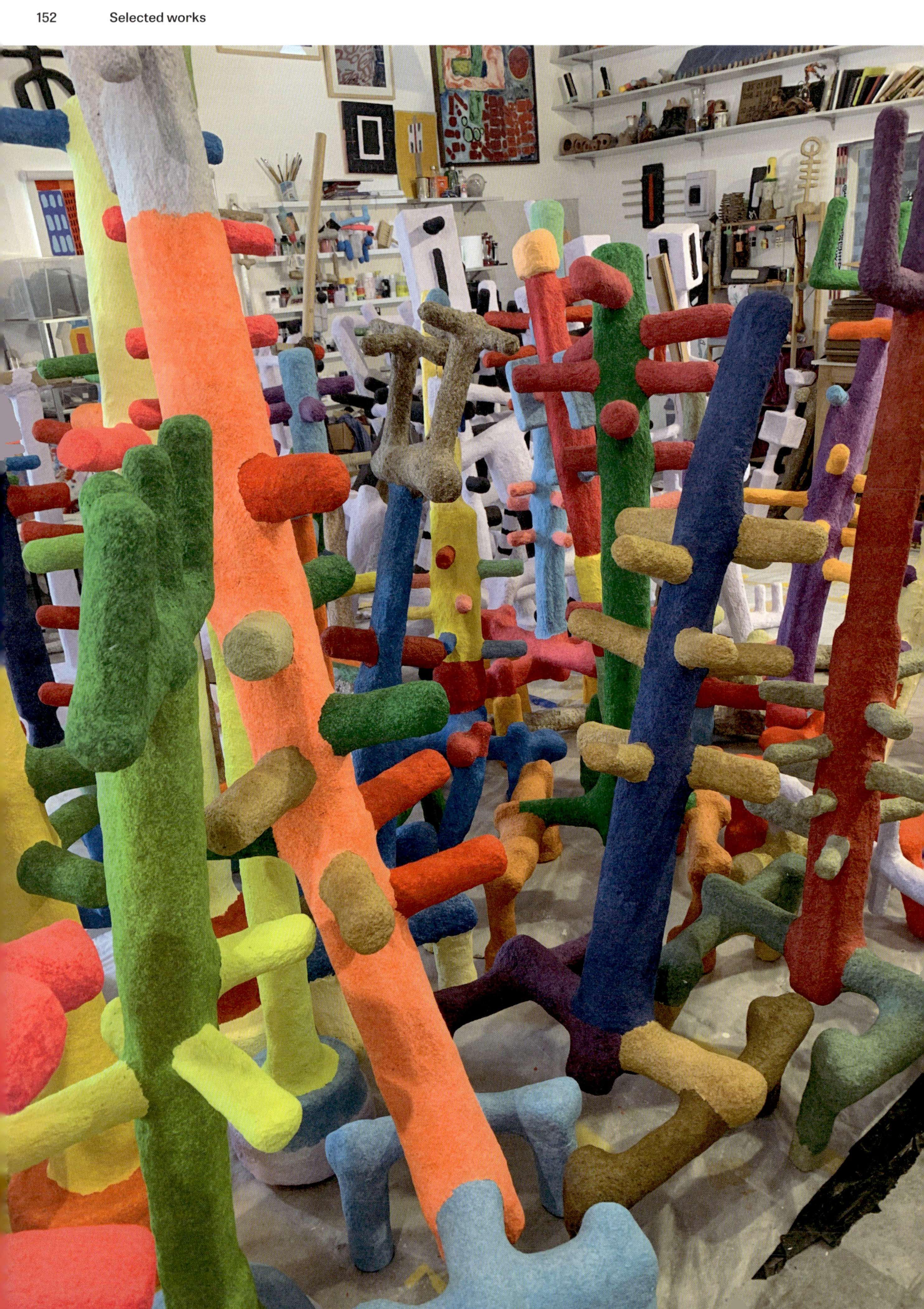

Work in progress view of *Between Sunrise and Sunset*, 2022, in the artist's studio

Between Sunset and Sunrise

Cristiana de Marchi

Between Sunset and Sunrise.
An Interview in Three Parts[1]

Part 1. Daylight

"I am still unable, as the Delphic inscription orders, to know myself; and it really seems to me ridiculous to look into other things until I have understood that."[2]

1. The interview was recorded in the artist's studio and various other locations in Khor Fakkan and Fujairah on June 18, 2021

2. Plato, *Phaedrus*, trans. Alexander Nehamas and Paul Woodruff (Indianapolis: Hackett Publishing Company, 1995), 5.

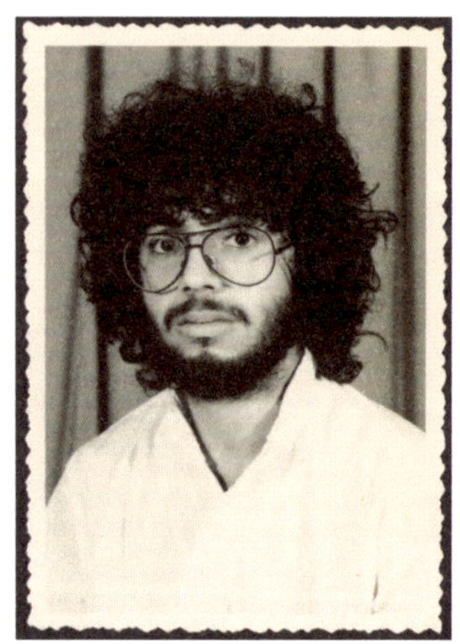

<u>**Cristiana de Marchi**</u> I have started thinking of this conversation with reference to Plato's Socratic dialogues[3] as a reflection on the role of conversations in the growing process and definition of a personality. Therefore, I am especially interested in the words and conversations that you had with some key figures in your life.

But let's start with your own words, those you recorded in writing and more specifically with your early experiments in poetry. Do you re-read your poems sometimes? Do you go back to them?

<u>**Mohamed Ahmed Ibrahim**</u> No, just now I found them again, while looking for the archive. I remembered that I had the poems but I didn't go back to look at them in a very long while.

When were they written?

They were written in the beginning of the 80s—1980–81 up to 1984.

I see there are also some notes, which look like a journal. Were you keeping a journal? Some of the pages have dates from 1990–91.

I cannot say I was keeping a diary. It was more like figuring out what I am doing, it's between conscious and unconscious writing, between the spontaneity of journaling and a more structured questioning. I would say it was an attempt to clarify ideas, to find directions, to start to look for myself, a self-searching.

Adel Khozam was saying that the poems have almost a visual kind of nature, they reflect your practice as an artist.

I would say that they reflect more my age at that time, because in that period I was thinking and writing about love, about "Woman," almost an idealization of womanhood. I believe it happens to everyone, it's a phase in life.

But you have continued this, somehow, through your artistic practice. Some of your paintings are very sensual, they have clear references to the attractiveness of the feminine. Maybe you have moved on from the ideals of love, but the softness associated with a woman's body has remained.

Yes, it's still there, there is a continuity, somehow developing from that quest.

Let's start with Ali Al Andal,[5] What was your relationship with him and what kinds of conversations would you have together?

"The Socratic Logos, ultimately, is not able to give birth to every soul, but only to the pregnant ones. […] But, then, who fertilizes the soul? Who makes it pregnant?"[4]

Ali was a friend, in the sense that, even if in some areas we didn't necessarily agree, we still shared many aspects, both in life and in our thoughts. He was a close friend from university. I could talk with him, and our conversations would frequently touch upon recurring subjects. He was writing poems and I liked writing, as well. He also knew that I was painting. After a few months, when he saw my paintings, he told me, "I will introduce you to Hassan,[6] my friend who just came back from the UK." So, Ali introduced me to Hassan.

How did he know Hassan?

Ali often frequented the Emirates Fine Arts Society (EFAS) and Ahmed Rashid[7] introduced him to Hassan. This was in the early 80s, maybe in 1981. Since then, he started visiting Hassan, every time Hassan came back from London.

Back to the conversations that you used to have with Ali. Were there any specific topics you were talking about, any subjects that he introduced you to, or writers, perhaps? Or is there anything that you would associate with him specifically, as a step in your self-discovery?

Yes, absolutely. Ali was studying Arabic literature and philosophy while I was studying psychology. We met in a class, which was common in our studies, "Islamic Philosophy." So, we had a talk in the cafeteria. I had noticed that he was different from the others. Then, we started to meet in the university cafeteria and have conversations like: who are you, who am I, what are you doing, what are you thinking … these kinds of existential questions without an answer. Afterward, we started meeting outside of the university. So, we developed this kind of friendship. We used to meet almost every day.

Were you talking about philosophy? You were reading philosophy at the time. Do you remember what were you reading?

3. Socrates (470–399 BCE), a seminal figure in Western philosophy, left no written record of his thoughts. He was presented by his student, Plato (c. 427–347 BCE), as the main speaker in a series of dialogues as well as by Xenophon and by at least nine other of his associates whose Socratic conversations are referred to in various sources, but most of which are now lost. In Plato's philosophical writing, Socrates is mostly the protagonist, discussing with one or more interlocutors. In parallel, the equally important role of the reader is also called into question as an absolutely irreplaceable interlocutor, because the reader is often left with the task of maieutically drawing the solution of many of the problems discussed.
4. Giovanni Reale and Dario Antiseri, *Il pensiero occidentale dalle origini ad oggi*, Vol. I (Brescia: Editrice La Scuola, 1983), 72 (my translation).
5. Ali Al Andal (1951–2004) was an Emirati poet.
6. Hassan Sharif (1951–2016) was an Emirati artist and writer.
7. Ahmad Rashid Thani (1963–2012) was an Emirati poet and researcher.

Besides the books that I had to read for university, I was reading books that I chose about a variety of subjects, but mostly novels, and modern visual art. Among the writers I read at that time, there were Tolstoy, Gabriel García Márquez, Jack London, and philosophers—Kant, Nietzsche, Sartre, Pavlov, but also the Ikhwan Al-Safa[8] and the Mu'tazila,[9] and of course, some comics like Tin Tin and Superman.

Ali Al Andal had a different way of thinking, a different mood. I liked his poems. I liked to spend time with him. I couldn't say that there were specific subjects or theoretical questions that were introduced through those conversations with Ali. I cannot recall anything in particular. We simply used to meet and I liked the way we talked: how we used to see and approach subjects. It's more like the way the conversation moved easily between the two of us. I felt I could have a smooth conversation with him. We were talking about poems, especially because the first time I met Ali, I was trying to write poems and then I started painting. I think it was in 1984, in Al Ain. At that time, when I started painting, I stopped writing for a while.

Did you feel like the two activities could not go together?

Exactly, they could not go together. Up until 1991, I was still writing poems. Then I realized that I cannot do both. I cannot be a writer and an artist at the same time.

Why not?

From my perspective they could not coexist. So, I was in the midst of a personal crisis and I felt like I had to find a solution. I already knew that I wanted to be an artist more than a writer. This is when I talked to Ahmed Rashid about this conflict and he told me "Then you have to stop writing and choose art." It felt like a relief! So, I left writing and I didn't write after that, until 2010 or 2011 when I wrote a few articles about artists that I met in France, which were published in *Al Khaleej* newspaper.[10]

But at the time—you are talking about the early 1990s—you already knew Hassan for quite some time, and Hassan was so active. I mean, he was an artist and an educator and he was writing, so the example of Hassan was that you can definitely do more than one thing at once. Did you have any conversations about that with Hassan?

No, not really. Even with Hassan, he was writing about art. He was not writing poems. My writing was different. When Hassan was writing, it was within the same field, the same area of his thinking. And I did that later on when I wrote about those French artists.

8. See page 26, footnote #5, for an explanation of *Ikhwān Al-Ṣafā*.

9. "Mu'tazila" (al-mu'tazilah) is an Islamic group that appeared in early Islamic history in the dispute over Ali's leadership of the Muslim community after the death of the third caliph, Uthman. Those who would neither condemn nor sanction Ali or his opponents but took a middle position, were called the Mu'tazila. By the tenth century the term had also come to refer to an Islamic school of speculative theology (kalām) that flourished in Basra and Baghdad (eighth–tenth century).

10. These articles were later translated to English and published in *Al Tashkeel*, no. 26 (2016): 82–85.

So, you felt the incompatibility between art and poetry, not between art and writing, in general?

> Yes, between art and literature. Writing about subjects that are not related to art, from my perspective, could not continue in parallel with developing an artistic practice.

Which poets were you reading at the time?

> Arabic poets and foreign poets translated into Arabic, like Baudelaire, *Les fleurs du mal* and Rimbaud. In Arabic, I read Ahmed Shawqi, Nizar Qabbani, Mahmoud Darwish, among others.

You said that you had your own books, that you were not only reading books that were available in the university library.

> Yes, these were poetry books that I bought. They were from my collection, I mean.

What about art books? Could you find art books in the UAE?

> Art books were not available in the UAE at that time. I could manage to get some from my brother-in-law, who was studying in the UK, and he sent them to me. On the other hand, the poetry books, I found them in Egypt and bought them by mail. I ordered them in bulk. I said I want this kind of book and they sent me around 500 books, both novels and poetry. At the time, it was very cheap in Egypt and they were publishing these editions for students.

Did they have art books in Al Ain University?

> At this time, I only had the books that my brother-in-law sent me. There were no art books, not even in the university. Not at all.

Which books did your brother-in-law send you? Do you remember?

> Yes, one book was like a critical reading of four European artists: Picasso, Salvador Dalí, Matisse, and Paul Klee in one book. And art history, especially a book overviewing art from the nineteenth century.

Were you asking your brother-in-law to get you specific books?

> No, anything he could find. He sent me a good number, but I can't remember how many books exactly. Whenever he could find them, he

would buy them and send four or five books at once. For me, four or five books were enough for almost a year.

How was your English at the time?

My English was ok, but I needed a dictionary for translating. We had the *Al-Mawrid* dictionary. I could spend two hours on one page or more, so it was a lengthy process.

What were you looking for in the text? Did you prioritize learning the vocabulary or did you want to learn about the practice of these artists?

I was trying to educate myself. I wanted to know everything which was available for me to know. There wasn't something specific in my reading, it was a curiosity about art in general.

Let's move on to Hassan Sharif. This is a huge chapter, of course.

"In Greek, what we call today "virtue" is called *areté* and means, what makes a thing good and perfect into what it is, or, better still, it means that activity or way of being that perfects each thing making it be what it must be, what it is meant to be."[11]

What are the first words that come to your mind when you think of conversations with Hassan?

I saw his work in an exhibition in Sharjah. I think it was the Emirates Fine Arts Society Annual Exhibition in 1986.

Which works was Hassan showing?

I remember *Cloth & Rope, Wire & Funneled Paper, Button & Cloth* and they were exhibited on the floor, directly.

11. Reale and Antiseri, *Il pensiero occidentale*, 62 (my translation).

What did you think of his work?

I thought, "This guy has a lot to say."

Did you see his works before or after meeting him?

Actually, I saw Hassan's works soon after I met him. When Ali Al Andal introduced me to Hassan, I didn't know about his practice. Hassan saw my work first, when I showed it to him. Later on, I saw Hassan's works in the exhibition.

Then, I am under the impression that, initially, the work spoke to you even more than the conversation that you had with Hassan.

This happened quickly, in a very short time. Maybe a few days after I met Hassan, there was the EFAS show. All of this—when I showed Hassan my work, when I saw Hassan's work in the exhibition and when we hung out together—it probably didn't take more than a week.

I am curious about this connection to the development of your practice because at the time you were painting, you were not making objects, yet. So, do you see a connection there?

No, there was no immediate, direct correlation. "After-painting" came later, after my solo show in 1991. From when I met Hassan up until this period I was painting.

I remember how we started to discuss painting and about my paintings. We used to go out together and we had these very clear, sincere conversations, very open to one another, about what he wants from art and what I want from art. I can still recall the main sentences, those that had a true impact on me. Hassan asked me, "Why are you painting like that?" or "Why do you want to paint like that?" He was investigating my reasons for painting in a certain way and trying to understand my perspective, not to look at my painting from his perspective.

Initially, when I first showed my works to Hassan, I didn't show him all of them. Later on, I showed him photographs of the recent ones, and I even brought one of my paintings to his studio in Dubai. Then, I started working there. At that time, I told him, "I want to draw or paint what I want, not what they like." This sense of freedom, which we were granting ourselves through our alliance, was an essential component of our relationship.

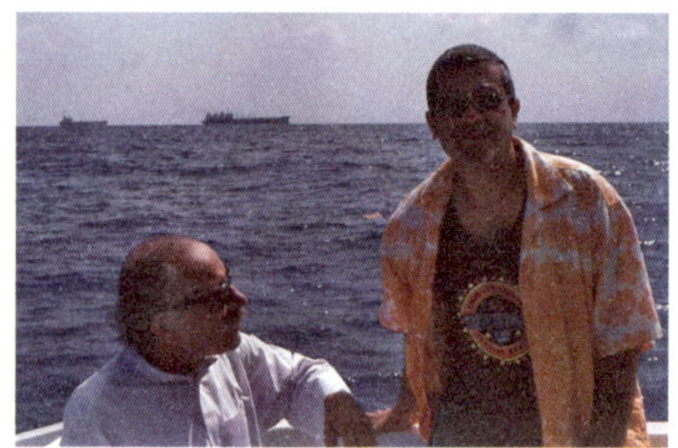

During this period, the audience in the UAE was still asking for conventional figurative art. They wanted something that they could read, that they could understand, but we were not interested in working in that direction.

So, were you aware at that time that you were not going to have an audience because of your decision to paint independently from the public understanding?

Yes, I was aware of that.

Hassan was also facing that same issue of not having an audience able to understand what he was doing. Did you ever have conversations with Hassan about this?

Not in those terms, although we were going through the same experience. Our approach was that, at least, we have one person to see our work and that was enough for us.

From left to right: Hassan Sharif
and Mohamed Ahmed Ibrahim
during the shooting of Mohammed
Kazem's *Directions 2002* project
in Fujairah

"Irony is the peculiar characteristic of the Socratic dialectic, and not only from the formal point of view, but also from the substantive one. In general, irony means "simulation."[12] In our specific case, it indicates the playful, multiple, and varied game of fictions and stratagems implemented by Socrates to force the interlocutor to give an account of himself."[13]

12. The ancient Greek word ειρωνεία originally means both "simulation" and "dissimulation."

13. Reale and Antiseri, *Il pensiero occidentale*, 69 (my translation).

Did you start sharing books with Hassan at that time? Did you
have readings or suggestions coming from Hassan?

> Yes, he started lending me books and then it became quite a regular
> occurrence.

You mentioned that you started with books that were about Picasso,
Matisse, and Klee from the modern movement of European art. Then
with Hassan, you were introduced to artists like Duchamp. I am
interested in that moment, when you were introduced to artists who
are totally different from the artists that you had studied by yourself
until that time.

> Yes, the books Hassan gave me were mostly about American masters,
> but he also gave me more books about Paul Klee or modern art. There
> were theoretical books, like the theory of art, and books with a rich visual
> apparatus, containing photographs and visual references to the works of
> European and American artists.
>
> I liked Duchamp's work, especially *The Bride Stripped Bare by Her
> Bachelors, Even*.[14] Hassan talked a lot about this work, so I found myself
> in this line of thinking, talking about artists like Duchamp, Paul Klee,
> Rauschenberg, Joseph Beuys, etc.

I am trying to retrace your education in art: what were the main steps,
knowing that it's in part a self-education, and then a kind of education
that developed through the conversations you had with artists and writers.
So, I am interested in knowing what your reaction was to artists like
Rauschenberg or Joseph Beuys. What did that open up for you? Did you
feel like there was a reaction in your work?

> Yes, my response or reaction to their work and practice was a sense of
> consonance, a correspondence. I found that this kind of thinking in art
> matched my thinking, so I found myself in this zone, in this area in art.
> I found a place that I could identify with, as an artist, after struggling
> "against," the current for quite some time.

How did you react to what Hassan wrote about you?[15] I am also interested
in the process he followed. I mean, you were having conversations and
then Hassan was writing about you or was it something that he was
writing independently from your conversations?

> No, what Hassan was writing emerged during our conversations together.
> It was something that we had already talked about. I felt absolutely

14. The original title in French is
*La mariée mise à nu par ses
célibataires, même* (1915–23),
by Marcel Duchamp.

15. Hassan Sharif has written
exclusively and repeatedly about
Ibrahim's practice, publishing
mostly articles in local newspapers.
See also Sharif's show, *Sharp
Tools for Making Art*, 1983–1995,
published by the Department of
Culture and Information, Sharjah.

confident, because I knew Hassan, and I trusted that he knew my way of thinking, that he could read me, and that he could read my work. The relationship between Hassan and me became a friendship, it wasn't simply an artist-to-artist relationship. Although art was connecting us, it was the element that brought us to meet and deepen our relationship. So, it was very clear to me what he would write, because the whole time he told me what he was writing.

So, when you were reading his articles about you, you found your own words in them, almost as if, while reading these texts that Hassan wrote about you, we are following some of your conversations with him, in a way … And then, there is Jos Clevers.[16] Would you like to tell me something about him before I start with my questions?

Sometimes you meet someone and you have that kind of conversation, that kind of communication, like you feel you are more than just in the present, as if you had known one another for a very long time. The communication flows easily because you immediately sense a connection. With Jos it was like that, a very easy, spontaneous kind of relationship. And not only with me, also with my friends, Mohammed Kazem and Hussain Sharif. When Hassan met Jos for the first time, we had the same feeling toward him.

Jos was very important to me and I started to visit him, to spend long periods of time at his place in Sittard. In 1994 we spent all summer and the beginning of autumn together. I felt a sense of freedom, just by being there, moving around the city. Imagine more than two months in a completely different environment, discovering myself as much as discovering the place. At that time, he also gave me a space in his art center,[17] just to focus on my practice and work.

Similar to an artist residency…

Yes, it was a kind of artist residency. There I did, for the first time, what I called, "Painting and Performance." In "Painting and Performance" I had 12 pages—because the sketchbook I bought had only 12 pages of oil pastel paper—so I hung two pages paired in six different places in the art center, from the table where we sat to drink our coffee up to my studio— two pages next to the table, two pages in the corridor, etc. I used to go back and forth. I kept on doing this for one week.

Were you intervening on the paper every time you passed by? (see pp. 168 –169 for images of this work).

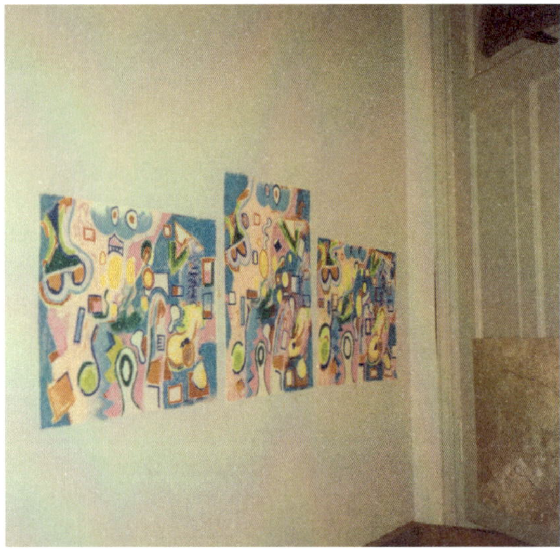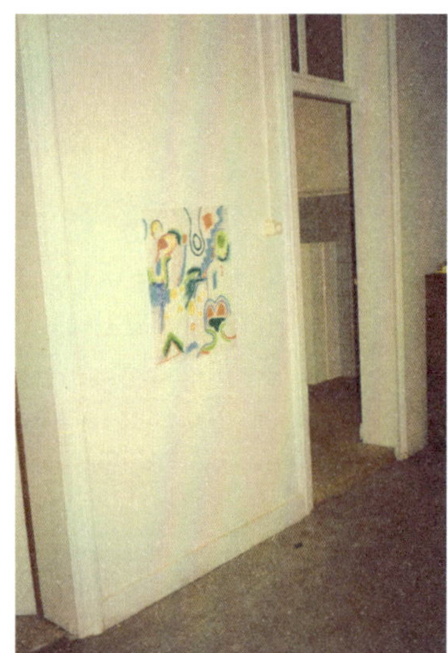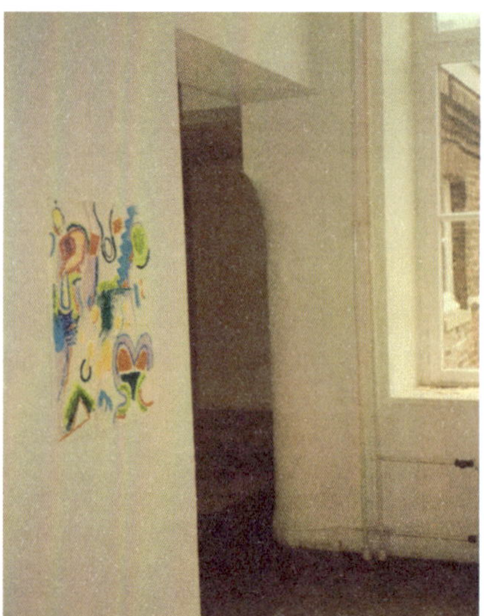

Documentation of Mohamed
Ahmed Ibrahim's performance
at the Sittard Art Center, the
Netherlands, 1994

Yes, whenever I passed the pages. I would draw a figure, and then I would move to the next one, drawing the same figure I drew before. For example, first I drew the same shape everywhere, let's say a square, and then I would change and move on to the circle. Then, I would repeat the circle on each paper, back and forth, repeatedly. In the end, the twelve sheets of paper became similar because of the saturation of repetition, but they were still different. What was the difference that I found? The surface of the wall had an effect on the paper. Out of the twelve papers, the differences came from the trace of the wall behind them, not only from my "gesture." For instance, when there is a ceramic tile, you will have a square in the background, and when the wall is rough, the paper becomes almost dotted, and so on.

I think this was my first performance. I see it that way. Even though there was no announcement and I just did it for myself. Because of that, sometimes I didn't call it a performance, and sometimes I did call it a performance. Only a few artists saw it. Nevertheless, you can say it's a performance…because at that time, I was still looking for the meaning of art or how I can express myself in art.

Have you found the answer?

Up until now, I didn't find it [laughing]. Really, you cannot find the answer. The only answer you can find is "Keep on creating," that's it. You can say "Keep on creating," but you cannot say "I found it."

After that time, what was your relationship with performance? Although intermittently, you have gone back to performance. I mean, I can see some of the works that you did as performative works, like the ones you did in France in 2009, for instance.

Yes, Hassan and I did a performance at a poultry farm in Umm Al Quwain. I remember it was a Friday morning when we woke up and

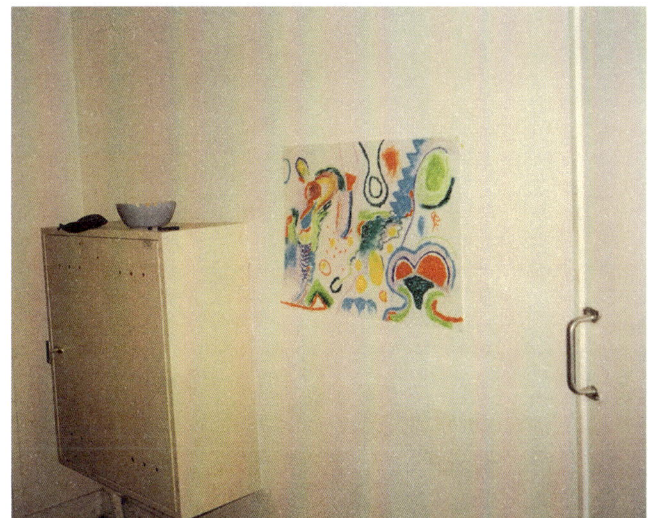
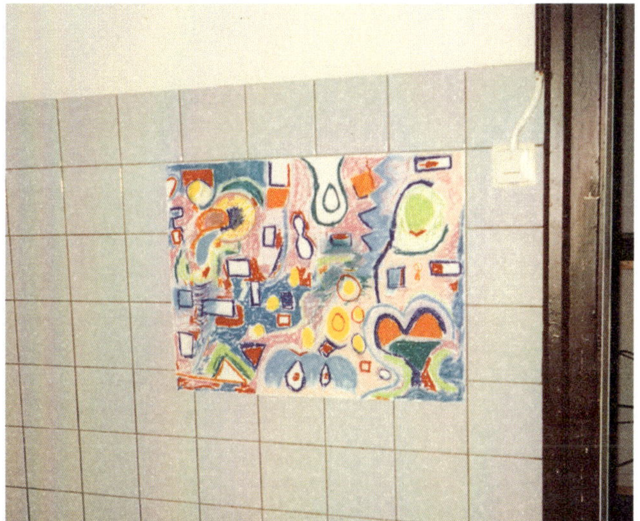

went outside. We didn't talk yet until we had the idea of doing this. The creative act brought with it the subject of the conversation. We started discussing the idea of trace, of our individual traces on the sand, and the role of the brushstroke, etc.

In the performance, Hassan was making a line with a wooden stick in the sand and I was behind him, brushing the line. Once we reached the limits of the farm, say after 200 meters, we inverted the roles, and we kept on repeating the action for more than half an hour.

Do you remember which year that was?

After 1990, I cannot remember exactly, but probably in 1993.

Is this the only time when you did something like that together?

Yes

Did you do anything like that with anyone else, like a joint performance?

No, only this one time with Hassan.

But you also had a joint project with Jos…

Yes, *Holy Places With No Creed* (see pp. 170–171 for images of this work). It started in 1994. The first time we were in Sittard, Jos and I were discussing the concept of art without documentation, of undocumented art, like performance and happenings. We were thinking about new tools in art and then we started to talk about religion. Every religion has a holy place. From that idea, as we were sitting in this restaurant called Tapas in Sittard, we called it a holy place.

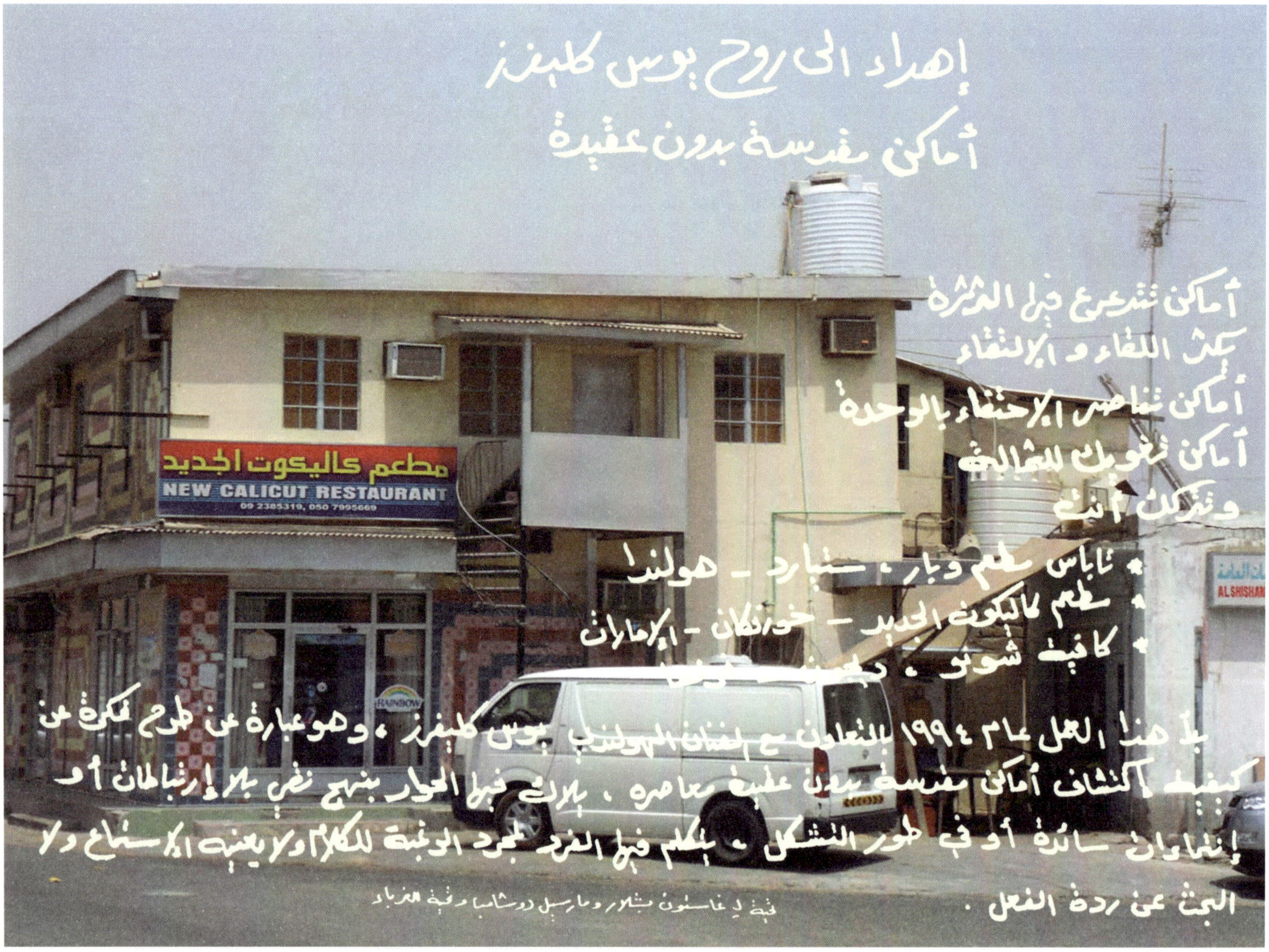

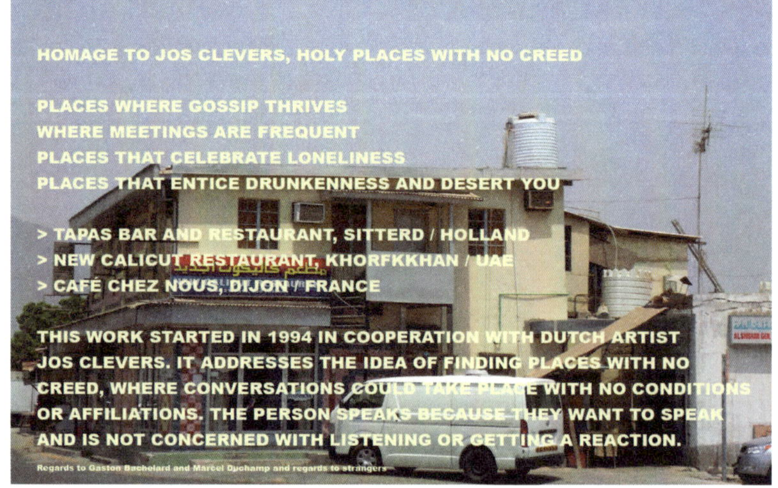

This page
Homage to Jos Clevers, Holy Places With No Creed, 1994–2009. Documentation of the New Calicut Restaurant in Khor Fakkan, UAE (Arabic)

Homage to Jos Clevers, Holy Places With No Creed, 1994–2009. Documentation of the New Calicut Restaurant in Khor Fakkan, UAE (English)

Next page
Homage to Jos Clevers, Holy Places With No Creed, 1994–2009. Documentation of Café Chez Nous, Dijon, France (French)

Homage to Jos Clevers, Holy Places With No Creed, 1994–2009. Documentation of Tapas Bar and Restaurant, Sittard, the Netherlands (English)

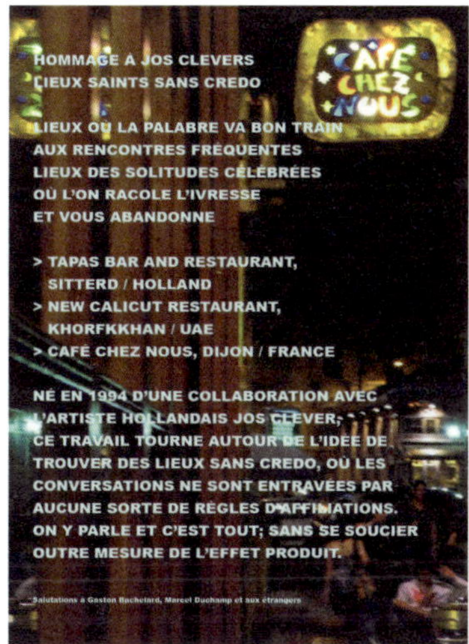

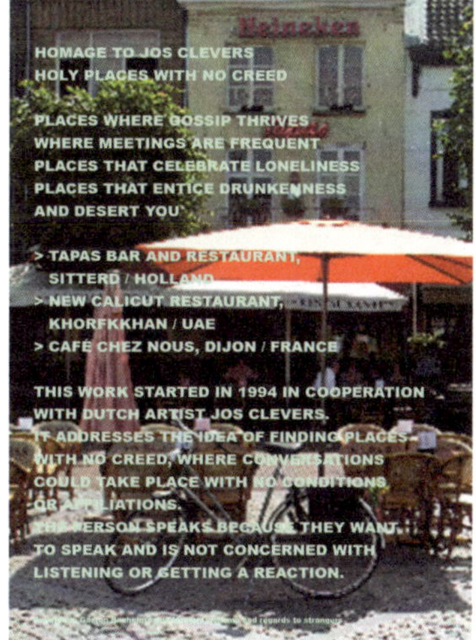

After a few years, Jos was visiting me in Khor Fakkan. I was working during the day and Jos was going around by himself. One day he came back home and told me that he found another holy place and I knew it was Calicut restaurant.

Finally, in 2009, in Dijon, I found another place with the same atmosphere, Café Chez Nous. I chose it as the third holy place and I made an announcement with an homage to Jos[18] and to Gaston Bachelard. I was reading Bachelard's *The Poetics of Space*[19] at the time and he taught in Dijon for a decade or so. I made a large poster of the three places with some writing and we made a small show in the same café. It was in collaboration with Le Consortium, where I was a resident artist. They even engraved a brass plate celebrating my project and they nailed it to the café wall.

I think this is the last holy place without a religion. With the commemoration and ultimately the documentation of the project, it is an homage to Jos' soul.

Is there any artist that you discovered for the first time when you went to The Netherlands? Did you happen to see exhibitions or books of artists you weren't familiar with?

Yes, Jos had a very good library, so I spent most of the time looking at art, either through images or photos or directly as artworks in exhibitions. If the books were written in English, I would also read them, but if they were in Dutch—and most of them were in Dutch—I would just look at the images. Through the simple exposure to the images, I could find the border between genres, for example, experimental and performance, or between erotica and photography. I could read them and I realized I didn't need a text to understand the works.

What became really clear to me, though, as I was looking at all those books, was that photography, the documentation through photography, was a potent instrument for artists. It was at this time that I understood that the camera can be a tool for artists, not only for documenting their work but also for circulating it. All of this was not accessible in the UAE. All the art books that I saw before traveling to The Netherlands were books about masters, published by scholars. But in Sittard, I realized how contemporary artists could use photography to document and circulate their own work. Hassan had already started to document my work, like the works of the other artists from the group. In a way, he was the first archivist of my work. But it was in Sittard that I started to open my mind and fully understand the importance of what he was already doing.

18. Jos Clevers died earlier, the
    same year.
19. First edition published 1958.
    Beacon Press editions 1969, 1994.

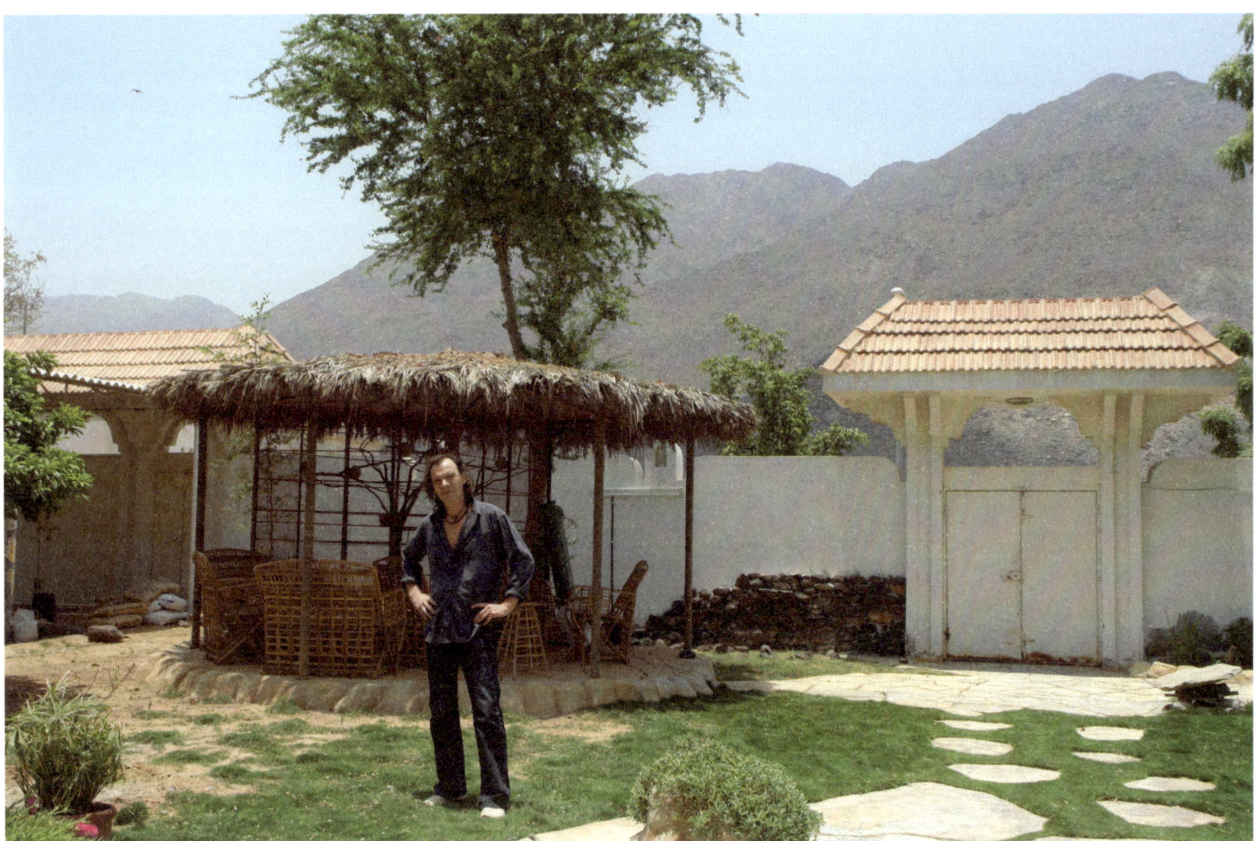

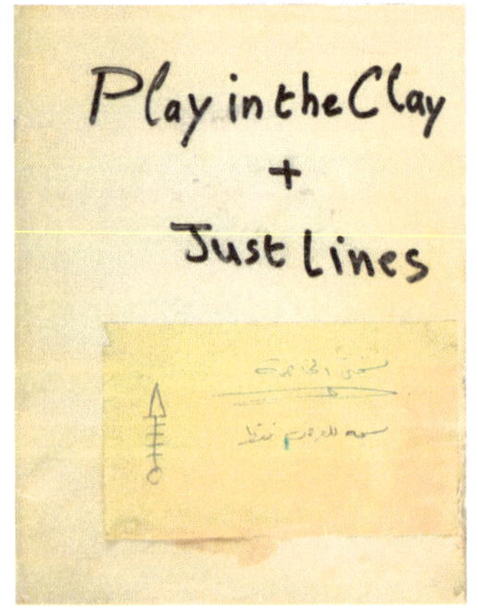

Besides the books, we were also visiting young artists and going to exhibition openings, not only in Sittard, but in Maastricht, where most of these activities were happening at the time.

Are there specific artists or places that you remember?

Now, not really, but at the time, all of them were special to me. All of them were interesting for me to see. I felt that almost all of those artists were similar to me in thinking.

A few years later, you attended Documenta[20] for the first time. What was your impression?

I have visited Documenta twice, in 1997 with Mohammed Kazem, and then in 2007 with Jos and Abdul-Raheem Sharif. While the first one had a very homogeneous rhythm and all the works were very consistent with one another, the second time[21] it was an awesome experience. The scale of the exhibition and the variety of works was astonishing, like being in a garden with different kinds of flowers and scents!

Jos Clevers at Mohamed Ahmed Ibrahim's home in Khor Fakkan, c. 2008

Play in the Clay + Just Lines (1997)
Handmade brochure,
21.5 x 16.5 cm

Part 3. Between Sunset and Sunrise

"Do we want to explain why something is beautiful? Well, to explain this "why" the Naturalist would refer to purely physical elements, such as color, figure and other elements of this kind. But—says Plato—these are not "true causes," but means or concauses. It is therefore necessary to postulate the existence of a further cause, which must be, to be a true cause, something not sensible but intelligible. It is the Idea, or pure "form" of Beauty in itself, which, with its participation or presence or community or, in any case, with a certain determining relationship, causes empirical things to be beautiful, that is, to be realized, through shape, color, and proportion, how they should be and how they must be precisely to be beautiful."

20. Documenta X, 1997, curated by
    Catherine David.
21. Documenta XII, 2007, curated by
    Roger M. Buergel and Ruth Noack.
22. Reale and Antiseri, *Il pensiero
    occidentale*, 98 (my translation).

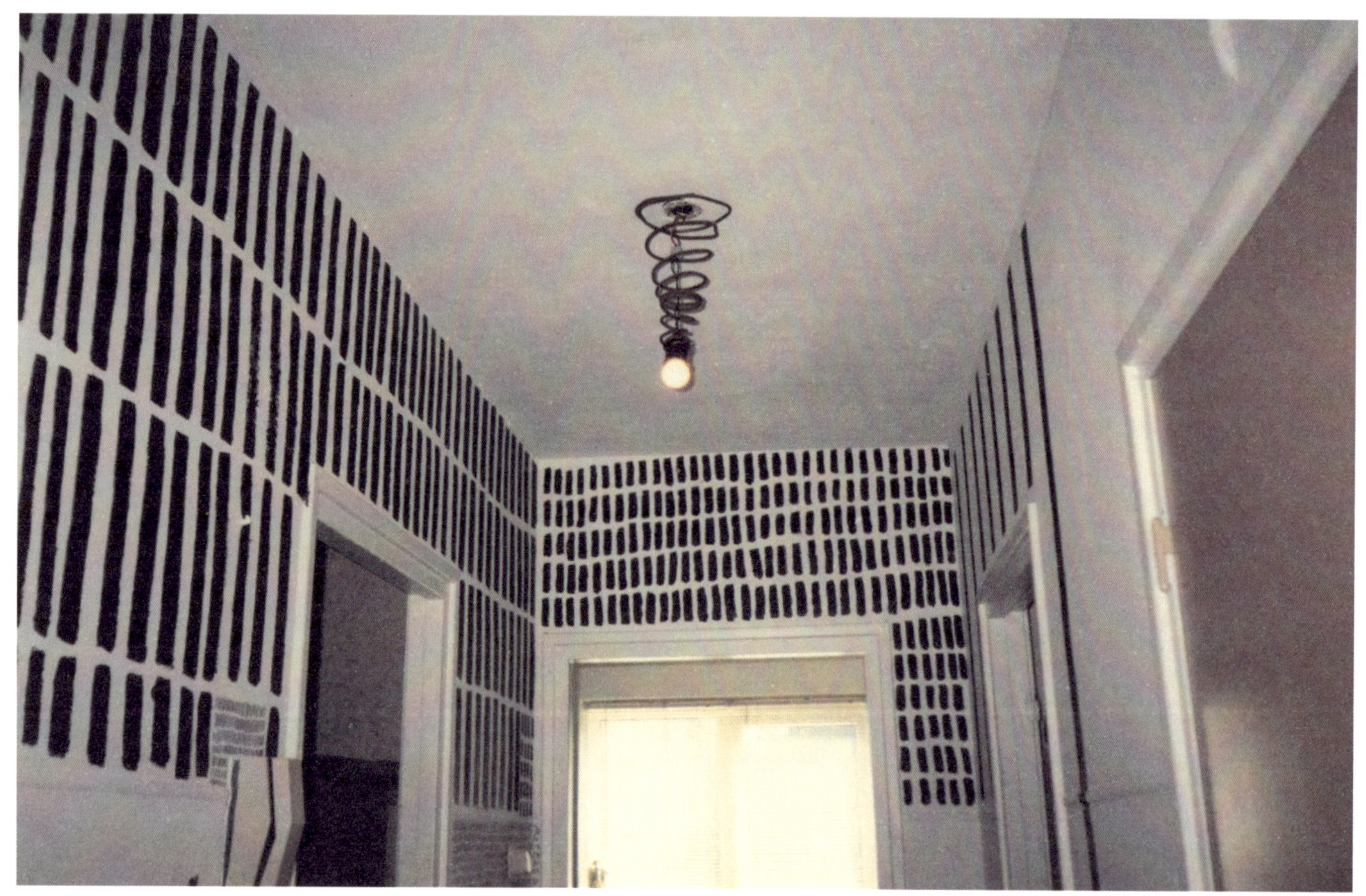

Shall we talk about the "Idea" in your creative process? What is the role of the "Idea" in the platonic sense?

I typically create more objects of the same kind, to fill the space. I place them in a bigger circle and I start by contouring the surface. Only later, I fill the gaps. There is a circularity, an idea of return, and each time in a different way, to define the space first, and then to substantiate it with more presence. Since they are similar in shape, I position the objects in different ways. For instance, one lying in a direction and then I put another one standing, etc., and because of their different orientation, they might seem different but, in the end, they are the same.

I follow a similar process in my drawings. In the drawings, I am filling the space, and I use ink and a brush. In the installations, I fill the space with the objects, because eventually, regardless of the material, the idea is similar. The only difference is perhaps the level of control. In drawing, I have more control, because it's two-dimensional, but when I work with three-dimensional pieces, they react to the environment, to the light, so the outcome is less predictable. They become almost alive, in relation with the viewers, who are not only guided by their eyes, but they have to deal with many dimensions, including their body, their sense of balance, etc.

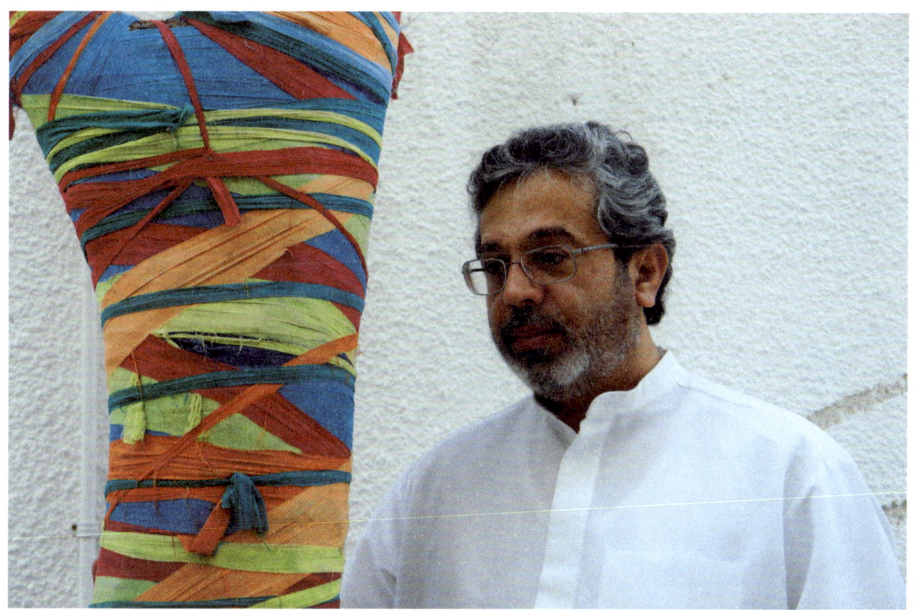

What is the generative process? How does the idea become embodied in the work?

> I will tell you with an example. Right now, we are four people,[23] sitting on a semi-square table, a very simple configuration. If I use a symbol for the square table, then maybe I call us circles: circle 1, circle 2, etc. Then, I get to add more shapes. Let's say two of us are drinking green tea. So, if I want to add another shape, I would add the same one for the two people, a triangle for instance, the third shape. For me and you, who are drinking black coffee, then coffee would be represented by a fork, so we would have one fork, and a second fork. I can continue to work like this, endlessly.

But you use a relatively limited number of symbols that you repeat in your drawings. Which means that, in each case, they represent an idea, in a referential way, to the specific context. They will represent something else when they are depicted in a different context. They seem to be more like alphabetical letters, that can be rearranged, rather than like words which can be composed.

> I don't want the viewer to read my paintings, I want them to have their own experience. I don't want them to decode the painting, it's not a language.

As far as I see it, it's all about your history. What you did before, is what gives you permission to do what you do next.

23. The recording of this segment of the interview took place in Khor Fakkan and Fujairah on June 18, 2021. Mohammed Kazem and Adel Khozam were also present.

Play in the Clay + Just Lines (1997)

Play in the Clay + Just Lines (1997)
Handmade brochure,
21.5 x 16.5 cm (overall)

Play in the Clay

+

Just Lines

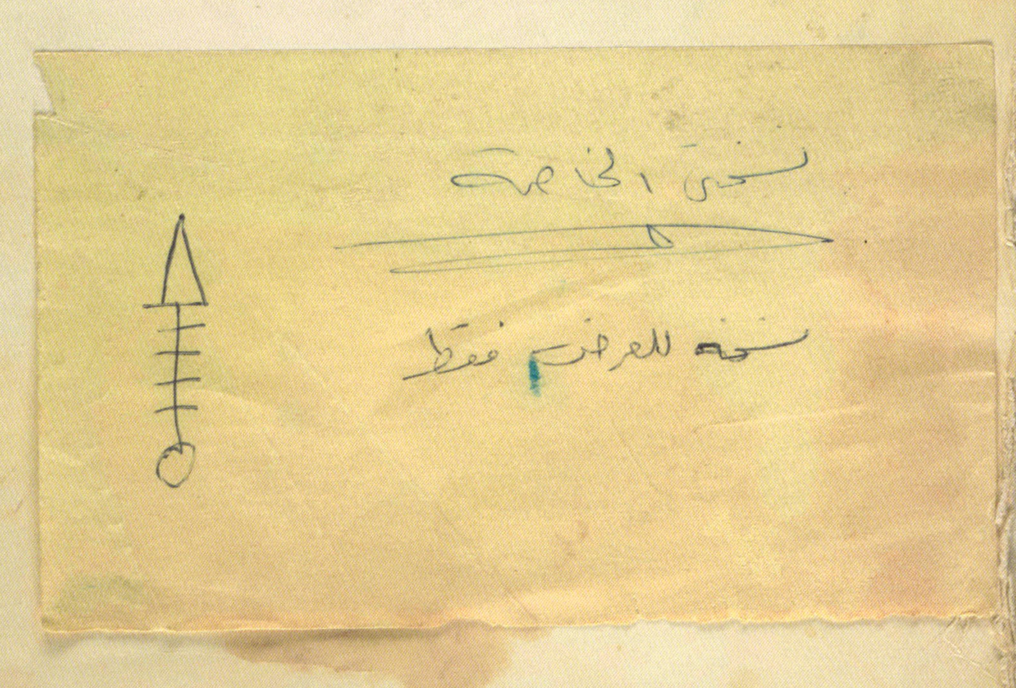

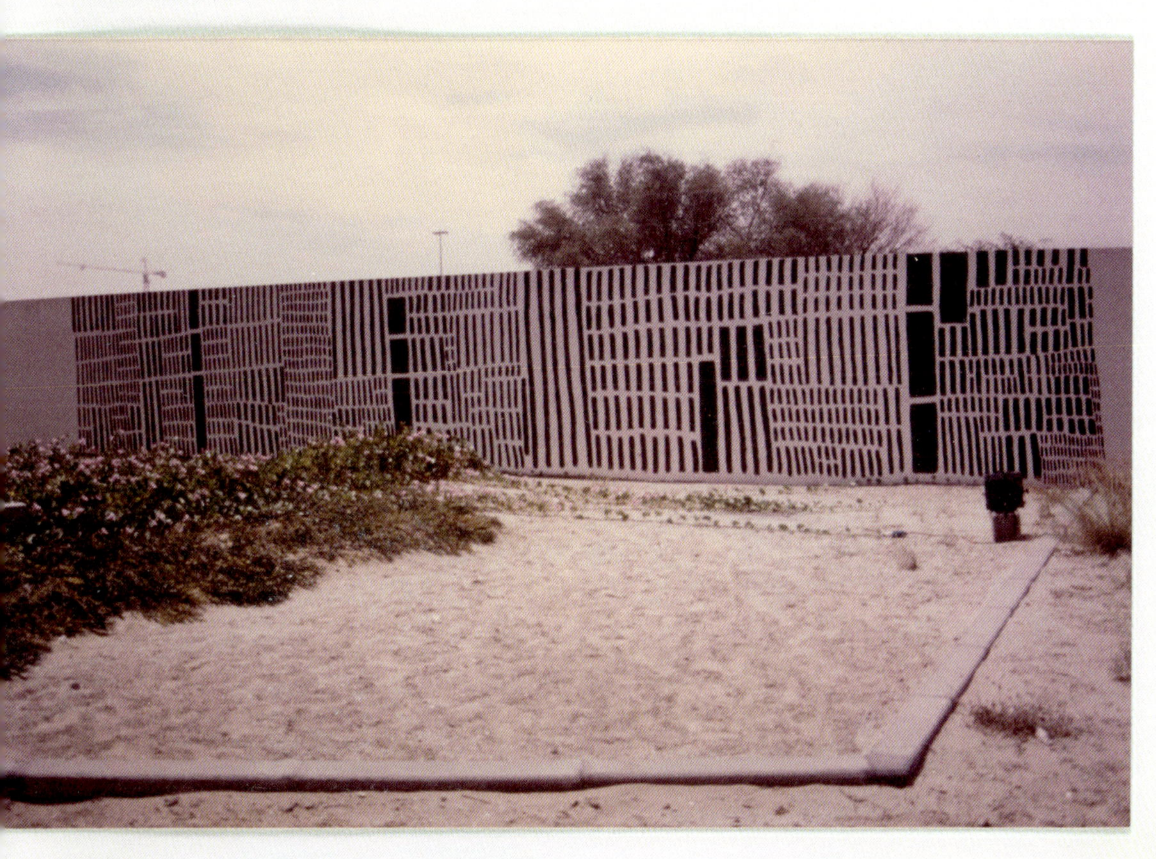

French colture Centr. Dubai - 1997

بناء حجري رقم ١

Piled rocks no.1

1995

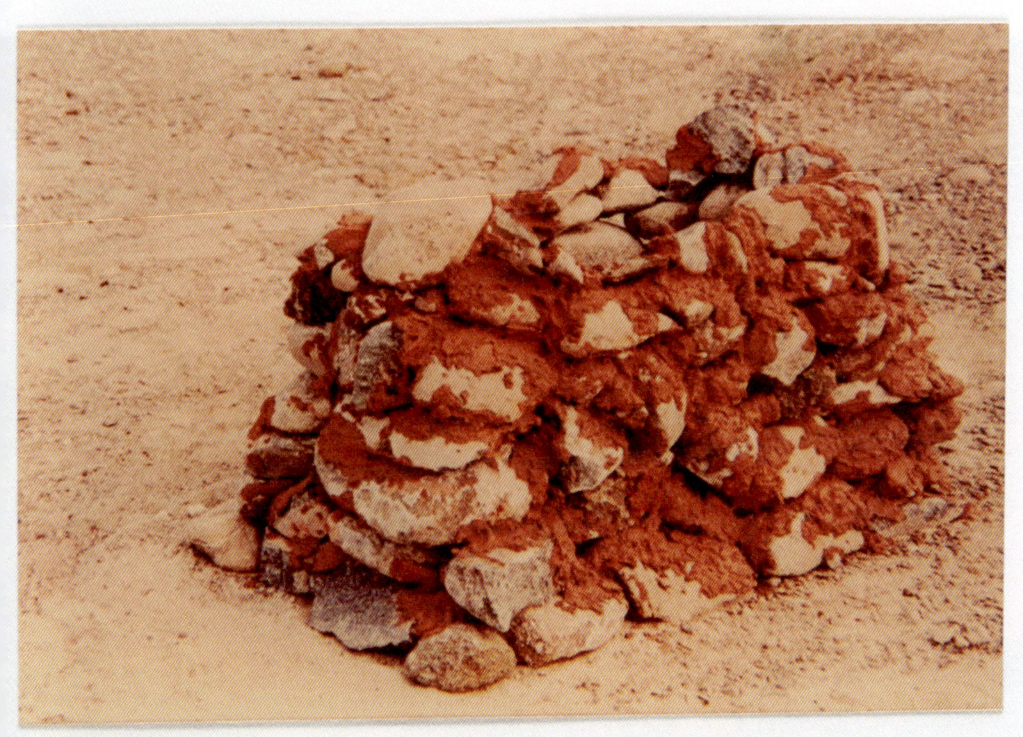

150 cm x 100 cm x 100 cm

- Mine

بناء حجري   رقم ٢

Piled rocks no.2

1995

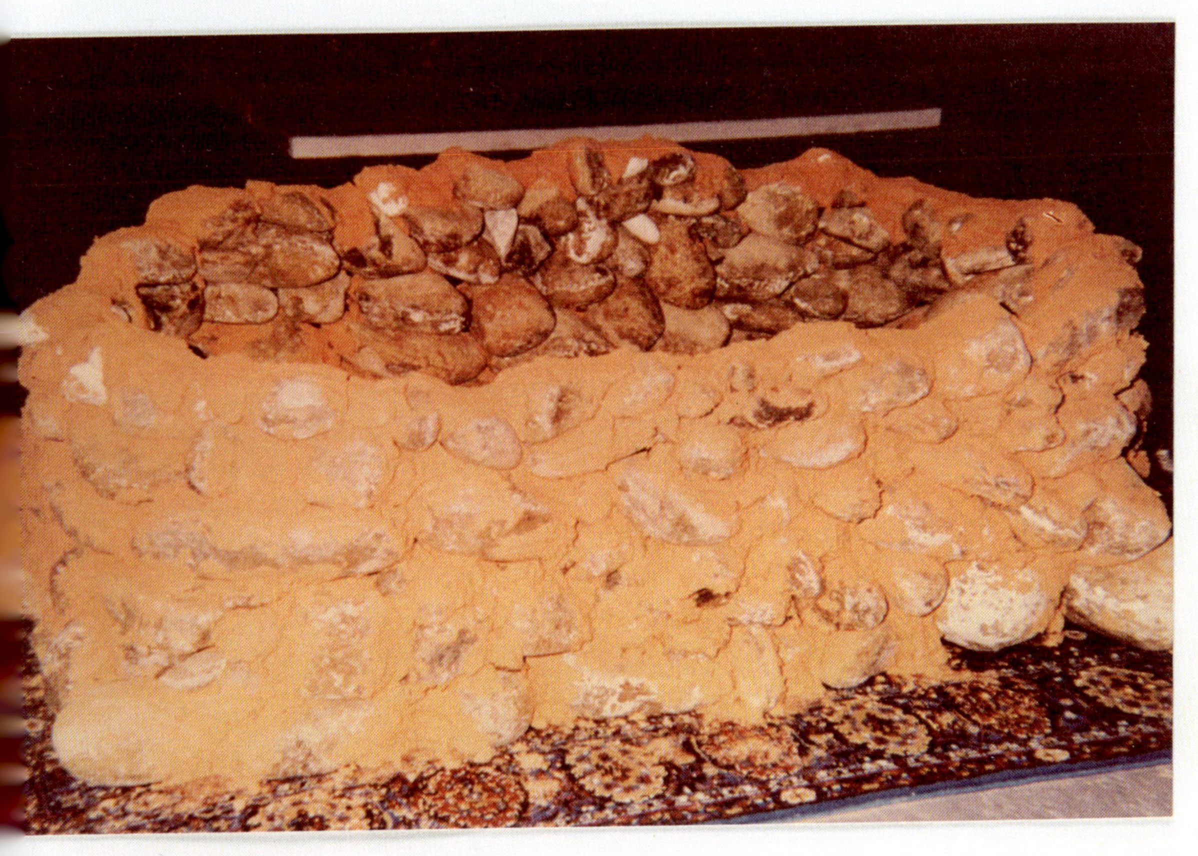

2nd Sharjah bennical — 1995

3m X 2m X 1m

أشجار مقمشة

Wrapped trees

1996

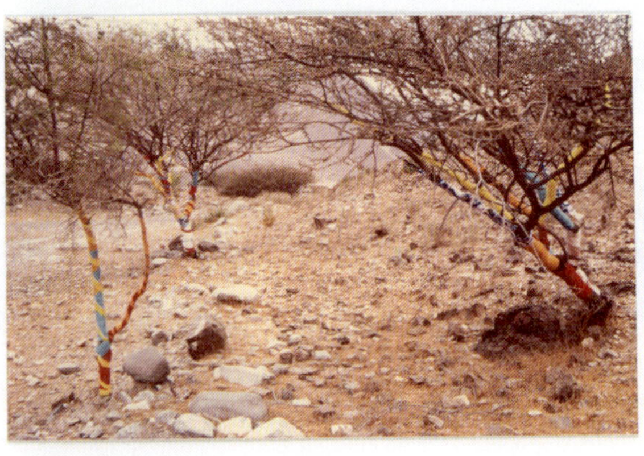

_between U.A.E and Oman
5 trees

السيارة المحطمة

Damaged car

1990

-Paulakry Farm-Ajman

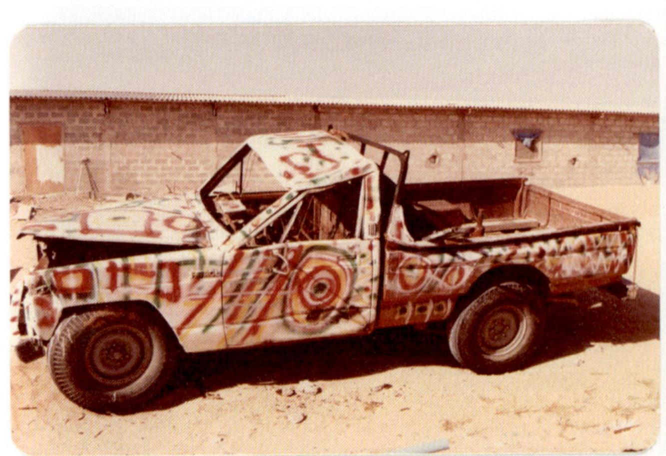

كرات ورقية

Paper balls

1992

1996

me + Hassan Sharif

Sharjah musum

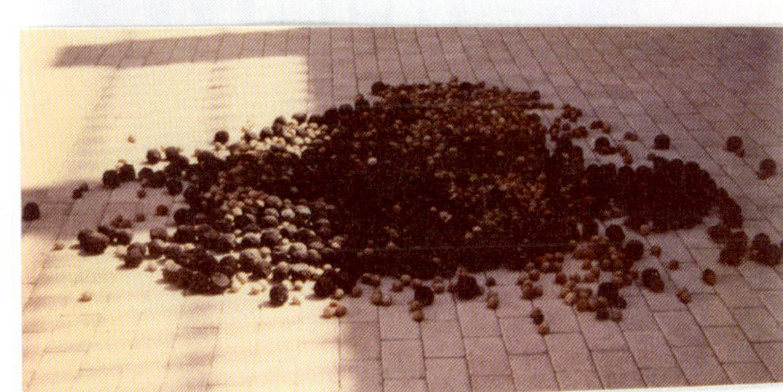

مركز مدينة سيتارد للفنون رقم ١

Sittard art center no. 1

1995

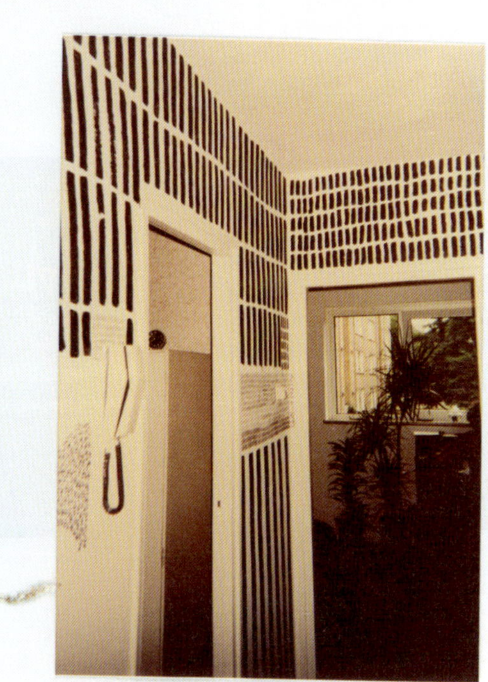

بيت الفنان / جوس كليفرز (هولندا)

The artist Jos Clevers's house (Holland).

1995

_ mine to

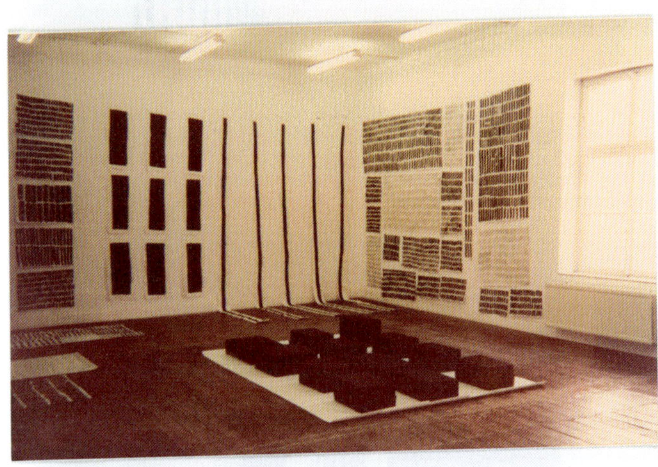

مركز مدينة سيتارد للفنون رقم ٢

Sittard art center no.2

1996

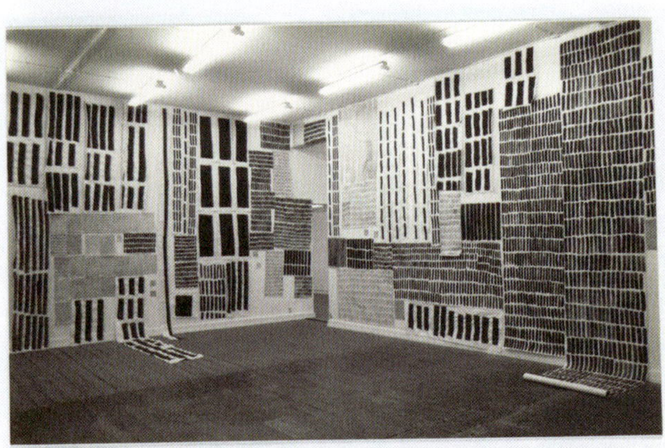

جبل خورفكان رقم ١

Khorfkhan mountain no.1
1990

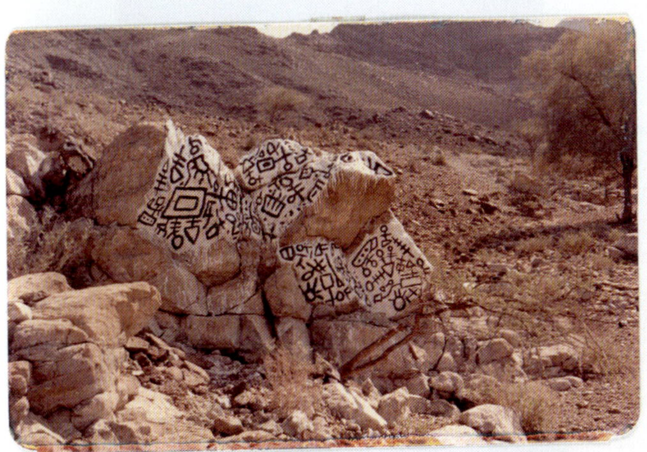

جبل خورفكان رقم ٢

Khorfkhan mountain no.2
1990

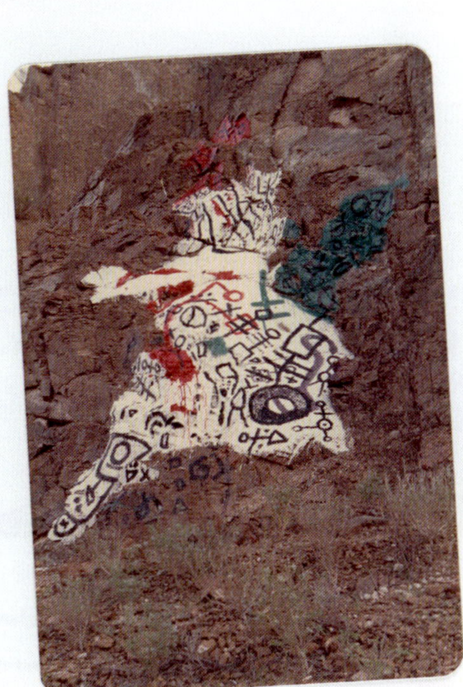

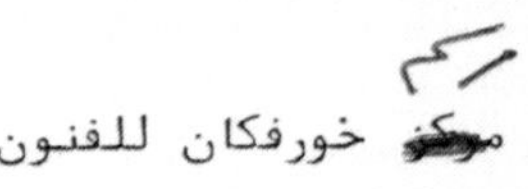

مركز خورفكان للفنون

Khofakhan art studio

1993

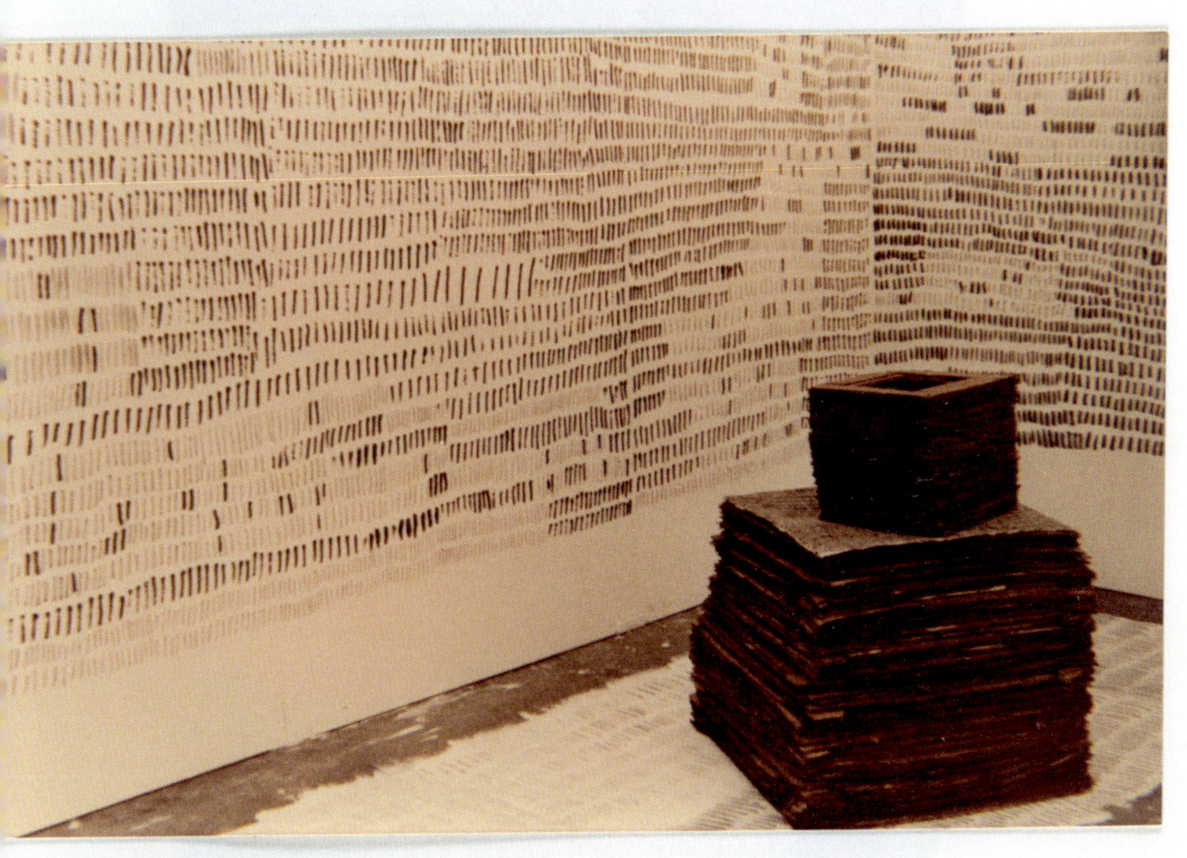

- bait mola duwood
- 1st Biennial

متحف الشارقة للفنون

Sharjah art museum

1996

- 6 Artst exb.

معرض ، ستة ،،

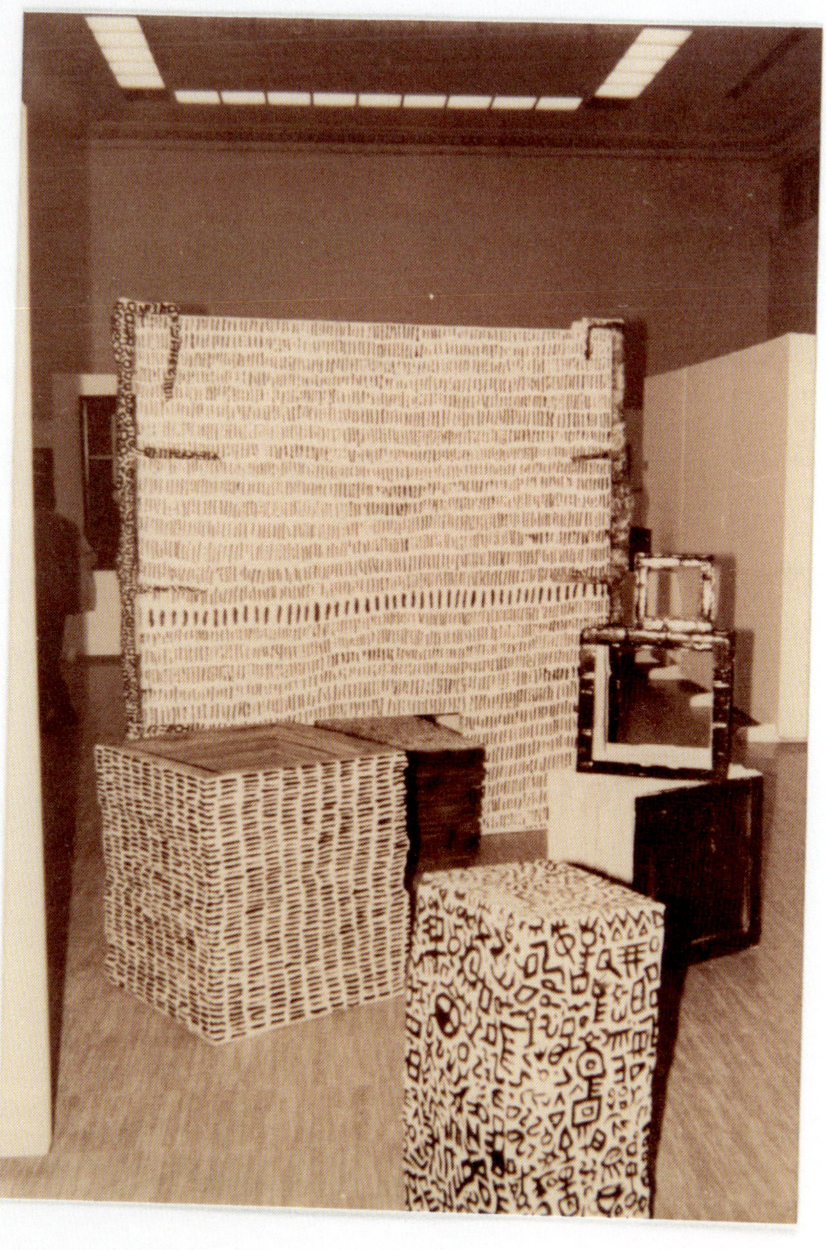

مكعب كرتوني (٤×٣×٦ فوت)

Cube (4 f x 3f x 6f).

1992

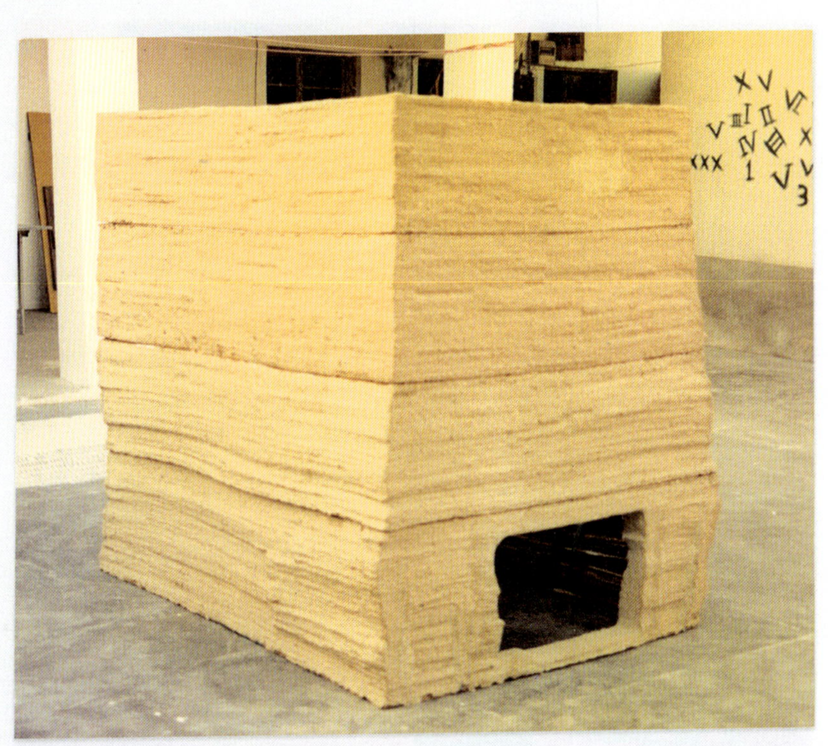

«كعبات كرتونية»
Cubes

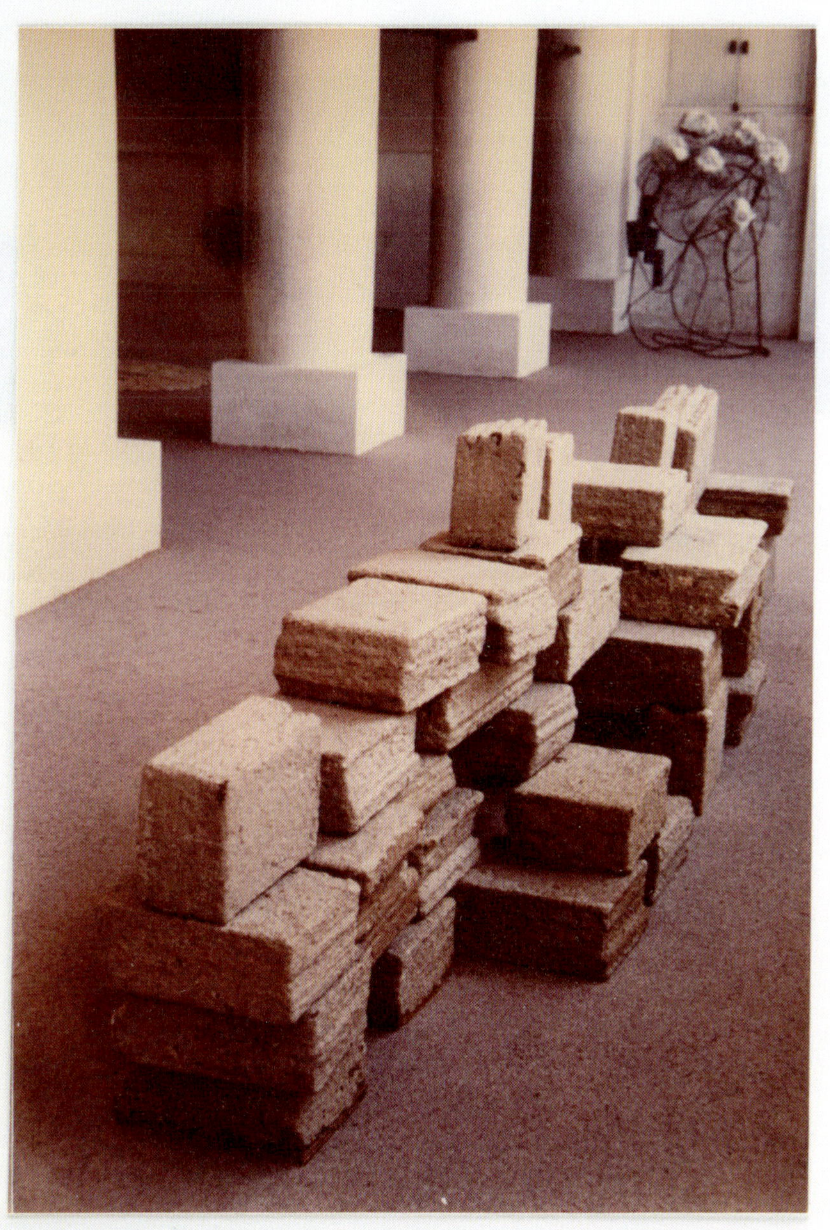

أحجار مربوطة

Tied stones.

1994

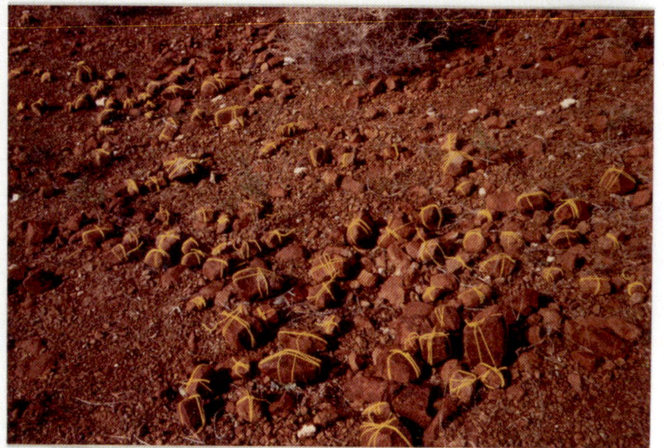

- dikal

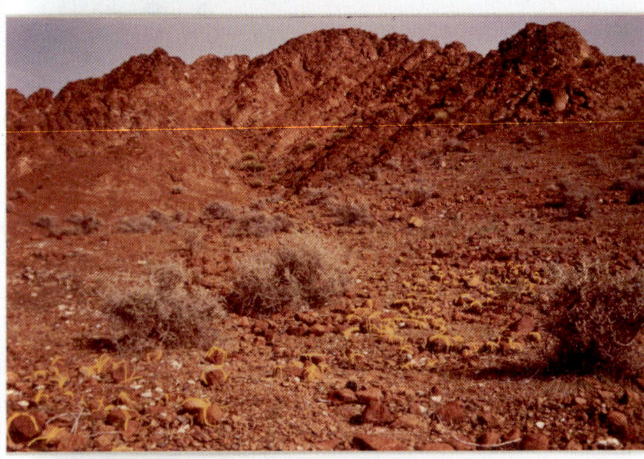

- Al ba'idya
- 2nd H-O

أحجار معلقه

Hanging stones.

1994

- 5 Artst exb.

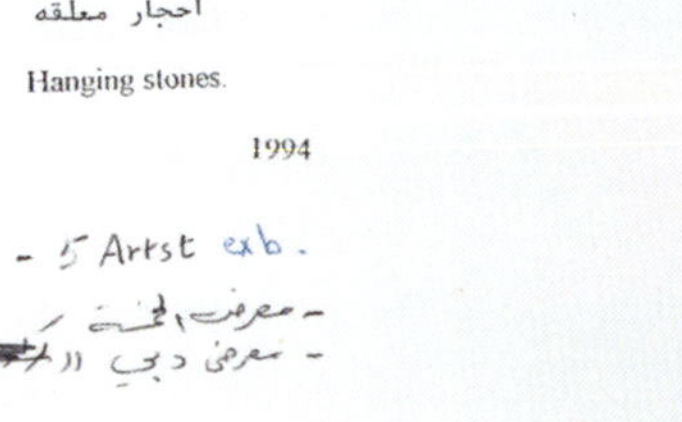

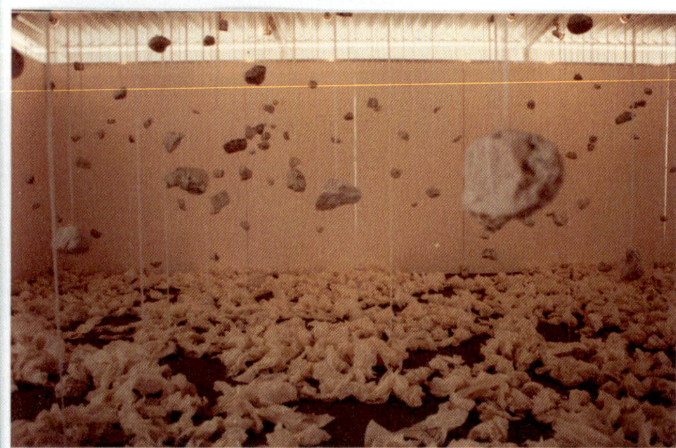

أشكال طينية رقم ١

Clay forms no. 1

1996

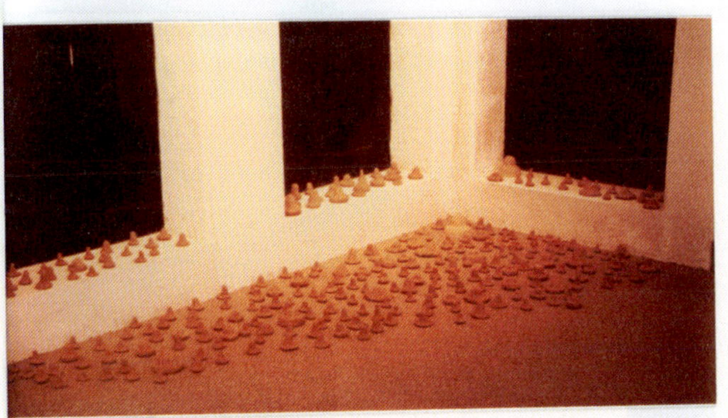

أشكال طينية رقم ٢

Clay forms no. 2

1996

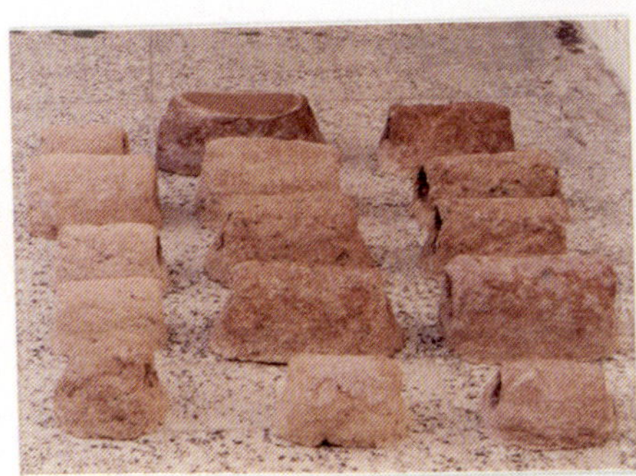

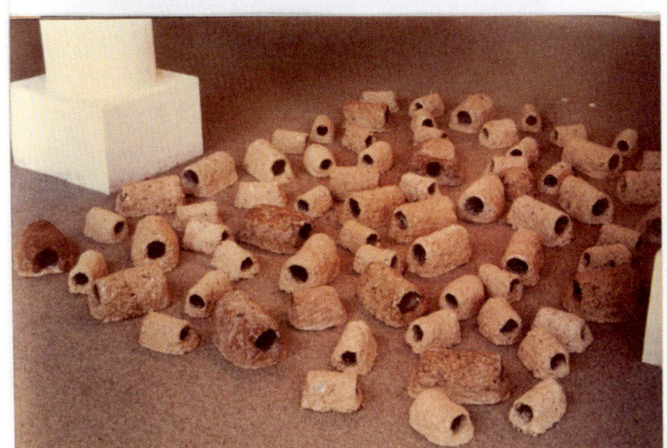

أشكال طينية رقم ٣

Clay forms no. 3

1996

(6th exh. Sharjah)

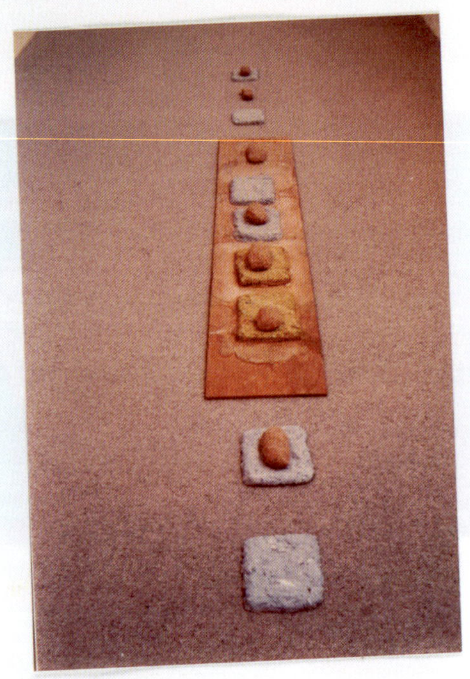

أشكال طينية رقم ٤

Clay forms no. 4

1997

Sharjah Int. Art Biennual

1997 -

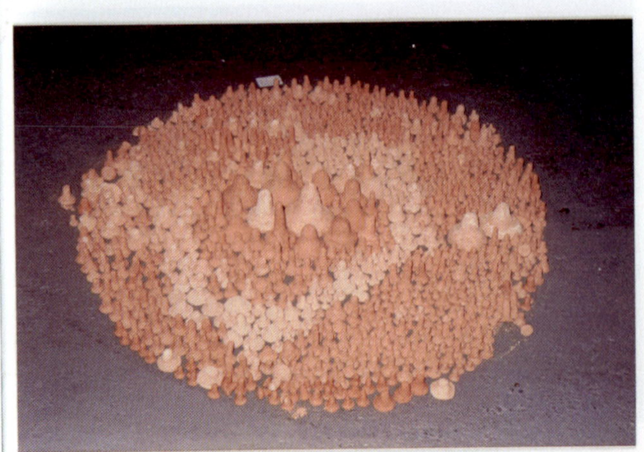

أشكال طينية رقم ٥

Clay forms no. 5

1997

Sharjah International Art
Biennial

1997-

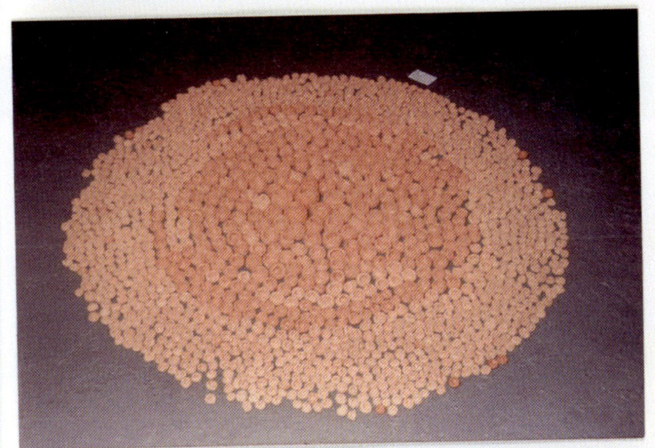

أشكال طينية رقم ٦

Clay forms no. 6

1997

— Sharjah International Art
Biennial

1997-

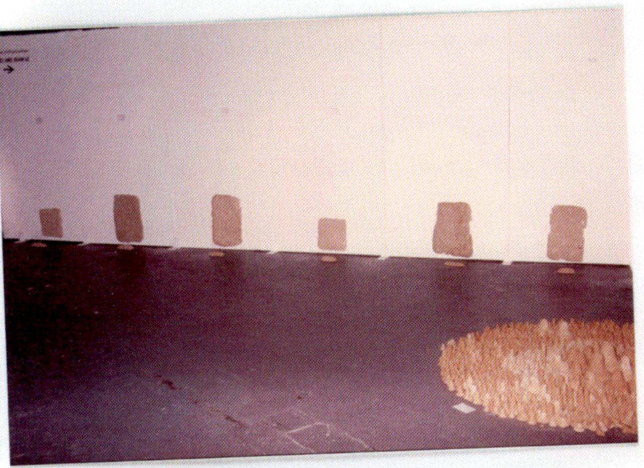

أشكال طينية رقم ٧

Clay forms no. 7

1997

— (Frinch cultur cinter — Dubai)

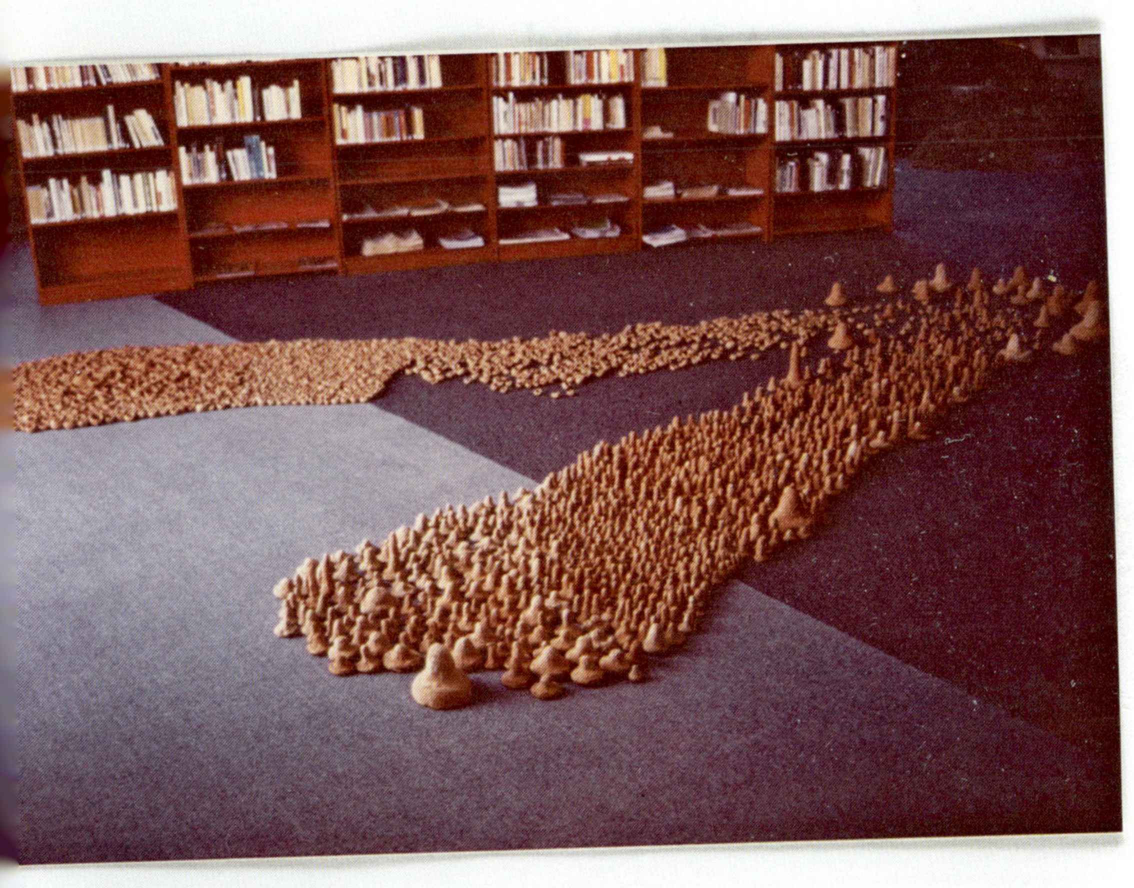

أشكال طينية رقم ٨

Clay forms no. 8

The original photo that had
been attached to this page
has been lost.

MOHAMED AHMED IBRAHIM
(b:1962, UAE)
Trained Archaeology in Pakistan (1980-81)
Studied Psychology in the UAE University (1982-86)
Member of the Emirates Fine Arts Society until 1994.
Individual Exhibitions
1991 - Sharjah
1991 - Abu Dhabi
1992 - Turkey
Joint Exhibitions (since 1987):
 UAE/Egypt/Kuwait/Bangladesh/Italy/India and Russia.

HoLLand - Sittard

MUHAMMAD AHMED IBRAHIM

"Artist Muhammed Ahmed Ibrahim starts forming his creations starting from ' the mother land', suggesting nobility and return to all the beginnings... and this experiment he calls 'the land art' in the UAE. What this artist added is that he wandered in those remote areas and left his traces in them. Then he painted them and brought them to an art exhibition.

"Works of Muhammed Ahmed Ibrahim give the opportunity to the viewer, and he is free to dearl with them by his body, the thing which you do not find in the painting which is hung in a frame on the wall" -

HASSAN SHARIF.

" The artist says 'My works search for their own scenes. The viewer is the one who writes down in his diary the date and the time of the exhibition.... I do not care for names or classifications. I have given up my doubt towards my works, and produce works I cannot call them anything other than 'ART'
MUHAMMED AHMED IBRAHIM.

محمد أحمد إبراهيم

- مواليد عام ١٩٦٢ - خورفكان
- أ. ع. م. درس علم النفس - جامعة الإمارات بين عامي ١٩٨٢ - ١٩٨٦
- شارك في المعارض الداخلية منذ عام ١٩٨٧.
- اما المعارض الخارجية فشارك في كل من القاهرة، الكويت، بنجلاديش، إيطاليا، الهند، موسكو، الكويت، فرنسا، ألمانيا وهولندا. أقام حتى الآن ثلاثة معارض شخصية الأول عام ١٩٩١ - المركز الثقافي بالشارقة، الثاني عام ١٩٩١ - المجمع الثقافي أبوظبي - الثالث عام ١٩٩٢ في تركيا. فاز بجائزة لجنة التحكيم في مهرجان دبي للفنون عام ١٩٩٤، مشرف المرسم الحر التابع لدائرة الثقافة والإعلام - خورفكان.

يبدأ الفنان محمد أحمد إبراهيم، في تشكيل إبداعاته إنطلاقا من "الأرض الأم"، إبحاراً منه بالأصالة والرجوع إلى كل البدايات .. وهذه التجربة، يطلق عليها "فن الأرض" في الإمارات، وجاءت إضافة هذا الفنان، أنه تجول في تلك المناطق النائية وترك أناره فيها، ثم قام بتصويرها وجلبها إلى معرض فني".

"تتيح أعمال محمد أحمد ابراهيم، الفرصة للمشاهد، وهو حر أن يتعامل بجسده معها، الأمر الذي لا تجده في اللوحة المعهودة المعلقة في إطار على الجدار".

حسن شريف

يقول الفنان :"أعمالي تبحث عن مشاهدها الخاصة، المشاهد هو الذي يدون بنكرته تاريخ ووقت المعرض .. فأنا لا تهمني التسميات ولا التصنيفات، لقد تجاوزت شكي تجاه أعمالي وأنتج أعمالاً لا أستطيع أن أسميها أي شيء آخر سوى "الفن"

محمد أحمد إبراهيم

Add:-

Khorfkhan art center
P. O. Box 10203
Khorfkhan
United Arab Emirates
(U.A.E.)
tel:00971-9-384655
fax:00971-9-382887

Mohamed Ahmed Ibrahim

Biographical Timeline

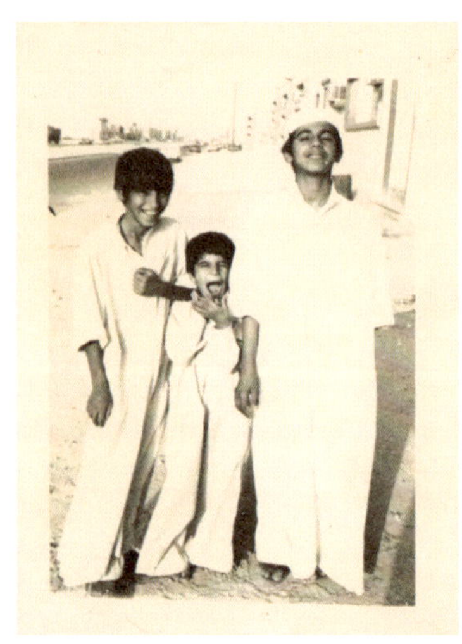

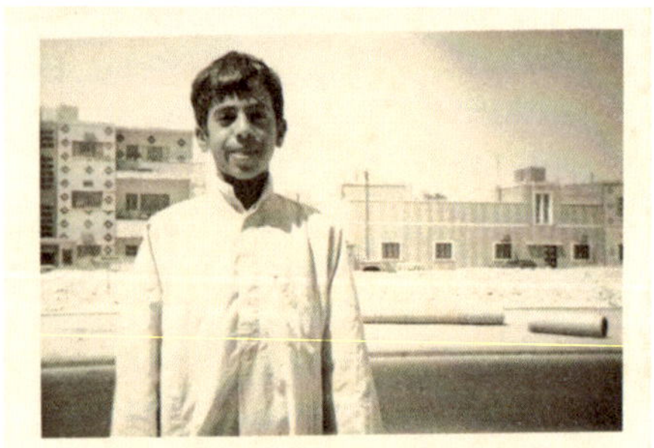

Mohamed Ahmed Ibrahim (right)
with his younger brother Ali
Ahmed Ibrahim (middle) and
neighbor Ibrahim Ali Issa (left).
Al Khaitan neighborhood, Kuwait,
1974

Mohamed Ahmed Ibrahim, in
front of the building where his
teacher lived. Mohammed lived
adjacent to these buildings, in the
neighborhood near the AlRandi
house, where a musical group
would play, n.d.

1962 Mohamed Ahmed Ibrahim is born on March 18, 1962, in Khor Fakkan, before the union of the UAE (1971).

1968–1976 His family relocates to Kuwait (Failaka Island, Freij Sharq, Khaitan), where he attends school, which includes art classes.

1976–1980 Upon the family's return to the UAE, Ibrahim spends his high school years between Khor Fakkan and Kalba, in Sharjah. Due to the fact that there aren't enough students in Khor Fakkan, they ride a bus to Kalba to attend school there. He continues to make art as part of his social activities.

1980–1985 Ibrahim graduates from high school. For university, he wants to study art in Cairo, but scholarships are no longer available. He briefly studies archaeology in Pakistan but returns within a year.

During this time, Ibrahim reads an announcement in a newspaper about a computer course that would take place in London, to be awarded after completion of a period of police service in the Abu Dhabi Police School. He enlists in the police service, and moves to Abu Dhabi. After some time, the management says that they can no longer send students to the UK. This is the beginning of Ibrahim's journey as a police officer.

During the first Book Fair at the Cultural Foundation in Abu Dhabi (1981), Ibrahim serves as an officer during the fair opening. At the end of the event, Sheikh Zayed, who was there, buys all of the books and tells the staff and officers to take as many as they want. Ibrahim fills up his car with books of all kinds.

Due to the contract he signs, Ibrahim is obliged to complete five years of police training. After receiving advice from a friend, he requests to be reposted in Al Ain, where there is a university, so he can simultaneously fulfill his duties as an officer and begin his studies.

Ibrahim moves to Al Ain as a police officer and as a college student at Al Ain University, majoring in psychology.

During this time, he begins actively reading and writing poetry. He receives books from multiple sources abroad. His brother-in-law, who is studying in London, sends him books about the history of art. From Egypt, he orders books that were translated into Arabic, including literature and philosophy.

These texts allow Ibrahim to deepen and clarify the role that art plays in his life.

At this time, Ibrahim connects with a group of creative students who are writers, actors, and, as he puts it, "generally people who are posing interesting questions." This group includes notable artists such as the actor Marei Al Halyan and poet Ali Al Andal.

1985   He takes an art workshop in Sharjah with Yaser Dweik to learn the fundamentals of painting.

During this year, Ibrahim has an accident and is confined to bed for three months in his mother's house. In this crucial period, he spends the entire time working with oil paints on canvas as well as pencil on paper. This episode marks the beginning of his journey into painting and drawing.

Mohamed marries his wife, Gharisa.

1986–1987   Ibrahim's first child, Ahmed, is born (July 20, 1986).

The poet Ali Al Andal sees Ibrahim's new artwork, and wants to introduce Ibrahim to his friend, the artist Hassan Sharif.

Al Andal plans a trip from Al Ain to the Emirates Fine Arts Society (EFAS), Sharjah, where Sharif has a solo show.

Ibrahim packs his artwork to show Sharif and leaves the works for him to look at. Soon, Sharif asks Ibrahim to come down to the Dubai Youth Atelier, where they have a conversation about Ibrahim's work. The conversation revolves around art and continues through the night. After this, Ibrahim begins to visit Sharif in Dubai weekly.

The next year, Ibrahim submits his work for the EFAS annual art exhibition, but it is rejected. Sharif insists that Ibrahim's work be in the exhibition, although it won't appear in the accompanying catalog.

The group show, *Exhibition for Tradition and The Arts, 27 Paintings by 10 Artists*, features Ibrahim's work at Sharjah Women's Club.

1988   Ibrahim's second son, Abdullah, is born (February 7, 1988).

Ibrahim considers this year as one of questions. He knows that it is time to leave the police force, but he needs to consider all of his responsibilities. He wants to focus more on his art practice and needs a job that would give him that time.

Ibrahim's artwork is formally accepted for the first time in the EFAS annual exhibition. He shows figurative works, still lifes, and landscape paintings. These works were produced during his time in Al Ain and at his mother's house in Khor Fakkan.

1989   Ibrahim still needs to complete four credits in order to graduate but when the poet Ahmed Rashid Thani calls him to take the position of Hall Supervisor at the Khor Fakkan Public Library, Ibrahim makes the immediate decision to move back to Khor Fakkan. He resigns from the police, and leaves the university.

His work is included in a group exhibition for the Kuwait National Day, at The Kuwaiti Co-op for Conceptual/Abstract Art.

1990   Ibrahim meets artist Abdullah Al Saadi at the Khor Fakkan Public Library.

He is given a studio space in the Khor Fakkan Public Library that is shared with Abdullah Al Saadi. This is where he produces work for his first solo exhibition the following year.

Ibrahim participates in *The Exhibition of the Emirates Fine Arts Society in the Soviet Union*, traveling to Moscow for the event.

He participates in the EFAS annual exhibition.

Next page
Abdullah Al Saadi (left) and Mohamed Ahmed Ibrahim (right) in Khor Fakkan, n.d.

Mohamed Ahmed Ibrahim's first solo exhibition, 1991. Opening reception at the Qasr Al Thaqafa

Mohamed Ahmed Ibrahim's first solo exhibition, 1991, which traveled to the Cultural Foundation Abu Dhabi, pictured here

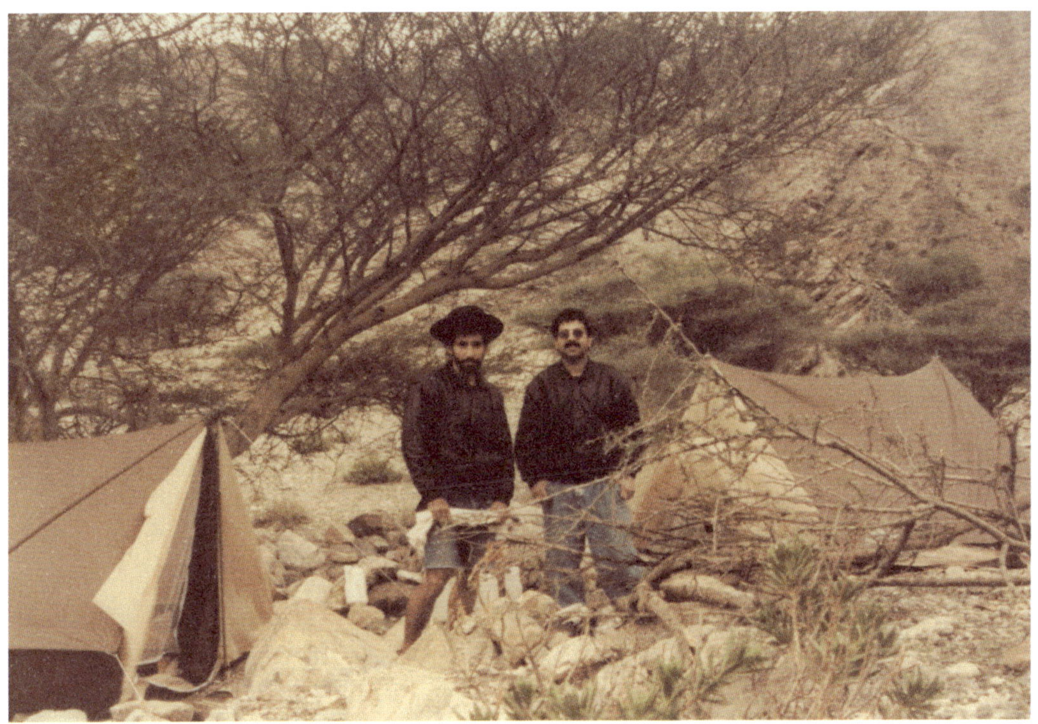

During this time, Asaad Arabi, an artist and professor living in France, is invited by the Sharjah Department of Culture and Information to visit and write about the annual EFAS exhibition. He pays particular attention to a group of conceptual artists, with a focus on the work of Ibrahim.

Ibrahim's third son, Khaled, is born (May 12, 1990).

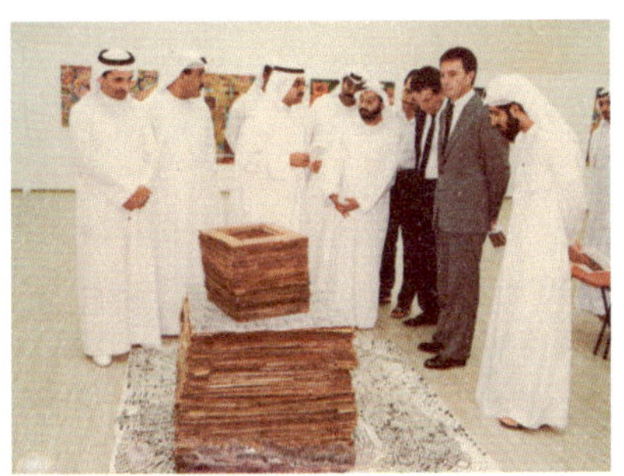

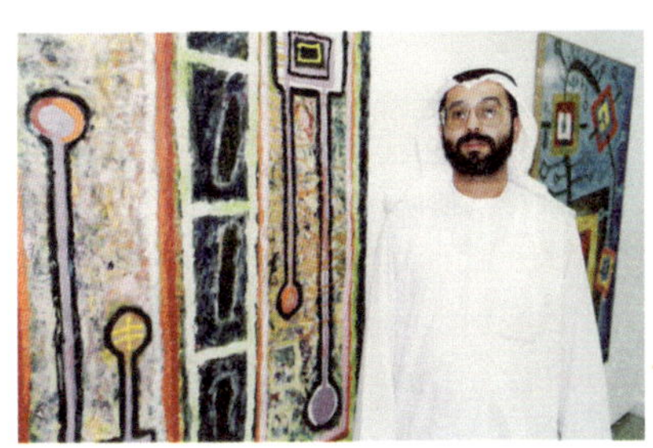

1991   Ibrahim's first solo exhibition opens at *Qasr Al Thaqafa*, part of Sharjah Department of Culture and Information (May 22–28, 1991). The exhibition travels to the Cultural Foundation, Abu Dhabi (July 9–17, 1991).

1992–1993   His first daughter, Salama, is born (November 7, 1992).

The Emirates Fine Arts Society opens a branch in Khor Fakkan, where Ibrahim plays a supervisory role.

The first edition of the Sharjah Biennial, UAE opens in 1993.

Ibrahim participates in a group exhibition marking the opening of the EFAS branch, timed to receive the visiting Sharjah Biennial audience. The exhibition also includes work by Abdullah Al Saadi and Erik Fabiyam. Ibrahim presents an installation of black lines on a white wall for this exhibition.

He participates in the 6th Asian Art Biennale in Dhaka, Bangladesh.

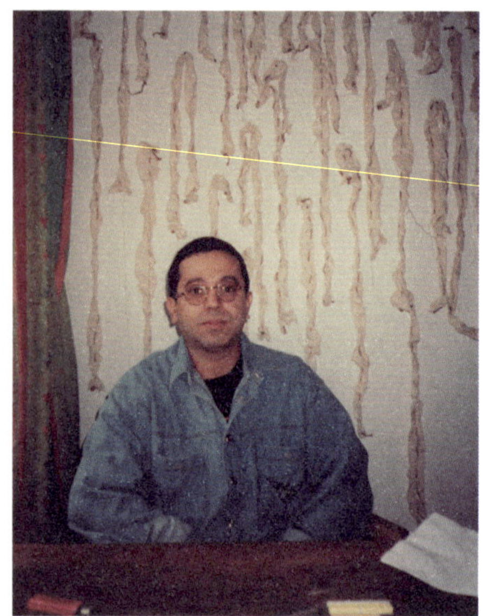

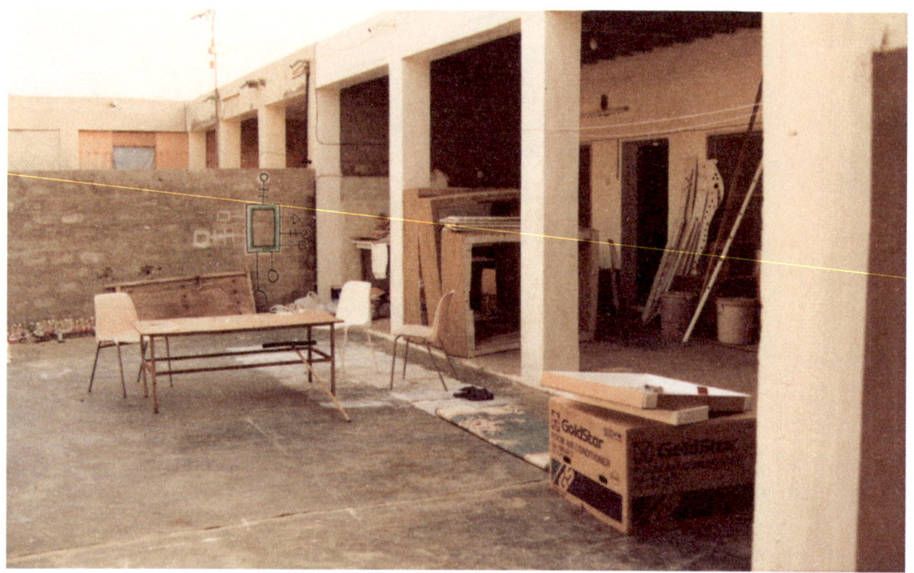

Mohamed Ahmed Ibrahim in
Sittard, sitting in front of Hassan
Sharif's wall installation, Sittard
Art Center, the Netherlands,
c. 1995

The Khor Fakkan branch of the
Emirates Fine Arts Society: it was
a two-bedroom and one majlis
shaabi house-turned studio.
Pictured here is the garage work
space, c. 1994

1994 Ibrahim participates in a group exhibition, entitled *The Five*, at the Emirates Fine Arts Society. This exhibition includes Hassan Sharif, Mohammed Kazem, Hussain Sharif, and Abdulraheem Salim.

Ibrahim meets Dutch artist and curator, Jos Clevers. Clevers is visiting to put together workshops as a part of the Children's Festival in Sharjah, Khor Fakkan, and Kalba, at the invitation of the Sharjah Department of Culture and Information. They ask Ibrahim to pick Clevers up and show him around. At that first meeting, Ibrahim makes an immediate connection with Clevers and decides to take him to meet Hassan Sharif and the rest of the group.

Jos Clevers invites Ibrahim to visit him in Sittard, Netherlands, where Clevers is the director of the Sittard Art Center. Clevers gives Ibrahim a big space to produce a work, which he does: black lines on paper, hung on the walls, soon take over the whole room. Clevers then asks Ibrahim to produce the same black lines on the walls of his home.

1995 Jos Clevers organizes the first European exhibition of art from the Emirates, which includes the artists Hassan Sharif, Hussain Sharif, Mohamed Ahmed Ibrahim, and Mohammed Kazem. Titled *Emirates Arts*, it opened at the Sittard Art Center (Kunstcentrum Sittard, Sittard, Netherlands) on December 17, 1995 and ran until January 21, 1996. Ibrahim presents the lines installation that he made there the year before, but now it is in dialogue with the work of his peers.

Along with his fellow artists Hussain Sharif, Hassan Sharif, and

Mohammed Kazem, Ibrahim resigns from the board committee of the Emirates Fine Arts Society. They publish their reasons in the *Al Khaleej* newspaper. As a consequence, EFAS removes their financial support of the Khor Fakkan branch. The space is then funded for two years by Ibrahim and Hassan Sharif, existing as its own separate entity, after which it closes.

Ibrahim participates in the second Sharjah Biennial, UAE.

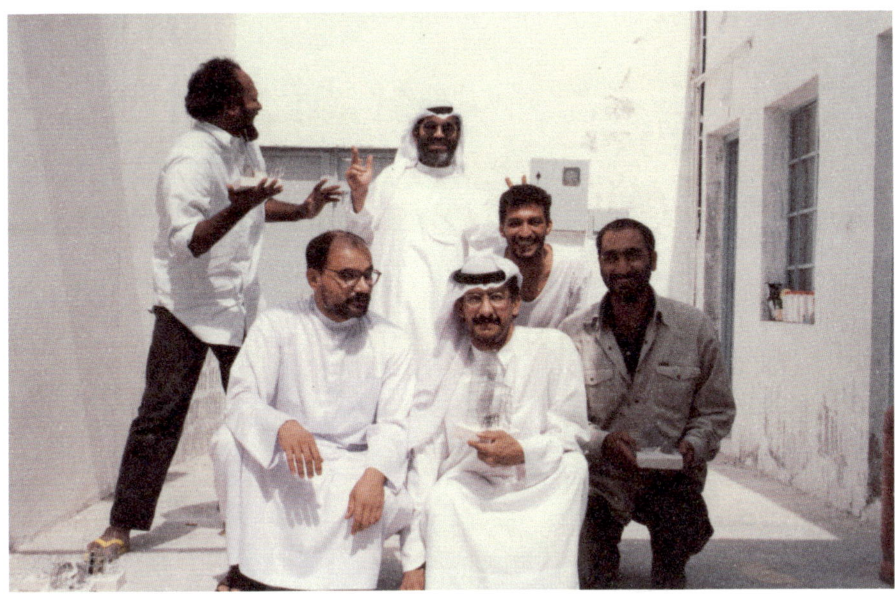

Left to right: Vivek Vilasini
(standing), Hussain Sharif (front),
Mohamed Ahmed Ibrahim (back),
Abdullah Abdelwahab (front),
Mohammed Kazem (back),
Mohamed Al Mazrouei (front).
In the courtyard of Hassan
Sharif's home in Dubai's Satwa
neighborhood, c. 1996

1996 The Khorfakkan Art Centre opens, hosted by the Sharjah Department of Culture and Information. Ibrahim leaves the Khor Fakkan Public Library and starts as the head of operations for the Khorfakkan Art Centre. That summer they give their first foundational workshop on art basics.

Ibrahim returns to the Sittard Art Center in the Netherlands, beginning a series of visits that will become an anchor point for his process in this period.

Ibrahim begins his Harley-Davidson motorcycle obsession after winning one as a prize.

He is included in a group exhibition, titled *Six Artists Exhibition*, at the Sharjah Art Museum, UAE, October 6–16, 1996. The other artists are: Hassan Sharif, Hussain Sharif, Mohammed Kazem, Vivek Vilasini, and Jos Clevers.

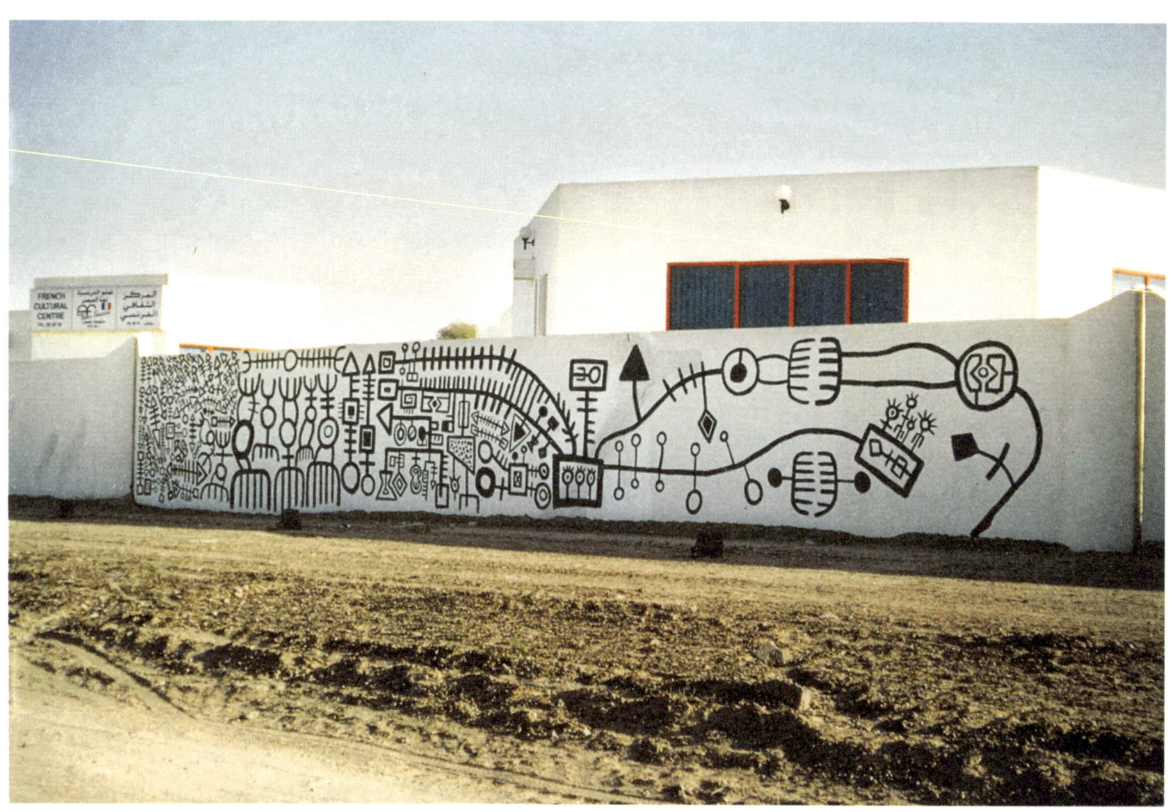

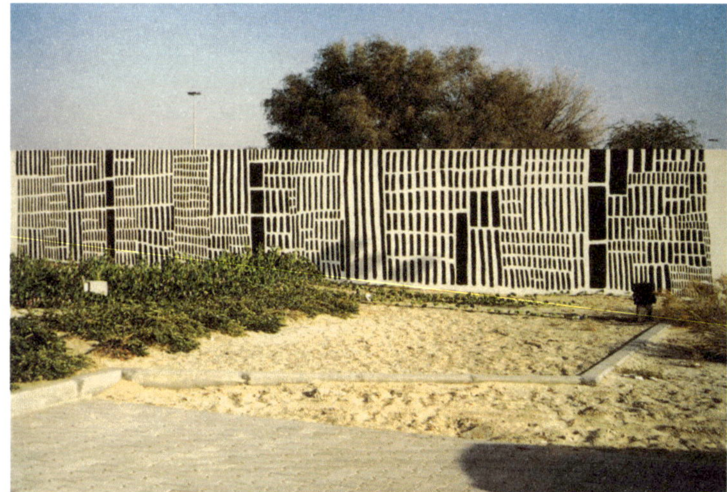

1997   Ibrahim participates in the exhibition *UAE Artists* at the Alliance Française Dubai, UAE. Other artists include Hassan Sharif, Hussain Sharif, Mohammed Kazem, Mohamed Ahmed Ibrahim, Jos Clevers, Vivek Vilasini, and Abdullah Al Saadi. Ibrahim presents work that is made of clay brought from the mountains of Khor Fakkan: over 100 pieces of clay in a circle. Outside the Alliance Française, he paints a mural of lines on one wall and symbols on another.

Ibrahim has a solo exhibition as part of the third Sharjah Biennial, UAE.

<table>
<tr><td>1998</td><td>Ibrahim's work is included in the UAE Contemporary Art exhibition at the Institut du Monde Arabe, Paris, France.

He participates in the 7th International Cairo Biennale, Egypt.</td></tr>
<tr><td>1999</td><td>Ibrahim's second daughter, Maryam, is born (February 18, 1999).

He participates in the fourth Sharjah Biennial, UAE, winning 1st place in the sculpture category.

Ibrahim's position with the Khorfakkan Art Centre ends. As a result, he is without storage for his work. He brings all of it into the mountains, where he burns it in a bonfire. The video documentation of the event is shown later at the Venice Biennale in 2009.

Afterward, he leaves for Sittard in the Netherlands where he spends the majority of the following year.</td></tr>
<tr><td>2000</td><td>In Sittard, he works at a variety of jobs while continuing his art practice.

When he returns to the UAE, Ibrahim begins working at Abu Dhabi Commercial Bank (ADCB) in Fujairah as an assistant clerk.

He participates in the 7th edition of the Havana Biennale, Cuba, curated by Nelson Herrera Ysla.

Ibrahim's work is also included in Emirates Identities at the Alliance Française Dubai, UAE.</td></tr>
<tr><td>2001</td><td>Once again, Ibrahim wins the Sharjah Biennial Prize, first place in the sculpture category.

He travels between the UAE and the Netherlands frequently during this year.</td></tr>
<tr><td>2002</td><td>Ibrahim participates in the 10th Asian Art Biennale, Dhaka, Bangladesh.</td></tr>
</table>

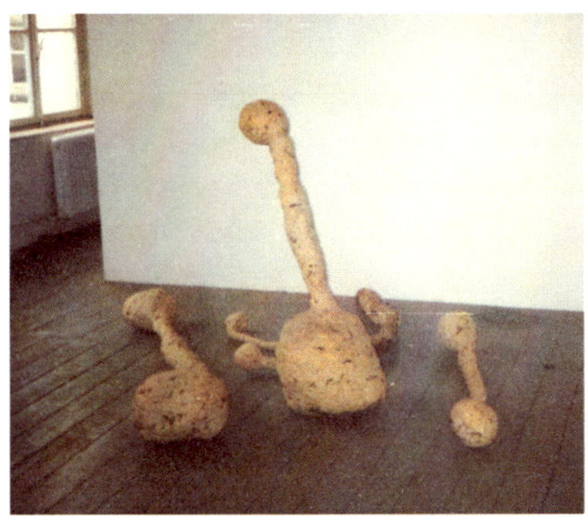

Sittard 1, 2001
Leaf, paper, and glue,
dimensions variable

The seminal exhibition, *5/U.A.E.* opens at the Ludwig Forum für Internationale Kunst, Aachen, Germany. Curated by Annette Lagler, it marks a pivotal institutional presentation of this community's work, as a result of the earlier work done by Clevers in Sittard. Ibrahim presents three clay sculptures, which remind him of the material used for building houses in Khor Fakkan.

The exhibition features five artists: Mohamed Ahmed Ibrahim, Hassan and Hussain Sharif, Mohammed Kazem, and Abdullah Al Saadi. As a result of the exhibition's title, they become known as "the five."

2003 Ibrahim participates in the 6th Sharjah Biennial, UAE, curated by Peter Lewis.

2004 Ibrahim's third daughter and youngest child, Shumookh, is born (September 13, 2004).

He is elected president of the Emirates Fine Arts Society.

2005 The work from the Ludwig exhibition is included in the *Languages of the Desert* exhibition, at the Kunstmuseum Bonn, Germany, curated by Dieter Ronte and Katrin Adrian Von Roques. Later, it will travel to the Institut du Monde Arabe, Paris, France.

Ibrahim's work is included in a special exhibition curated by Mohammed Kazem for the Emirates Fine Arts Society, titled *Cultural Diversity*, in parallel with the Sharjah Biennial.

2006 During the exhibition at the Institut du Monde Arabe, Ibrahim meets Dominique de Varine who will later give Ibrahim space to work in Brittany, France.

Mohammed Kazem curates an exhibition at Dubai Total Art Gallery, titled *Window*, with 16 UAE artists, including Mohamed Ahmed Ibrahim.

The filmmaker Valsalan Kanara creates an interview-based documentary on Hassan Sharif and the group of "five," titled *Objects. A documentary on Hassan Sharif* (English, 67 min).

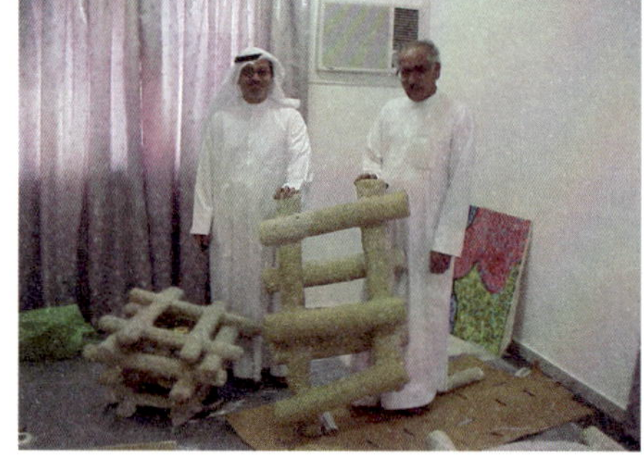

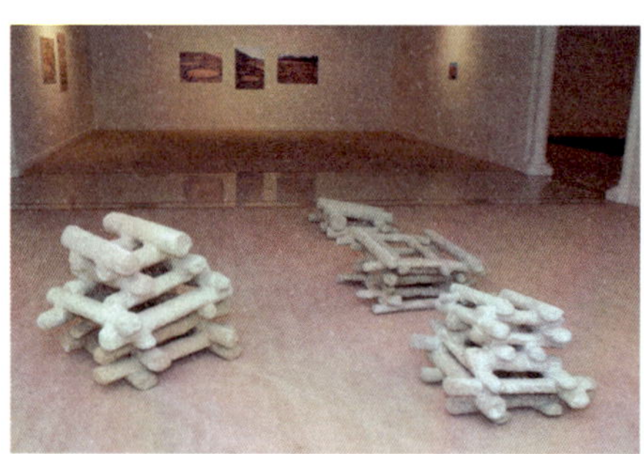

Mohamed Ahmed Ibrahim (left) and Hassan Sharif (right) at Mohamed's home in Khor Fakkan

Fujairah, 2001
Flower seeds, paper, glue, dimensions variable. As installed at the Sharjah Art Museum, *Cultural Diversity* exhibition, 2005

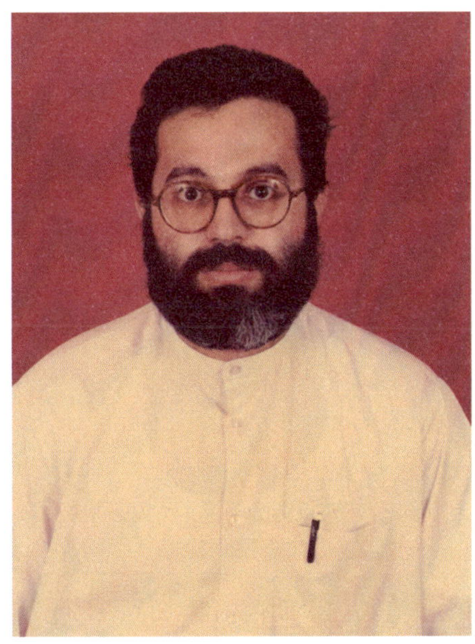

A portrait of Mohamed upon his return to Khor Fakkan from Al Ain in the early 1990s. His Compo Pen is visible in his pocket: he used this pen in his work until the pen stopped being produced. This image was taken during his time working at the Khorfakkan Library.

From left to right: Mohamed Ahmed Ibrahim, Jos Clevers, Mohammed Kazem. Art Dubai, 2008

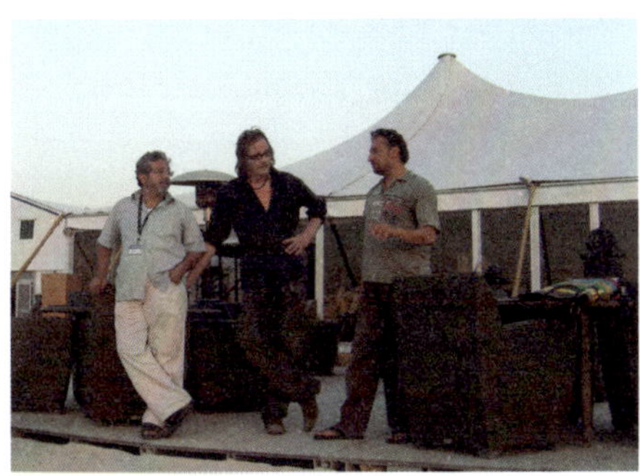

This is produced by Hassan Sharif's brother, Abdul-Raheem Sharif, who had been playing an important role in archiving the work of the group of "five."

2007   Ibrahim participates in the 8th Sharjah Biennial, UAE.

This year is a turning point for Ibrahim and his community of artists.

Abdul-Raheem Sharif and Mohamed Ahmed Ibrahim go to Documenta where they meet with Jos Clevers. Together, they come up with a plan to create a venue to display the group's work. Abdul-Raheem would convert his villa in the Al Quoz neighborhood of Dubai, where he had been storing their artwork, and would name it The Flying House after a painting by Clevers of the same title (a house painted upside down).

The group collaborates to open The Flying House.

Ibrahim participates in several exhibitions that year, including *The Masters* at the Royal Mirage Hotel, Dubai, UAE, and *The Emirates and its renowned Arab Artists* at Dubai Community Theatre & Arts Centre (DUCTAC), UAE, focusing on seven contemporary UAE artists.

At the end of the year, Ibrahim resigns from his ADCB bank job and begins work as the area manager of the Umm Al Quwain National Bank Fujairah branch.

2008   Ibrahim resigns from his post as the area manager at the Umm Al Quwain National Bank, Fujairah, UAE.

Mohammed Kazem and Jos Clevers curate shows on behalf of The Flying House. In March, they curate *Season of Art* at DIFC, UAE and *The Flying House at The Creek Art Fair*, The Creek Art Fair, Al Bastakiya, Dubai, UAE.

Cristiana de Marchi joins The Flying House and begins curating with the group.

The Mashreq Bank Dubai hosts a Flying House group show, curated by Cristiana de Marchi and Jos Clevers, which includes work by Ibrahim.

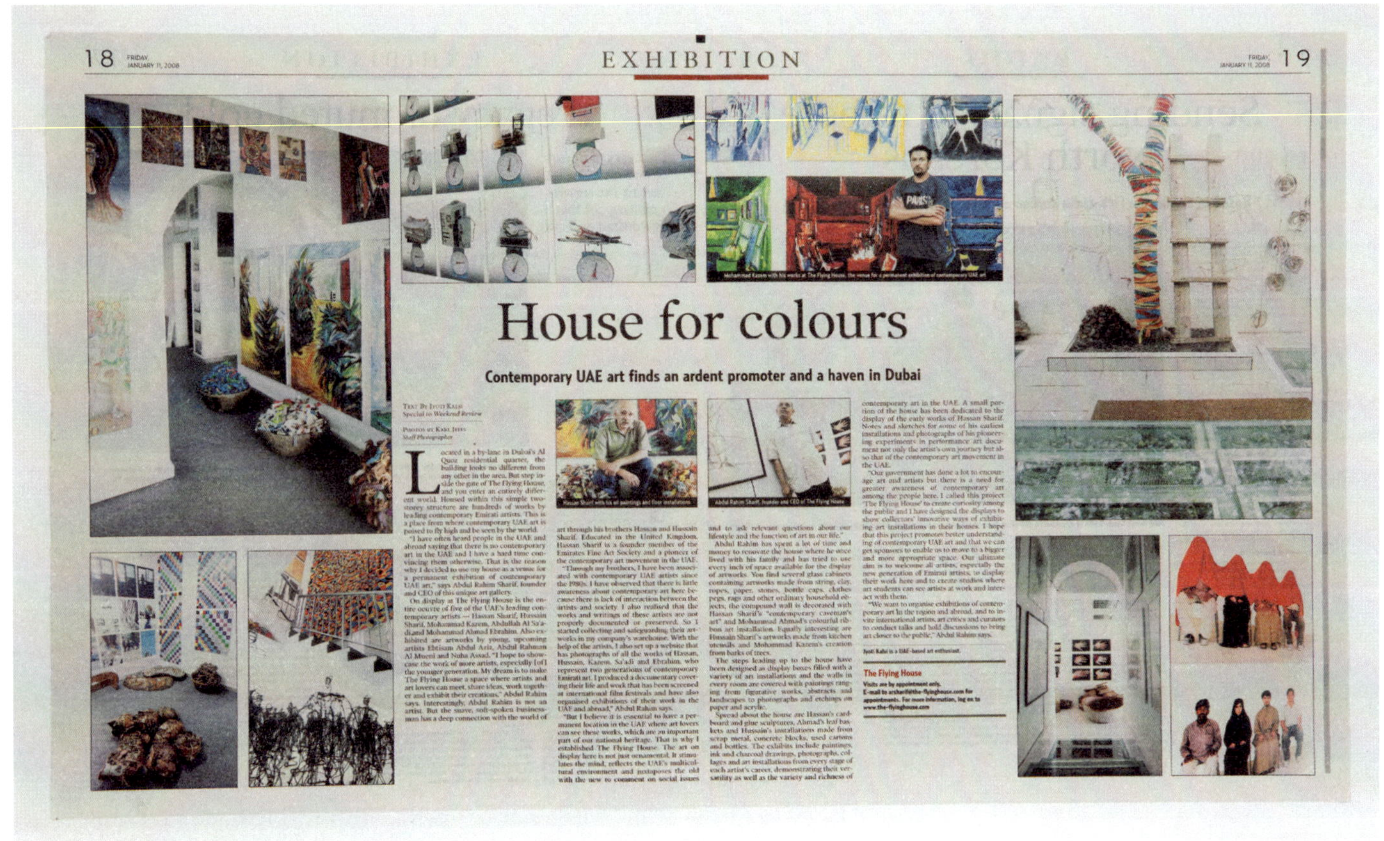

Clip of "House for Colours: Contemporary UAE Art Finds an Ardent Promoter and a Haven in Dubai" by Jyoti Kalsi in *Gulf News, Weekend Review*, January 11, 2008

Jos Clevers returns to the Netherlands, due to illness.

That summer, Ibrahim is included in *Selected UAE Contemporary Artists Expo*, Expo 2008, Zaragoza, Spain, curated by Mohammed Kazem.

In Abu Dhabi, the Salwa Zeidan Gallery hosts the exhibition *Contemporary Emirati Art*, curated by Mohammed Kazem.

2009   Jos Clevers dies in January.

Ibrahim's video of burning his art is included in the 53rd Edition of the Venice Biennale, Italy, for the Abu Dhabi Authority for Culture & Heritage (ADACH) Platform for Visual Arts. It is curated by Catherine David.

Ibrahim is granted a six-month residency at Le Consortium, in Dijon, France supported by the Emirates Foundation Abu Dhabi. During this residency, he has a heart attack. Regardless of being hospitalized, he continues to make work. During his Dijon period, he begins marking and redacting magazines, in a style related to his series of lines paintings.

Ibrahim goes for an extended stay in Lumière, Brittany, France, as the guest of Dominique de Verine. There he creates three performances, tracing circles in the landscape between the house and the sea. He talks about the remnants of the performance, saying: "In the morning, the work was no longer what it was, it lived only for that night."

At the end of this year, Ibrahim begins working as an administrator in the Khorfakkan Hospital.

He has a solo exhibition at the Khorfakkan Art Centre, Sharjah, UAE.

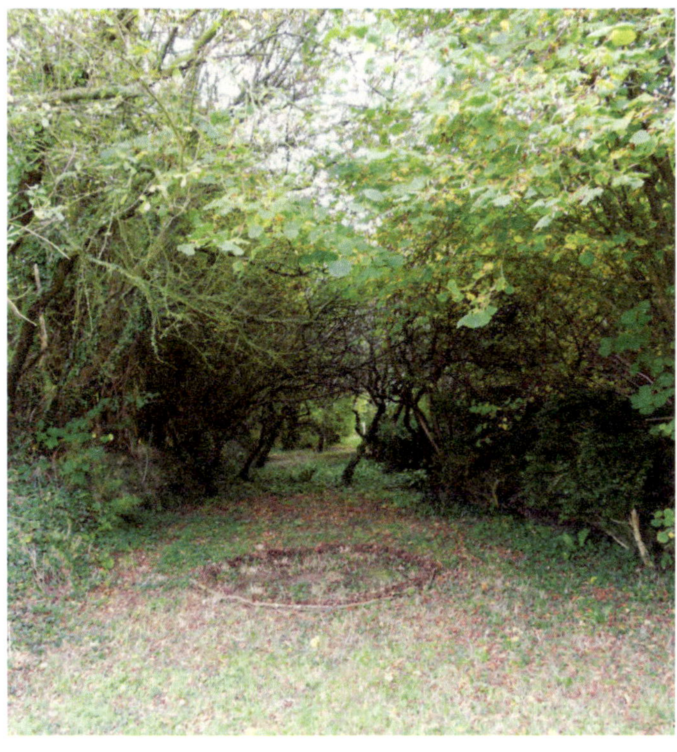

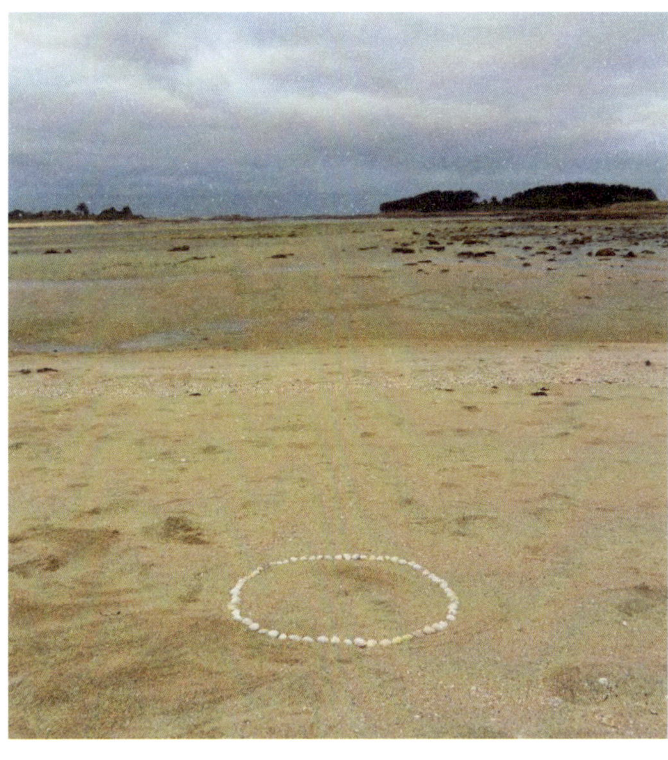

Both
Documentation of Mohamed Ahmed Ibrahim's performances in Lumière, Brittany, France, 2009

2010   Ibrahim is included in two exhibitions curated by Cristiana de Marchi and Mohammed Kazem: *Vis Roboris* at AB Gallery, Luzern, Switzerland, and *Dropping lines* at Salwa Zeidan Gallery, Abu Dhabi, UAE.

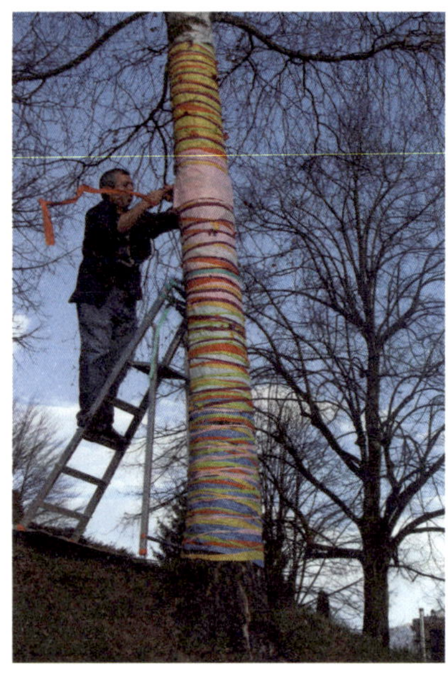

2011–2012 By this time, international attention has turned to the group of artists surrounding Ibrahim. This is a result of many factors, including the inauguration of The National Pavilion UAE for the Venice Biennale in 2009, as well as the ongoing work of The Flying House in promoting their art.

Ibrahim is included in *MinD—Dubai Contemporary* (2012), a survey of the art scene in the UAE, curated by Mohammed Kazem at DUCTAC, Dubai, UAE.

2013 Ibrahim is selected to produce a major new commission as part of *Emirati Expressions: Realised*, Manarat Al Saadiyat, Abu Dhabi, UAE, curated by Reem Fadda with assistant curator Maisa Al-Qassimi.

He has his first commercial solo exhibition, *Primordial* at Cuadro Gallery, Dubai, UAE.

2014 Ibrahim's work *Stones Wrapped in Copper* is included in *On Site: The Inaugural Exhibition* at The NYU Abu Dhabi Art Gallery, UAE, curated by Maya Allison.

2015 Ibrahim is selected for the A.i.R Dubai residency, a Tashkeel project in partnership with the Delfina Foundation, Art Dubai, The Dubai Culture & Arts Authority. Curator Lara Khaldi expands this to include a series of commissions for Art Dubai. During this period, he works with Munira Al Sayegh and develops the installation *Land Swap* (discussed in Al Sayegh's essay in this volume).

In this period, Ibrahim begins to produce his black lines on paper or canvas as three-dimensional objects.

His work is included in *Urban:ness: Encountering the City* at DUCTAC, UAE, curated by Mukta Ahluwalia Bedi. Cristiana de Marchi publishes an article about this exhibition in *Al Tashkeel* magazine titled "The Disappearance of Fish and Other Stories."

Ibrahim is included in *The Unbearable Lightness of Being*, at YAY Gallery, Baku, Azerbaijan.

Mohamed Ahmed Ibrahim
creating his artwork for the
Vis Roboris exhibition in Luzern,
Switzerland, 2010

Ibrahim formally joins Cuadro Gallery, Dubai, UAE, for his second solo exhibition with them, titled *Turab*. This is a turning point in his career. After 30 years of developing his practice in a non-commercial milieu, his work begins to be collected more consistently.

He makes a Land Art installation, titled *The Qubba Project*. The following year, it is commissioned as a photographic series by the Abu Dhabi Music & Arts Foundation (ADMAF), UAE.

2016   Ibrahim has a third solo show at Cuadro Gallery, Dubai, UAE, in March, *Primordial II*.

He participates, as a guest of honor, in the exhibition *Al Haraka Baraka*, curated by Alexandra MacGilp, at Maraya Art Center, Sharjah, as part of the "UAE Unlimited" platform founded and supported by His Highness Sheikh Zayed bin Sultan bin Khalifa Al Nahyan.

Ibrahim is commissioned for *Portrait of a Nation* by the Abu Dhabi Music and Arts Foundation (ADMAF). The exhibition is hosted in Abu Dhabi's Emirates Palace to celebrate the 20th anniversary of ADMAF. For this commission, he produces a photographic series of his Land Art, *The Qubba Project* (2015).

Ibrahim is awarded a residency in Kochi, India, with the "Trans-Indian Ocean Artist Exchange," supported by the Kochi Biennale Foundation, India in collaboration with the Maraya Art Centre, Sharjah, UAE.

While in Kochi, Ibrahim reunites with artist Vivek Vilasini for the first time since Vilasini departed the UAE in 1999.

Hassan Sharif dies in September.

The residency exhibition, titled *Residuals and the Anthology of Narcissis*m, is a two-person show with Mohammed Kazem curated by Mo Reda, in the Mandalay Hall, Kochi, India. Ibrahim presents a new body of work, derived from locally-sourced materials, in earth tones, developing his lines series into a sculptural wall collage.

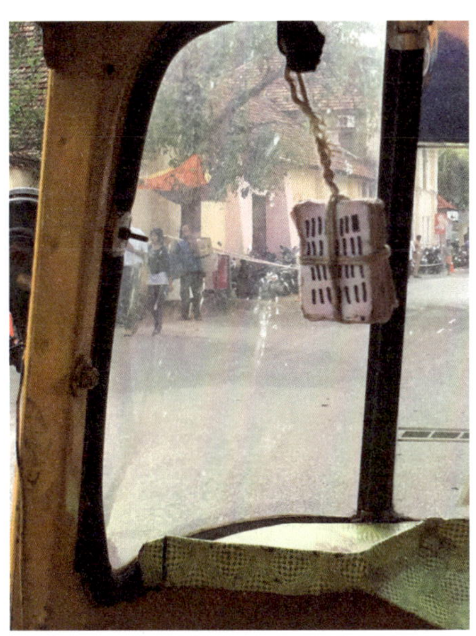

One of Ibrahim's artworks in the window of a Tuk-Tuk in Kochi, India, 2016

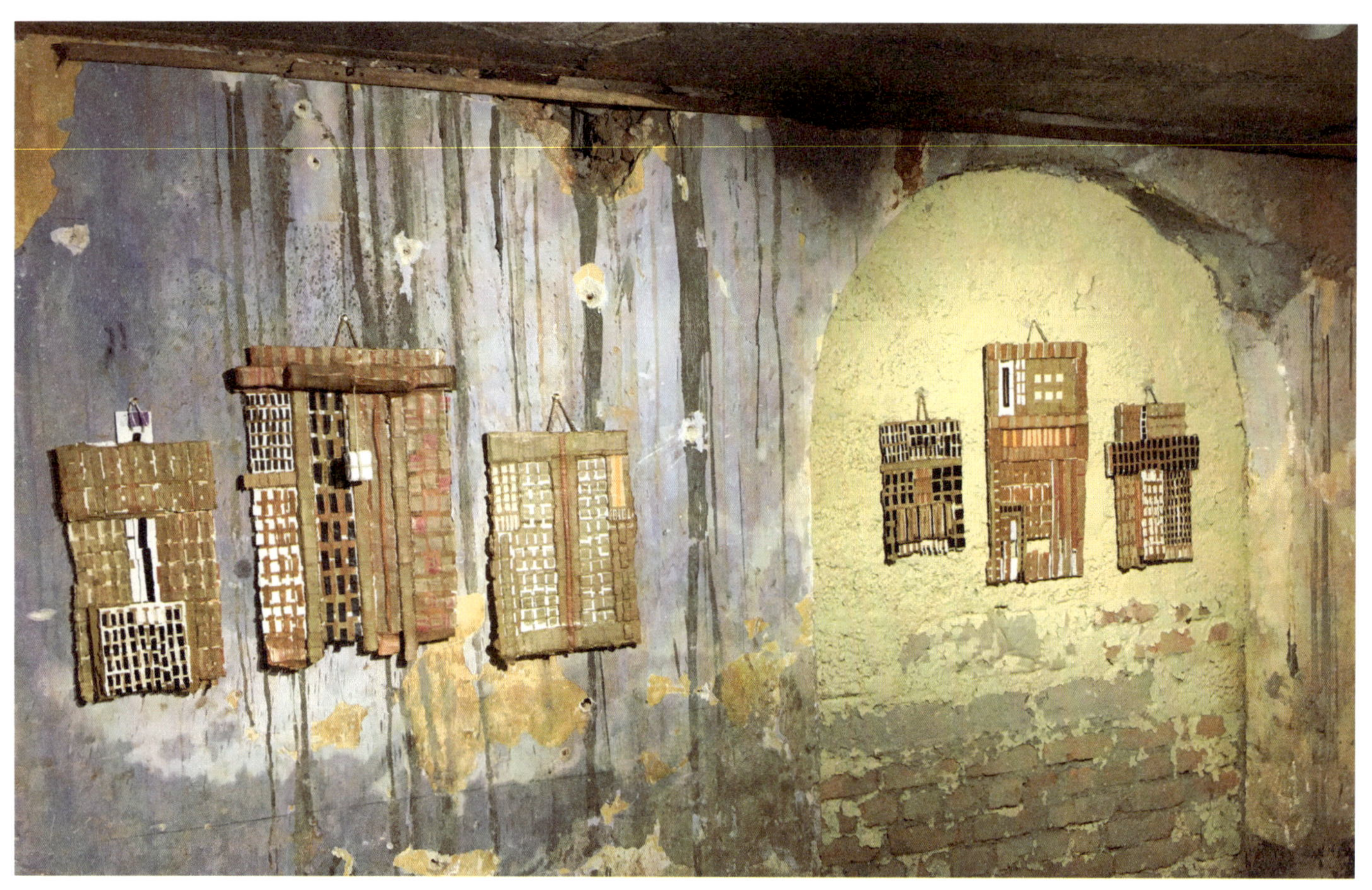

2017 Ibrahim participates in an exhibition curated by Cristiana de
Marchi and Muhanad Ali, in which emerging artists are asked
to produce work in dialogue with the group known as "the five."
Is Old Gold? opens at DUCTAC in Dubai, UAE on February 21,
2017.

In March, a second exhibition that delves into the history of
"the five" opens: *But We Cannot See Them: Tracing a UAE Art
Community, 1988–2008*, curated by Maya Allison at The NYU
Abu Dhabi Art Gallery, UAE. The accompanying book includes
interviews with Ibrahim and his fellow artists, as well as Cristiana
de Marchi, covering the period leading up to the opening of The
Flying House.

Ibrahim is included in *Homage without an Homage*, an exhibition
in memory of the late Hassan Sharif, curated by Cristiana de
Marchi, Art Dubai, UAE.

As part of the Abu Dhabi Music and Arts Foundation (ADMAF)
exhibition, *Portrait of a Nation*, the commissioned *The Qubba
Project* travels to the Collectors Room in Berlin, Germany.
Ibrahim attends this opening.

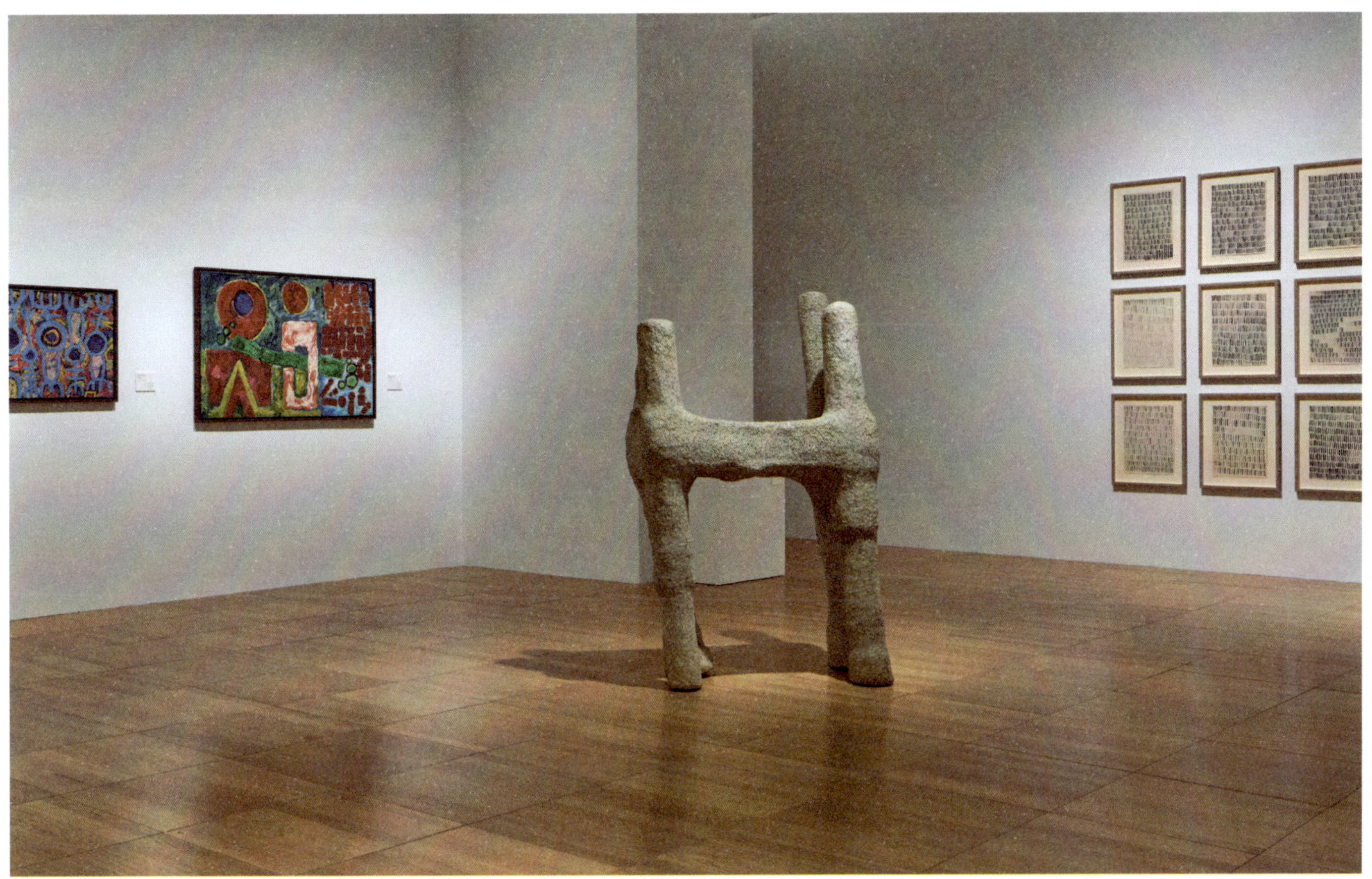

During this year, he is featured in a two-person exhibition with Martin Holzschuh at Lange Strasse 31 Studio Space in Frankfurt, Germany.

Ibrahim is commissioned to create a new iteration of the installation from the 1995 Sittard exhibition, as part of a group exhibition titled *Gateway: Line* at Manarat Al Saadiyat, Abu Dhabi, UAE. This exhibition is curated by Maya Allison as part of Abu Dhabi Art and remains on view until January 27, 2018.

Ibrahim decides to retire and resigns from the Khorfakkan Hospital. This period marks a new and open-ended relationship with his practice. As he puts it, "Now, you have to punch in and out from your own time and work, which never happens."

He begins to build his new studio that takes over part of the land around his home in Khor Fakkan.

Installation view of *But We Cannot See Them: Tracing a UAE Art Community, 1988–2008*, 2017, at The NYUAD Art Gallery, Abu Dhabi, UAE

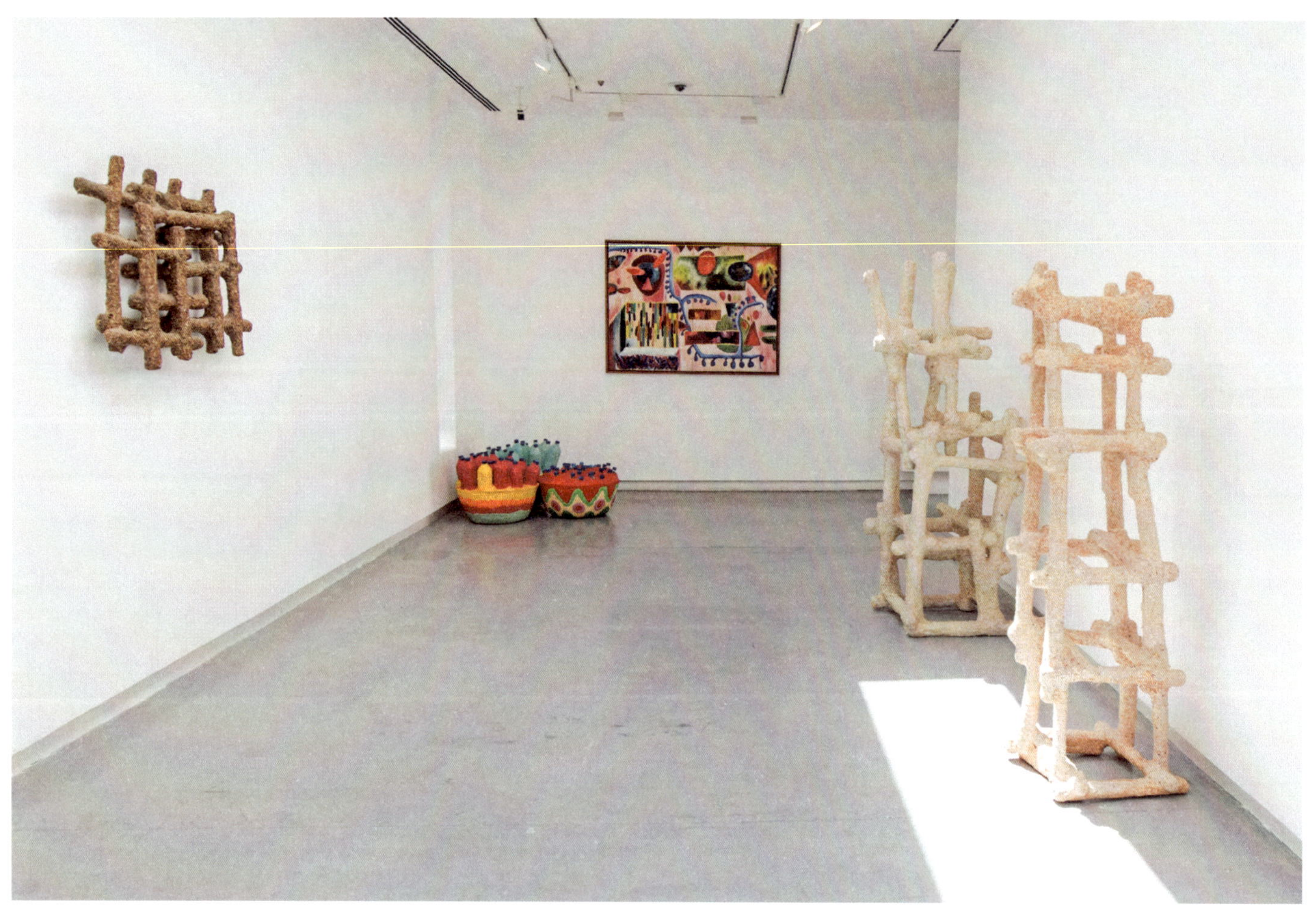

2018 Ibrahim has his first major institutional solo show, *Elements*, curated by Sheikha Hoor Al-Qassimi, at the Sharjah Art Foundation, UAE.

His early work and a new commission are included in *Artists and The Cultural Foundation: The Early Years*, curated by Maya Allison at the Cultural Foundation, Abu Dhabi, UAE.

Ibrahim paints a mural in Reem Park, Abu Dhabi, UAE, commissioned by Aldar Properties.

2019 Ibrahim signs with the gallery Lawrie Shabibi, Dubai, UAE, where he has a solo show titled, *The Space Between the Eyelid and the Eyeball*, and a group exhibition, *Materialize*, during that year.

The "For Abu Dhabi Initiative" commissions him to paint a mural, a project named *GROCERY*, at Madinat Zayed fruit market in Abu Dhabi, UAE.

Ibrahim begins discussions with *Desert X AlUla*, a Land Art exhibition in Saudi Arabia.

2020   *Desert X* opens to extensive international coverage featuring Ibrahim's colorful work that is embedded in the landscape, titled *Falling Stones Garden*.

Ibrahim has a solo show in New York City, USA, at the Aicon Art Gallery, titled *Mixed Lines*.

The Minister of Culture, H.E. Noura Al Kaabi, visits Ibrahim's studio and writes an article about the experience that is published in the *Ittihad* newspaper.

He participates in *Upsurge: Waves, Colour and Illusion*, a group exhibition at Lawrie Shabibi gallery, Dubai, UAE.

With the COVID-19 crisis closing borders and halting exhibition activity, Ibrahim embarks on an intensive period of production in his studio. This ultimately leads to his project for The National Pavilion UAE at the Venice Biennale. Ibrahim participates in a virtual exhibition, titled *Vernacular Automatisms*, a two-artist show with Victor Ekpuk, curated by Murtaza Vali for Aicon Art Gallery.

Ibrahim has his second solo show at Lawrie Shabibi, Dubai, UAE, titled *Memory Drum*.

In September, the announcement is made that Ibrahim will represent the UAE for the Venice Biennale 2022.

2021   Ibrahim participates in a series of exhibitions with Lawrie Shabibi, Dubai, UAE, including *Under Construction* (group exhibition), *Dusk Till Dawn* (solo show), and *Under Construction Part II* (group exhibition).

Munira Al-Sayegh curates his work in two exhibitions. The first is *Hair Mapping Body; Body Mapping Land*, at ICD Brookfield Place, Dubai. In December, *Between the Sky and the Earth: Contemporary Art from the UAE*, a group exhibition, opens at The Middle East Institute Arts and Culture Center, Washington, D.C., United States, in collaboration with The NYU Abu Dhabi Art Gallery, UAE, on the occasion of the 50th anniversary of the founding of the United Arab Emirates.

As far as I see it, it's history. What you di what gives you perr what you do next.

ll about your
before is
ission to do

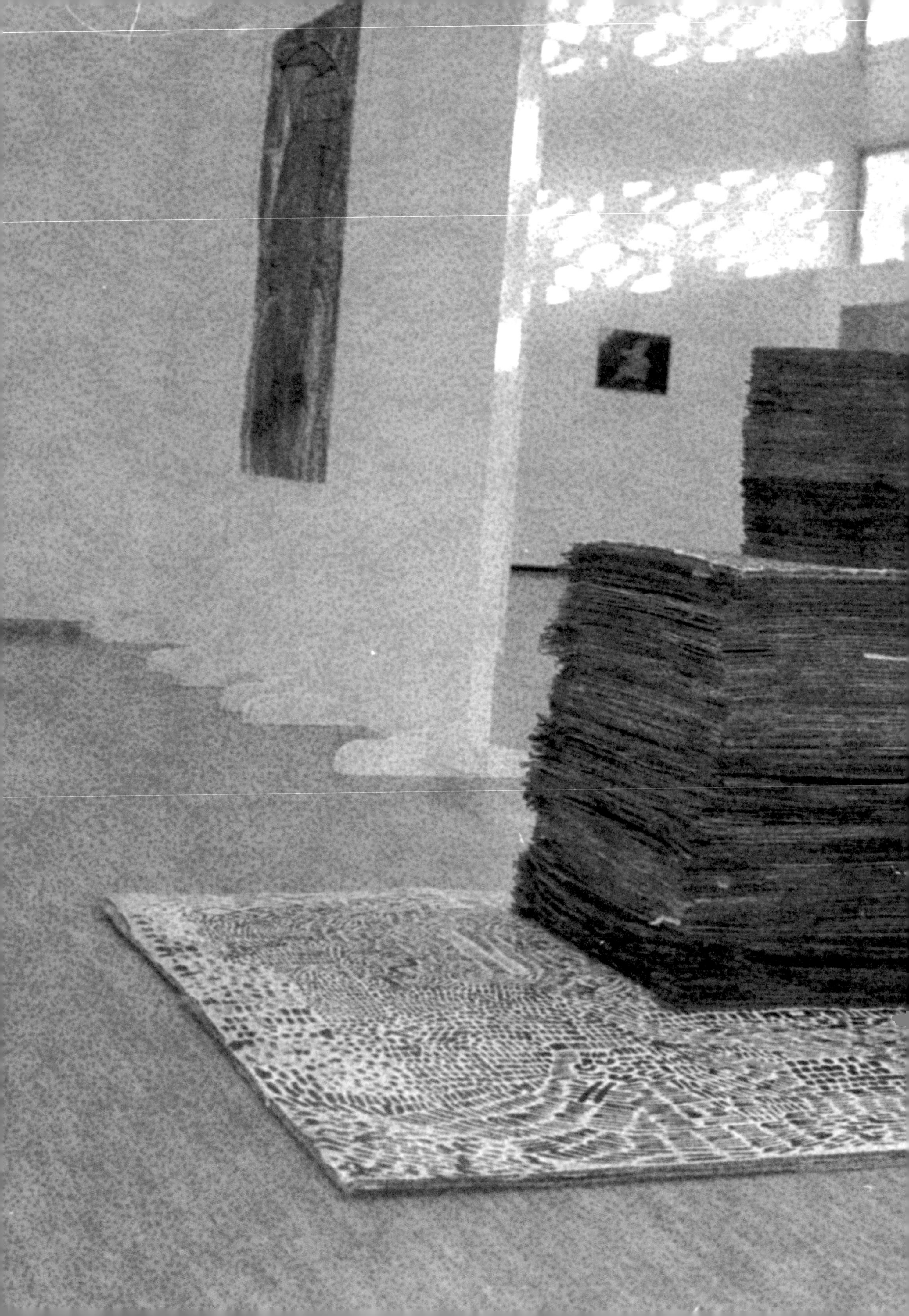

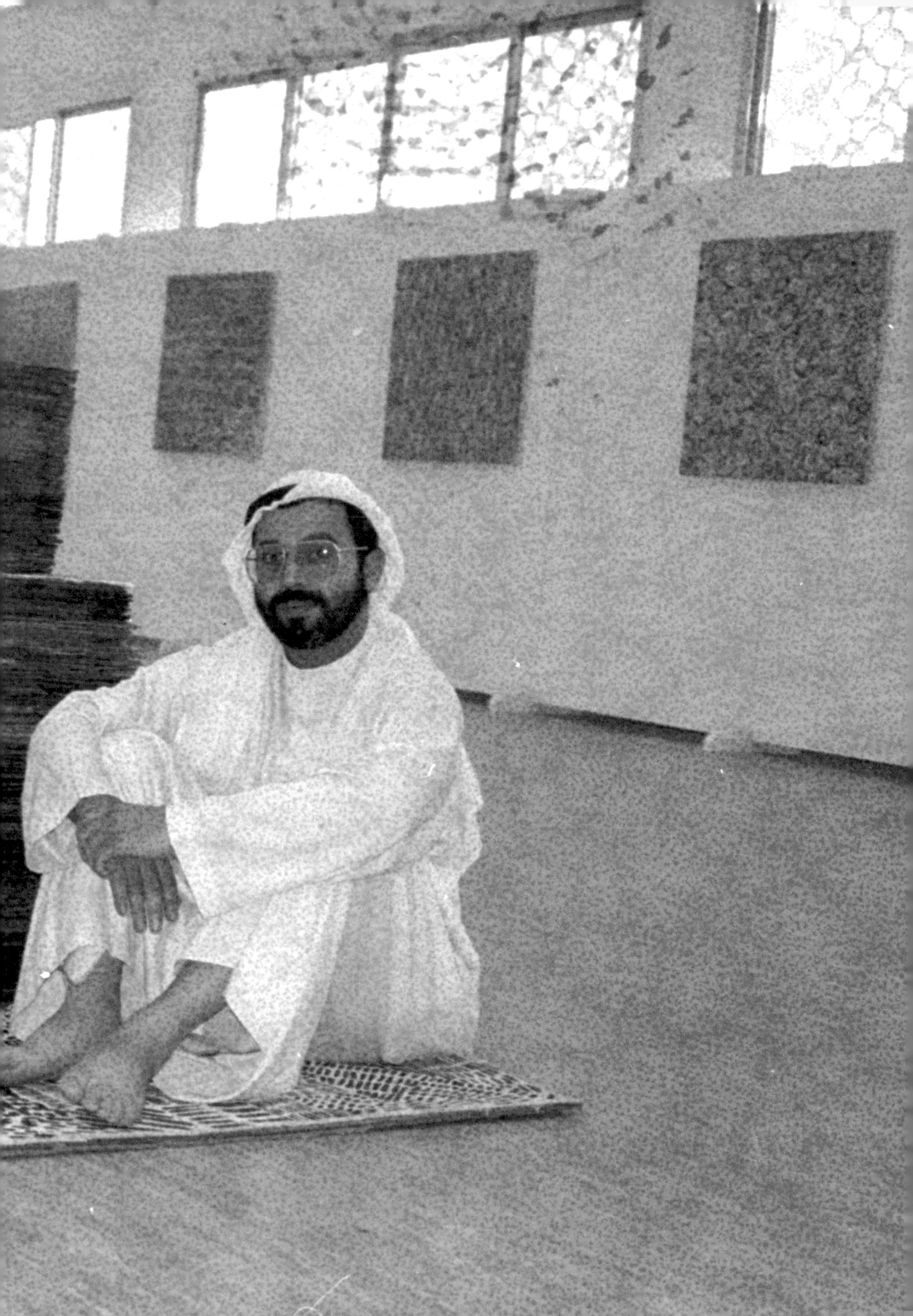

Image Credits

All images courtesy of the artist unless otherwise stated.

Front cover, pages 4–5, 25, 71, 77, 132–133, 134–135, 226: Photo: Shanavas Jamaluddin. Courtesy of Sharjah Art Foundation

Page 26: Collection of HH Sheikh Zayed bin Sultan bin Khalifa Al Nayhan

Pages 27, 38, 41, 42, 60, 61 (bottom), 74, 100, 101, 126, 127, 128, 129, 136, 137, 138–139, 140, 142, 143, 144, 145, 150, 151: Courtesy of Lawrie Shabibi

Pages 29, 31: Photo: John Varghese. Courtesy of the National Pavilion UAE La Biennale di Venezia

Pages 33, 225: Photo: John Varghese. Courtesy of The NYUAD Art Gallery

Pages 45, 47: Photo: Cheb Moha. Courtesy of the National Pavilion UAE La Biennale di Venezia

Pages 55–59, 68–69, 70, 75, 89, 96, 98, 99, 106, 130–131, 141, 146, 147, 175, 216, 219 (bottom), 220: Courtesy of the archive of The Flying House

Page 51 (top): From the private collection of Mohammed AlQassab. Courtesy of the Emirates Fine Arts Society

Pages 51 (bottom), 52, 53: Courtesy of the Emirates Fine Arts Society

Page 61 (top): Photo: Pia Shobha Shamdasani

Page 76: Photo: Abdul-Raheem Sharif. Courtesy of the artist

Pages 78–79: Courtesy of the artist and the Abu Dhabi Music & Arts Foundation Art Collection

Page 80 and back cover: Photo: Lance Gerber. Courtesy of the artist, Lawrie Shabibi, RCU, and Desert X

Pages 85, 86, 87, 88: Courtesy of Fumio Nanjo

Page 107 (top): Photo: Mohamed Al Mazrouei

Pages 111, 112: © Photo: Haupt & Binder

Pages 114, 115, 116: Courtesy of Tashkeel

Pages 124–125: Courtesy of Abu Dhabi Art

Page 149: Photo: Ismail Nour. Courtesy of Alserkal Advisory and ICD Brookfield Place

Pages 152, 223, 224: Photo: Maya Allison

Pages 164, 218 (bottom), 222: Photo: Mohammed Kazem

Page 215: Photo: Hassan Sharif

Page 218 (top): Photo: Abdul-Raheem Sharif

Previous page
Mohamed Ahmed Ibrahim's first solo exhibition, 1991. Opening reception at Emirates Fine Arts Society